INSTRUMENTS OF THE MONEY MARKET

SIXTH EDITION

edited by
Timothy Q. Cook and Timothy D. Rowe

Federal Reserve Bank of Richmond
Richmond, Virginia
1986

First Edition 1968

Second Edition 1970

Third Edition, First Printing 1974

Third Edition, Second Printing 1975

Fourth Edition, First Printing 1977

Fourth Edition, Second Printing 1979

Fifth Edition, First Printing 1981

Fifth Edition, Second Printing 1982

Fifth Edition, Third Printing 1984

Sixth Edition, First Printing 1986

Sixth Edition, Second Printing 1988

Library of Congress Catalog Card Number: 74-75991

CONTENTS

FOREWORD

This is the sixth edition of *Instruments of the Money Market*. The new edition reflects the rapid change and innovation that has occurred in the money market in recent years. It contains three articles on subjects not included in the last edition: short-term interest rate futures, options on interest rate futures, and short-term municipal securities. All but two of the articles in this edition are completely new, and the other two have been thoroughly revised.

The articles were all written during 1986. Two of the authors, Stephen A. Lumpkin and Michael J. Moran, are economists at the Board of Governors of the Federal Reserve System. Another author, Jeremy G. Duffield, is with The Vanguard Group of Investment Companies. The other authors are with the Research Department of the Federal Reserve Bank of Richmond.

Numerous market participants and Federal Reserve staff members generously provided information that was helpful in writing this edition of *Instruments of the Money Market*. These include Kathy Alba, Union Bank, Los Angeles; Jackson L. Blanton, Federal Reserve Bank of Richmond; Galen Burghardt, Jr., Chicago Mercantile Exchange; Kevin J. Conery, Shearson Lehman Brothers, Inc.; Robert J. DeMichiel, Smith Barney, Harris Upham and Co., Inc.; Steven A. Englander, Federal Reserve Bank of New York; Charles W. Grant, Central Fidelity Bank, Richmond; Frances R. Hurdle, Federal Reserve Bank of Richmond; Frederick H. Jensen, Board of Governors of the Federal Reserve System; Joseph J. Kelly, Securities Data Company, Inc.; Thomas A. Lawler, Federal National Mortgage Association; Alan D. Marks, Smith Barney, Harris Upham and Co., Inc.; Christopher Mates, Prudential-Bache Securities, Inc.; David E. Maynard, Fidelity Management and Research; Christopher J. McCurdy, Federal Reserve Bank of New York; Thomas J. Murray, Merrill Lynch and Co., Inc.; Patrick M. Parkinson, Board of Governors of the Federal Reserve System; Nicholas Ronalds, Chicago Mercantile Exchange; James W. Slentz, Chicago Mercantile Exchange; Robert Smith, First Boston Corporation; and F. Parry Young, Standard & Poor's Corp. This edition also benefited from suggestions made by the staff of the Board of Governors of the Federal Reserve System.

A number of employees of the Federal Reserve Bank of Richmond provided invaluable assistance in the production of the book. These include Patricia G. Rhodes, who served as managing editor; Linda B. Almeida, who coordinated production of the output; Kenneth H. Anderson, who did the charts; and Susan R. Cash, who helped locate reference material used in the book. Michael Maryn at the Board of Governors provided research assistance for the article on federally sponsored credit agencies.

1

THE MONEY MARKET

Timothy Q. Cook and Timothy D. Rowe

FUNCTION OF THE MONEY MARKET

The purpose of financial markets is to transfer funds from lenders to borrowers. A common distinction made by financial market participants is between the "capital market" and the "money market," with the latter term generally referring to borrowing and lending for periods of a year or less. The United States money market is very efficient in that it enables large sums of money to be transferred quickly and at a low cost from one economic unit to another for relatively short periods of time.[1]

The need for a money market arises because receipts of businesses, governments and other economic units do not coincide with their expenditures. These units can hold money balances—that is, transactions balances in the form of currency, demand deposits, or NOW accounts—to insure that planned expenditures can be maintained independently of cash receipts. Holding these balances, however, involves a cost in the form of foregone interest. To minimize this cost, economic units usually seek to keep their money balances at a minimum required for their day-to-day transactions. They supplement these balances with holdings of money market instruments that can be quickly and relatively costlessly converted to cash and that have low price risk due to their short maturities. Economic units can also meet their short-term cash demands by maintaining access to the money market and raising funds there when required.

A special need for the money market arises from the requirement that banks and other depository institutions hold non-interest bearing deposits at Federal Reserve Banks to satisfy reserve requirements. These institutions have an incentive to keep their non-interest bearing deposits at a minimum by investing excess reserves in the money market. They can also raise funds quickly to satisfy reserve requirements by borrowing in the money market.

The money market brings together economic units who want to borrow large sums of money for short periods of time with those who want to lend them. The

---

[1] For more detail on the role of financial markets in the economy see Van Horne [1984, Chapter 1].

money market instruments created in this process are generally characterized by a high degree of safety of principal and are most commonly issued in units of $1 million or more. Maturities range from one day to one year, although the most common are three months or less. There are active secondary markets for most of the instruments that allow them to be sold prior to maturity. Unlike organized securities or commodities markets, the money market has no specific location. Although it is centered in New York, it is primarily a telephone market that is easily accessible from all parts of the nation as well as from foreign financial centers.

Of course, the money market and the long-term capital market are not completely separate. Borrowers can finance longer term projects by repeatedly borrowing in the money market rather than by issuing long-term bonds. Investors with funds to invest for a long period can do so by rolling over their holdings of money market instruments rather than by investing in long-term bonds. Also, in recent years there has been a proliferation of financial instruments that have features of both short-term and long-term securities. Nevertheless, the concept of a money market in which borrowers and lenders meet to transfer large sums of money for short periods of time is still a useful one that continues to be widely employed in the financial markets.

OVERVIEW OF THE MONEY MARKET

The money market encompasses a group of short-term credit market instruments, futures markets instruments, and the Federal Reserve's discount window. The table summarizes the instruments of the money market and serves as a guide to the chapters in this book. The major participants in the money market are commercial banks, governments, corporations, federally sponsored credit agencies, money market mutual funds, futures market exchanges, brokers and dealers, and the Federal Reserve.

Commercial Banks Commercial banks are major participants in many parts of the money market. Banks borrow in the money market to fund their loan portfolios and to acquire funds to satisfy reserve requirements. Banks are active in the market for Federal funds, which are very short term—chiefly overnight—loans of immediately available money; that is, funds that can be transferred between banks within a single business day. Reserves of banks are efficiently distributed throughout the banking system in the funds market. The borrowing and lending of reserves takes place at a competitively determined interest rate known as the Federal funds rate. Banks and other depository institutions can also borrow on a short-term basis at the discount window of the twelve regional Federal Reserve Banks and pay a rate of interest set by the Federal Reserve called the discount

THE MONEY MARKET

Instrument	Principal Borrowers
Federal Funds	Banks
Discount Window	Banks
Negotiable Certificates of Deposit (CDs)	Banks
Eurodollar Time Deposits and CDs	Banks
Repurchase Agreements	Securities dealers, banks, thrift institutions, nonfinancial corporations, governments (principal participants)
Treasury Bills	U.S. Government
Municipal Notes	State and local governments
Commercial Paper	Nonfinancial and financial businesses
Bankers Acceptances	Nonfinancial and financial businesses
Federal Agency Discount Notes and Coupon Securities	Farm Credit System, Federal Home Loan Banks, Federal National Mortgage Association
Shares in Money Market Instruments	Money market funds, local government investment pools, short-term investment funds
Futures Contracts	Dealers, banks (principal users)
Futures Options	Dealers, banks (principal users)

rate. A bank's decision to borrow at the discount window depends on the relation of the discount rate to the Federal funds rate, as well as on administrative arrangements surrounding the use of the window. In recent years total outstanding borrowing at the discount window has ranged from $200 million to $3 billion, which is only a small part of total depository institution reserves and a miniscule part of the money market. Nevertheless, because of their role in the implementation of monetary policy, the discount window and the discount rate are of widespread interest to the financial markets.

Banks also borrow funds in the money market for longer periods by issuing large negotiable certificates of deposits (CDs) and by acquiring funds in the Eurodollar market. A large denomination CD is a certificate issued by a bank as evidence that a certain amount of money has been deposited for a period of time—usually ranging from one to six months—and will be redeemed with interest at maturity. Eurodollars are deposit liabilities denominated in United States dollars of banks outside the United States (or of International Banking Facilities in the United States). They can be either large CDs or nonnegotiable time deposits. United States banks raise funds in the Eurodollar market through their overseas branches and subsidiaries.

A final way banks raise funds in the money market is through repurchase agreements (RPs). An RP is the sale of securities with a simultaneous agreement by the seller to repurchase them at a later date. In effect this agreement (when properly executed) is a short-term collateralized loan. (For the lender—that is, the buyer of the securities in such a transaction—the agreement is often called a reverse RP.) Most RPs involve United States government or federally sponsored agency securities. Banks are an active participant on the borrowing side of the RP market.

Governments   The United States Treasury and state and local governments both raise large sums in the money market. The Treasury raises funds in the money market by selling short-term obligations of the United States government called Treasury bills. Bills have the largest volume outstanding and the most active secondary market of any money market instrument. Because bills are generally considered to be free of default risk they typically have the lowest interest rate at a given maturity. State and local governments raise funds in the money market through the sale of both fixed and variable rate securities. A key feature of these securities is that their interest income is generally exempt from Federal income taxes, which makes them particularly attractive to investors in high income tax brackets.

Corporations   Nonfinancial and financial businesses raise funds in the money market primarily by issuing short-term unsecured promissory notes called commercial paper. In recent years an increasing number of firms have gained access to this market. As a result, commercial paper has grown at a rapid pace and now has an amount outstanding exceeding every other money market instrument except Treasury bills. Business enterprises—generally those involved in international trade—also raise funds in the money market through bankers acceptances.

4

Stripped of the procedural details involved in its creation, a bankers acceptance is simply a vehicle that facilitates short-term loans, particularly between importers and investors. The name refers to the fact that in their creation a bank "accepts" the responsibility of repaying the loan, thereby shielding the investor from default risk.

Federally Sponsored Credit Agencies   The federally sponsored credit agencies are a group of privately owned financial intermediaries with certain unique ties to the federal government. These agencies borrow funds in the financial markets and channel these funds primarily to the farming and housing sectors of the economy. They raise a substantial part of their funds in the money market through the sale of discount notes and coupon securities.

MMFs and Other Short-Term Investment Pools   Short-term investment pools are a highly specialized group of money market intermediaries that includes money market mutual funds, local government investment pools, and short-term investment funds of bank trust departments. These intermediaries purchase large pools of money market instruments and sell shares in these instruments to investors. In doing so they enable individuals and other small investors to earn the yields available on money market instruments. These pools, which were virtually nonexistant before the mid-1970s, had over $375 billion in assets as of mid-1986.

Futures Exchanges   Another major development in the money market since the mid-1970s has been the introduction of futures contracts and futures options in money market instruments. A money market futures contract is a standardized agreement to buy or sell a money market security at a particular price on a specified future date. There are active futures markets for three-month Treasury bills and three-month Eurodollar time deposits. A money market futures option gives the holder the right, but not the obligation, to buy or sell a money market futures contract at a set price on or before a specified date. Options are currently traded on both Treasury bill and Eurodollar futures contracts. Money market participants use futures contracts and futures options to hedge against the risk of unexpected changes in interest rates. Futures contracts and futures options are traded on organized exchanges which set and enforce trading rules.

Dealers and Brokers   The smooth functioning of the money market depends critically on brokers and dealers, who play a key role in marketing new issues of money market instruments and in providing secondary markets where outstanding issues can be sold prior to maturity. Dealers use RPs to finance their inventories of securities. Dealers also act as intermediaries between other participants in the RP market by making loans to those wishing to borrow in the market and borrowing from those wishing to lend in the market. The participants in these transactions include nonfinancial corporations, state and local governments, banks, and thrift institutions. Securities dealers also do a huge amount of transactions with the Federal Reserve, which uses the RP market as a means of temporarily increasing or decreasing the supply of bank reserves.

Brokers match buyers and sellers of money market instruments on a commission basis. Brokers play a major role in linking borrowers and lenders in the Federal funds market and are also active in a number of other markets as an intermediary in trades between dealers.

Federal Reserve   The Federal Reserve is a key participant in the money market. The Federal Reserve controls the supply of reserves available to banks and other depository institutions. By controlling this supply, the Fed is able to influence the Federal funds rate that institutions pay in the market to borrow and lend reserves. Movements in this rate, in turn, can have pervasive effects on other money market rates. For this reason the Federal funds rate is widely viewed as the key money market rate. The Federal Reserve affects the reserve positions of banks primarily through the purchase and sale of Treasury bills, either outright in the bill market or on a temporary basis in the market for repurchase agreements. These "open market operations" are carried out by the Open Market Trading Desk at the Federal Reserve Bank of New York. The Trading Desk frequently buys or sells billions of dollars of Treasury bills or RPs in a single day.

The Federal Reserve's administration of the discount window can also influence the supply of reserves and the Federal funds rate. Further, under certain Federal Reserve operating procedures, changes in the discount rate can have a strong direct effect on the Federal funds rate and other money market rates.

SOME FEATURES OF THIS BOOK

The purpose of this book is give a detailed description of the various money market instruments and the markets in which they are used. Where possible the book tries to explain the historical forces that led to the development of an instrument, influenced its pattern of growth, and led to new forms of the instrument. Much of the discussion focuses on the period from the early 1970s through the early 1980s which was one of particularly rapid change in the money market. Factors underlying this change include high and extremely volatile interest rates, major changes in government regulations affecting the markets, and rapid technological change in the computer and telecommunications industries. These developments strongly influenced the pattern of growth of many of

6

the money market instruments and stimulated the development of several new instruments.

Another subject discussed in the book is the relationships between the yields on different money market instruments. The rates of return on money market instruments tend to fluctuate together because these instruments are close substitutes for each other in many investment portfolios. Differentials between money market rates occur, however, because investor decisions are based on after-tax interest rates adjusted for default risk. The effect of default risk on interest rate differentials can change with the state of economic activity and the health of the financial system. The effect of taxes depends on the level of interest rates and on changes in tax regulations. A number of chapters discuss the effects of these and other factors on interest rate relationships in the money market.

Finally, a major focus in the book is on the roles played by the Federal Reserve in the money market. The Fed carries out its monetary policy goals primarily by influencing money market rates, and changes in monetary policy are first evident in the behavior of very short-term money market rates. For this reason participants throughout the financial markets closely watch the behavior of these rates to perceive possible changes in policy. As explained in the Federal funds chapter—and also discussed in the discount window and Treasury bill chapters—the Fed influences money market rates through its control of the supply of reserves available to depository institutions and, at times, through its manipulation of the discount rate. In addition to its monetary policy role the Fed plays an important role as a regulator in a number of the markets.

Reference

Van Horne, James C. *Financial Market Rates and Flows.* Englewood Cliffs, NJ: Prentice Hall, Inc., 1984.

2

FEDERAL FUNDS

Marvin Goodfriend
William Whelpley

Federal funds are the heart of the money market in the sense that they are the core of the overnight market for credit in the United States. Moreover, current and expected future interest rates on Federal funds are the basic rates to which all other money market rates are anchored. Understanding the Federal funds market requires, above all, recognizing that its general character has been shaped by Federal Reserve policy. From the beginning, Federal Reserve regulatory rulings have encouraged the market's growth. Equally important, the Federal funds rate has been a key monetary policy instrument. This chapter explains Federal funds as a credit instrument, the funds rate as an instrument of monetary policy, and the funds market itself as an instrument of regulatory policy.

CHARACTERISTICS OF FEDERAL FUNDS

Federal funds have three distinguishing features. First, they are short-term borrowings of immediately available money—funds which can be transferred between depository institutions within a single business day. The vast majority, roughly 80 percent, of Federal funds are overnight borrowings. The remainder are longer maturity borrowings known as term Federal funds. Second, Federal funds are liabilities of those depository institutions required to hold reserves with Federal Reserve Banks as defined by the Monetary Control Act of 1980. They are: commercial banks, savings banks, savings and loan associations, and credit unions. Third, historically Federal funds borrowed have been distinguished from other depository institution liabilities because they have been exempt from both reserve requirements and interest rate ceilings.[1] Depository institutions are also

---

[1] This distinction has been blurred since passage of the Depository Institutions Dereg-ulation and Monetary Control Act of 1980. Reserve requirements have been eliminated on some personal time deposits and interest rate controls have been removed on all liabilities except traditional demand deposits. However, interbank deposits are still re-servable and explicit interest is still prohibited on interbank demand deposits. In addition, our definition should be qualified because repurchase agreements (RPs) at banks have

the most important eligible lenders in the market. The Federal Reserve, however, also allows depository institutions to classify borrowings from Federal agencies and nonbank securities dealers as Federal funds.[2]

The supply and demand for Federal funds arises in large part as a means of efficiently distributing reserves throughout the banking system. On any given day, individual depository institutions may be either above or below their desired reserve position. Reserve accounts bear no interest, so banks have an incentive to lend reserves beyond those required plus any desired excess. Banks in need of reserves borrow them. The borrowing and lending of reserves takes place in the Federal funds market at a competitively determined interest rate known as the Federal funds rate.

The Federal funds market also functions as the core of a more extensive overnight market for credit free of reserve requirements and interest rate controls. Nonbank depositors supply funds to the overnight market through repurchase agreements (RPs) with their banks. The overnight repurchase agreement is a collateralized one-day loan, which in most cases requires actual transfer of title on the loan collateral. Under an overnight repurchase agreement, a depositor lends funds to a bank by purchasing a security, which the bank repurchases the next day at a price agreed to in advance. Overnight RPs account for about 25 percent of overnight borrowings by large commercial banks. Banks use RPs to acquire funds free of reserve requirements and interest controls from sources, such as corporations and state and local governments, not eligible to lend Federal funds directly. Total daily average gross RP and Federal funds borrowings by large commercial banks are roughly 200 billion dollars, of which approximately 130 billion dollars are Federal funds. Competition for funds among banks ties the RP rate closely to the Federal funds rate. Normally, the RP rate is around 25 basis points below the Federal funds rate; the lower rate being due to the reduced risk and additional transaction cost of arranging an RP.

METHODS OF FEDERAL FUNDS EXCHANGE

Federal funds transactions can be initiated by either the lender or borrower. An institution wishing to sell (loan) Federal funds locates a buyer (borrower) directly through an existing banking relationship or indirectly through a Federal funds broker. Federal funds brokers maintain frequent telephone contact with active funds market participants and match purchase and sale orders in return for

---

not had interest rate ceilings or reserve requirements. Strictly speaking, RPs are not Federal funds. Yet as we explain below, their growth and use have had much in common with the Federal funds market. And the point of view of this article is that they are close functional equivalents.

[2] A more complete list of eligible lenders is found in Board of Governors of the Federal Reserve System, *Federal Reserve Bulletin* vol. 56 (January) 1970, p. 38.

a commission. Normally, competition among participants ensures that a single funds rate prevails throughout the market. However, the rate might be tiered, higher for a bank under financial stress. Moreover, banks believed to be particularly poor credit risks may be unable to borrow Federal funds at all.

Two methods of Federal funds transfer are commonly used. The first involves transfers conducted between two banks. To execute a transaction, the lending institution authorizes the district Reserve Bank to debit its reserve account and to credit the reserve account of the borrowing institution. FEDWIRE, the Federal Reserve System's wire transfer network, is employed to complete a transfer.

The second method simply involves reclassifying respondent bank demand deposits at correspondent banks as Federal funds borrowed. Here, the entire transaction takes place on the books of the correspondent. To initiate a Federal funds sale, the respondent bank simply notifies the correspondent of its intentions. The correspondent purchases funds from the respondent by reclassifying the respondent's demand deposits as "Federal funds purchased." The respondent does not have access to its deposited money as long as it is classified as Federal funds on the books of the correspondent. Upon maturity of the loan, the respondent's demand deposit account is credited for the total value of the loan, plus an interest payment for use of the funds. The interest rate paid to the respondent is usually based on the nationwide effective Federal funds rate for the day. In practice, the correspondent frequently resells the reclassified funds in the Federal funds market itself, earning the Federal funds rate in the process.

TYPES OF FEDERAL FUNDS INSTRUMENTS

The most common type of Federal funds instrument is an overnight, unsecured loan between two financial institutions. Overnight loans are, for the most part, booked without a formal, written contract. Banks exchange verbal agreements based on any number of considerations, including how well the corresponding officers know each other and how long the banks have mutually done business. Brokers play an important role evaluating the quality of a loan when no previous arrangement exists. Formal contracting would slow the process and increase transaction costs. The verbal agreement as security is virtually unique to Federal funds.

In some cases Federal funds transactions are explicitly secured. In a secured transaction the purchaser places government securities in a custody account for the seller as collateral to support the loan. The purchaser, however, retains title to the securities. Upon termination of the contract, custody of the securities is returned to the owner. Secured Federal funds transactions are sometimes requested by the lending institution.

10

Continuing contract Federal funds are overnight Federal funds loans which are automatically renewed unless terminated by either the lender or borrower. This type of arrangement is typically employed by correspondents who purchase overnight Federal funds from a respondent bank. Unless notified by the respondent to the contrary, the correspondent will continually roll the interbank deposit into Federal funds, creating a longer term instrument of open maturity. The interest payments on continuing contract Federal funds loans are computed from a formula based on each day's effective Federal funds rate. When a continuing contract arrangement is made, the transactions costs (primarily brokers fees and funds transfer charges) of doing business are minimized because the entire transaction is completed on the books of the correspondent bank. In fact, additional costs are incurred only when the agreement is terminated by either party.

DETERMINATION OF THE FEDERAL FUNDS RATE

To explain the determinants of the Federal funds rate, we present a simple model of the bank reserve market which incorporates the actions of both private banks and the Federal Reserve.[3] In this model, the funds rate is competitively determined as that value which equilibrates the aggregate supply and demand for banking system reserves.

The aggregate demand for bank reserves arises primarily from the public's demand for checkable deposits against which banks hold reserves. The aggregate quantity of checkable deposits demanded by the public falls as money market interest rates rise, raising the opportunity cost of holding checkable deposits. Hence, the derived demand for bank reserves is negatively related to market interest rates. The aggregate demand schedule for bank reserves is shown in Figure 1, where f is the funds rate and R is aggregate bank reserves.

The aggregate stock of reserves available to the banking system is determined by the Federal Reserve. In principle, the Federal Reserve could choose to provide the banking system with a fixed stock of reserves. If the Federal Reserve chose this strategy, a fixed stock of reserves, $\bar{R}$, would be provided through Federal Reserve purchases of government securities. The resulting funds rate would be f* in Figure 1, or the rate which equilibrates the aggregate supply and demand for bank reserves.

Such a Federal Reserve operating procedure, known as total reserve targeting, is the focus of hypothetical textbook discussions of monetary policy. The hallmark of total reserve targeting is that shifts in the market's demand for

---

[3] Goodfriend [1982, pp. 3–16].

Figure 1

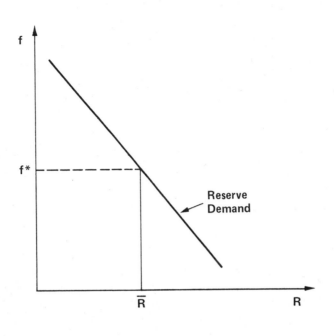

Figure 2

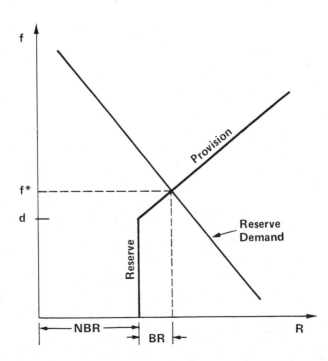

reserves are allowed to directly affect the funds rate. In practice, however, the Federal Reserve has never targeted total reserves. Instead, it has adopted operating procedures designed to smooth funds rate movements against unexpected reserve demand shifts.[4] The simplest smoothing procedure is Federal funds rate targeting, which involves selecting a narrow band, often 50 basis points or less, within which the funds rate is allowed to fluctuate. Explicit Federal funds rate targeting was employed by the Federal Reserve during the 1970s.

The funds rate can be targeted directly by supplying, through open market purchases of U.S. Treasury securities, whatever aggregate reserves are demanded at the targeted rate. For example, if the Federal Reserve chose to peg the funds rate at f* in Figure 1, it would have to accommodate a market demand for reserves of $\bar{R}$. In principle, either total reserve or funds rate targeting could yield the ex ante desired funds rate, f*, so long as the Federal Reserve had precise knowledge of the position of the reserve demand locus. There is, however, an important difference between these procedures. With a total reserve target, market forces directly influence the funds rate. They have no direct effect under a funds rate target. Instead, they affect the volume of total reserves.

Federal Reserve operating procedures become more complicated when reserves are provided by bank borrowing at the Federal Reserve discount window. Figure 2 shows the relationship between reserve provision and the Federal funds rate when there is discount window borrowing. The locus has a vertical and a nonvertical segment because reserves are provided to the banking system in two forms, as nonborrowed and as borrowed reserves. Nonborrowed reserves (NBR) are supplied by the Federal Reserve through open market purchases, while borrowed reserves (BR) are provided by discount window borrowing.

The distance between the vertical segment of the reserve provision locus and the vertical axis is determined by the volume of nonborrowed reserves. The reserve provision locus is vertical up to the point where the funds rate (f) equals the discount rate (d) because when the funds rate is below the discount rate, banks have no incentive to borrow at the discount window. Conversely, when the funds rate is above the discount rate borrowers obtain a net saving on the explicit interest cost of reserves. This net saving consists of the differential (f − d) between the funds rate and the discount rate. In administering the discount window the Federal Reserve imposes a noninterest cost of borrowing which rises with volume. In practice, higher borrowing increases the likelihood of triggering costly Federal Reserve consultations with bank officials. Banks tend to borrow up to the point

[4] Goodfriend [1986], contains a theoretical rational expectations model of interest rate smoothing and discusses its implications for money stock and price level trend-stationarity.

where the marginal expected noninterest cost of borrowing just offsets the net interest saving. Consequently, borrowing tends to be greater the larger the spread between the funds rate and the discount rate. Hence, the reserve provision locus is positively sloped for funds rates above the discount rate.

Discount window borrowing plays a role in determining the funds rate whenever the Federal Reserve restricts the supply of nonborrowed reserves so that the funds rate exceeds the discount rate. In that case, the banking system's demand for reserves is partially satisfied by borrowing at the discount window. If the Federal Reserve chooses to keep nonborrowed reserves fixed in response to an unexpected shift in either reserve demand or the demand for discount window borrowing, then the procedure is called nonborrowed reserve targeting. Nonborrowed reserve targeting is a kind of cross between funds rate and total reserve targeting in the sense that the reserve provision locus is diagonal, rather than horizontal or vertical, thereby partially smoothing the funds rate against aggregate reserve demand shifts. The Federal Reserve employed nonborrowed reserve targeting between October 1979 and the fall of 1982.

By contrast, the Federal Reserve may choose to respond to a shift in reserve demand or the demand for discount window borrowing by adjusting the provision of nonborrowed reserves to keep aggregate discount window borrowing unchanged. The latter procedure, known as borrowed reserve targeting, is closely related to funds rate targeting. This is because, for a given level of the discount rate, targeting borrowed reserves determines the funds rate except for unpredictable instability due to shifts in the demand for discount window borrowing. Borrowed reserve targeting has been the predominant operating procedure since late 1982. An analytically similar procedure, known as free reserve targeting, was employed throughout the 1920s and in the 1950s and '60s.[5]

As can be seen in Figure 2, Federal Reserve discount rate policy plays an important role in determining the funds rate when f is greater than d under either nonborrowed or borrowed reserve targeting. As is easily verified diagrammatically, with a borrowed reserve target a discount rate adjustment changes the funds rate one-for-one. The effect is smaller with nonborrowed reserve targeting. Keep in mind, however, that the discount rate would be irrelevant for determination of the funds rate if the Federal Reserve were to supply a stock of nonborrowed reserves sufficiently large so that the funds rate fell below the discount rate, and banks had no incentive to borrow at the discount window. It is also irrelevant when the Federal Reserve targets the funds rate directly. Discount rate adjustments have played an important role since October, 1979 in both the

---

[5] Free reserves are defined as excess reserves minus borrowed reserves, or equivalently nonborrowed reserves minus required reserves. Net borrowed reserves are negative free reserves.

14

nonborrowed and borrowed reserve targeting periods, as they did in the 1920s, '50s and '60s under free reserve targeting. In contrast, discount rate adjustments had no direct impact on the funds rate when the funds rate itself was targeted during the 1970s. In that period, however, the announcement effect associated with discount rate changes sometimes signaled Federal Reserve intentions to change the funds rate target in the future.

THE FEDERAL RESERVE, THE FEDERAL FUNDS RATE, AND MONEY MARKET RATES

The Federal Reserve's operating procedures in the reserve market have varied greatly over the years. As we have seen, however, the Federal Reserve has always exercised a dominant influence on the determination of the Federal funds rate through setting the terms upon which it makes nonborrowed and borrowed reserves available to the banking system.

The funds rate is the base rate to which other money market rates are anchored. Market participants determine money market rates according to their view of current and expected future Federal funds rates. In practice, because Federal Reserve monetary policy smooths funds rate movements, such views depend heavily on anticipated Federal Reserve policy intentions. As an example, consider bank certificates of deposit (CDs), which are generally arranged for a few months. CD rates, adjusted for reserve requirements, are roughly aligned with an average of expected future funds rates over the term of the CD. Banks can raise funds either through CDs or Federal funds and therefore choose whichever option is expected to be cheaper. Likewise, corporations considering a Treasury bill purchase have the option of lending their funds daily over the term of the bill at the overnight repurchase rate, which is closely tied to the Federal funds rate. As shown in Chart 1, arbitrage such as described above among alternative money market instruments generally keeps their yields in line, abstracting from differences due to transaction costs and risk differentials.

Such considerations on the part of market participants make current and expected future Federal Reserve policy toward the Federal funds rate the key determinant of money market rates in general. Having made this point, we must realize that it provides only a partial explanation of money market rates. A full explanation requires an understanding of Federal Reserve monetary policy. In particular, economy-wide variables such as unemployment and inflation do ultimately play an important role in the evolution of the funds rate through their effect on the Federal Reserve's monetary policy actions over time.

15

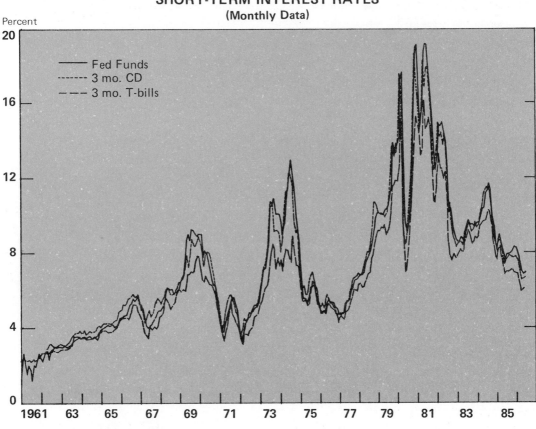

Chart 1
SHORT-TERM INTEREST RATES
(Monthly Data)

Percent

20

16

12

8

4

0

——— Fed Funds
------- 3 mo. CD
– –– 3 mo. T-bills

1961 63 65 67 69 71 73 75 77 79 81 83 85

Source: *Federal Reserve Bulletin.*

HISTORY OF THE FEDERAL FUNDS MARKET

The birth of widespread trading in Federal funds is roughly pinpointed by a *New York Herald Tribune* article appearing in April 1928.[6] That article described the growing importance of Federal funds trading in the money market, reporting a typical daily volume of $100 million.[7] The primary purpose of the article was to announce the inclusion of the Federal funds rate in the *Tribune's* daily table of money market conditions.

As the *Tribune* described it, Federal funds transactions involved the exchange of a check drawn on the clearing house account of the borrowing bank for a check drawn on the reserve account of the lending bank. The reserve check cleared immediately upon presentation at the Reserve Bank, while the clearing

[6] *New York Herald Tribune* [1928].
[7] Willis [1970, p. 12] contains evidence of market activity as far back as 1922.

house check took at least one day to clear. The practice thereby yielded a self-reversing, overnight loan of funds at a Reserve Bank; hence the name, Federal funds. By 1930, the means of trading Federal funds had expanded to include book-entry and wire transfer methods.[8]

The emergence of Federal funds trading constituted a financial innovation allowing banks to minimize transactions costs associated with overnight loans. By their very nature, Federal funds could be lent by member banks only, since only member banks held reserves at Reserve Banks. The beneficiaries on the borrowing side were also member banks, which could receive funds immediately through their Reserve Bank accounts. Federal funds offered member banks a means of avoiding reserve requirements on interbank deposits if they could be classified as "money borrowed" rather than deposits.

In September, 1928 the Federal Reserve Board ruled that Federal funds should be classified as nonreservable money borrowed.[9] A further decision in 1930 found that Federal funds created by book-entry and wire transfer methods should also be nonreservable. These decisions provided the initial regulatory underpinnings for the Federal funds market of today. In both the 1928 and 1930 rulings, the Board indicated that it viewed Federal funds as a substitute for member bank borrowing at the Federal Reserve discount window. It argued that because discount window borrowing was not reservable, Federal funds borrowing should not be either. This view seemed appropriate because the mechanics of a Federal funds transaction restricted participation in the Federal funds market to member banks alone.

The Federal Reserve Board's decision to make Federal funds nonreservable is best understood as a means of encouraging the Federal funds market as an alternative to the two conventional means of reserve adjustment then in use: the discount window and the call loan market. Following World War I, aggregate Federal Reserve discount window borrowing generally exceeded member bank reserves. There was relatively little Federal Reserve discouragement of continuous borrowing at the window. Member banks could adjust their reserve positions directly with the Federal Reserve by running discount window borrowing up or down. In addition, banks had a highly effective means of reserve adjustment in the call loan market. Since the middle of the nineteenth century, banks had made a significant fraction of their loans to stock brokers, secured by stock or bond

---

[8] Board of Governors of the Federal Reserve System, *Federal Reserve Bulletin* vol. 16 (February) 1930, p. 81.

[9] Board of Governors of the Federal Reserve System, *Federal Reserve Bulletin* vol. 14 (September) 1928, p. 656.

collateral on a continuing contract, overnight basis.[10] A bank could obtain reserves on demand by calling in its broker loans, and it could readily lend excess reserves by increasing its supply of call loans. The call loan market was the functional equivalent of the Federal funds market for reserve adjustment purposes.

By 1928, however, the Federal Reserve had begun discouraging both the discount window and the call loan market as means of reserve adjustment. Since 1922, substantial open market purchases had reduced borrowed reserves to less than one-third of total reserves.[11] Moreover, in an apparent effort to further reduce the highly visible subsidy that member banks appeared to receive at the window, the Federal Reserve began actively discouraging continuous discount borrowing by individual banks.[12] Both policy actions tended to make discount window borrowing less effective for routine reserve adjustment purposes. This was particularly true for banks with undesired reserves, because with borrowing usually low or zero, they could not dispose of reserves by running down borrowings from the discount window. In addition, the Federal Reserve came to see the call loan market as an inappropriate means of financing security speculation during the stock market boom of the late 1920s. It went so far as to bring "direct pressure" on individual banks to restrict call loans.[13]

Apart from providing a substitute for the discount window and call loans, Federal funds helped to offset the increased cost of membership due to the more restrictive discount policy and the discouragement of call lending. Membership in the Federal Reserve System is voluntary, and throughout most of its history the Federal Reserve has been concerned about membership attrition. One of the significant costs of membership was the requirement that banks hold more noninterest bearing reserves than nonmember banks had to hold. In making Federal funds nonreservable, the Federal Reserve reduced a cost of membership by providing member banks a means of more effectively competing for overnight interbank deposits.

Banking legislation in the 1930s further enhanced the attractiveness of Federal funds by enabling banks to continue to pay market interest on overnight interbank balances even after the Banking Act of 1933 prohibited explicit interest on demand deposits. This benefit was to prove particularly important in the high

---

[10] See chapters 7 and 13 in Myers [1931].

[11] Board of Governors of the Federal Reserve System, *Banking and Monetary Statistics, 1914–1941*, pp. 368–96.

[12] *Fifteenth Annual Report of the Federal Reserve Board Covering Operations for the Year 1928*, (Washington : GPO) 1929, pp. 7–10.

[13] See the discussion in Friedman and Schwartz [1963, pp. 254–66].

interest rate environment of the 1960s and '70s. In order to prevent excessive use of stock market credit, the Securities and Exchange Act of 1934 authorized the Federal Reserve Board to set margin requirements for both brokers and banks, and others if necessary, on loans collateralized by listed stocks and bonds. Relatively high margin requirements, coupled with other restrictions, brought about a permanent decline in the call loan market.[14]

Extremely low interest rates in the 1930s greatly reduced the interest opportunity cost of holding excess reserves. Consequently, banks held a large volume of excess reserves during this period and Federal funds trading virtually disappeared. Federal Reserve pegging of Treasury bill rates between 1942 and 1947 rendered the funds market superfluous for reserve adjustment purposes. Under this policy the Federal Reserve freely converted Treasury securities into reserves at a fixed price. Therefore, banks could use their inventory of Treasury bills for reserve adjustment purposes just as they had used their discount window borrowings in the early 1920s. The Federal Reserve abandoned its Treasury bill price peg in 1947 and Federal funds trading gradually reemerged as the most efficient means of reserve adjustment. Furthermore, higher market interest rates prevailing in the 1950s increased the opportunity cost of holding excess reserves, making more frequent reserve adjustment desirable. Consequently, the volume of trading in Federal funds grew sharply, with daily average gross purchases of large reserve city banks reaching about $800 million by the end of 1959.[15]

In the 1960s, the Federal funds market began to take on a broader role beyond that of reserve adjustment borrowing. Banks made more extensive use of Federal funds as a means of avoiding the reserve requirement tax and the interest prohibition on demand deposits, both of which became more burdensome as inflation and interest rates rose throughout the period. Although the Federal Reserve was responsible for enforcing both of these legislative restrictions, it had to be concerned throughout this period with offsetting the increased burden of membership in the System, and its actions during the period reflected this concern.[16]

The Board's first significant ruling with regard to the Federal funds market in this period was made in 1964 when it decided that a respondent bank, whether member or not, could request a correspondent member bank to simply reclassify

---

[14] The historical margin requirement series is reported in Board of Governors of the Federal Reserve System, *Banking and Monetary Statistics*.

[15] Board of Governors of the Federal Reserve System, *Federal Reserve Bulletin* vol. 50 (August) 1964, p. 954.

[16] Goodfriend and Hargraves [1983] document in detail how the membership problem dominated reserve requirement reform throughout this period.

a deposit as Federal funds, instead of having to transfer Federal funds through a Reserve Bank account.[17] This ruling probably had its major effect on smaller respondent banks, who had previously found use of Federal funds too costly for the size of their transactions. Allowing banks to simply reclassify their correspondent balances as Federal funds enabled smaller institutions to benefit from Federal funds, as large banks had already been doing. Moreover, it allowed Federal Reserve member correspondent banks to compete more effectively for interbank funds, thereby reducing a disincentive to membership. In 1986, for example, aggregate interbank reservable deposits at large commercial banks were only 25 to 30 percent of aggregate Federal funds borrowings.

Banks in the 1960s also had increasing incentive to give their nonbank depositors access to nonreservable, market interest-paying overnight loans. Nonbanks had always been prohibited from participating in the Federal funds market. But during the 1960s, widespread use of overnight repurchase agreements (RPs) by banks became popular as a means of allowing their nonbank depositors to earn an overnight rate only slightly below the Federal funds rate. As mentioned earlier, the lower rate is due to the reduced risk and additional transaction cost of arranging an RP. RPs do not allow nonbanks to lend Federal funds proper. Because RPs allow nonbanks to approximately earn the Federal funds rate, however, the RP market together with the Federal funds market constitutes a unified overnight loan market.

Obviously, nonbank depositors did not need access to a relatively unregulated overnight rate for reserve adjustment purposes. But the need to facilitate reserve adjustment had been the rationale for waiving reserve requirements and interest rate controls on Federal funds. Nevertheless, the Federal Reserve chose not to make RPs at banks subject to reserve requirements or interest rate controls, probably because doing so would have worsened the competitive position of member banks relative to nonmembers and increased membership attrition.

It was necessary, however, to face up to two consequences of allowing widespread use of RPs at banks. First, RPs were not covered by deposit insurance. Second, shifts from deposits to RPs reduced the reserve requirement tax base and consequently cost the U.S. Treasury tax revenue. A 1969 Federal Reserve rule restricting eligible bank RP collateral to direct obligations of the United States or its agencies, e.g., Treasury bills, responded to those concerns. In principal, requiring RPs to be collateralized with liabilities of the United States

---

[17] Board of Governors of the Federal Reserve System, *Federal Reserve Bulletin* vol. 50 (August) 1964, pp. 1000–1001.

made them free of default risk.[18] In addition, restricting bank RP paper exclusively to U.S. liabilities may have enhanced the demand for U.S. debt, offsetting somewhat the loss of reserve requirement tax revenue.

A 1970 Board ruling formally clarified eligibility for participation on the lending side of the Federal funds market. Eligibility was restricted to commercial banks whether member or nonmember, savings banks, savings and loan associations, and others.[19] In effect, the ruling explicitly segmented the overnight bank loan market into two classes of institutions, those that could lend Federal funds, and those that were required to pay somewhat more substantial transactions costs, through RPs, to earn a rate on overnight loans free of reserve requirements and interest rate controls. Because RPs were uneconomical in smaller volumes, smaller firms and households were unable to obtain nonreserveable market yields on overnight money until the emergence of money market mutual funds in the late 1970s.

CONCLUSION

It is interesting to note how far the Federal funds market has come from its beginnings in the 1920s. Initially, the regulatory rationale for making Federal funds nonreservable was to provide member banks with a substitute for the discount window and call loans for reserve adjustment purposes. Participation in the Federal funds market was limited to member banks, i.e., banks holding required reserves at Reserve Banks. By the 1970s, however, that initial participation principle was effectively overturned. Nonbanks were not allowed to participate directly in the Federal funds market, but they were allowed to earn approximately the Federal funds rate through RPs at banks. Reserve adjustment obviously no longer provided a rationale for sanctioning access to an overnight loan rate free of reserve requirements and interest rate controls. Rather, the granting of such access is better explained as a means by which, in order to minimize membership attrition, the Federal Reserve allowed member banks and their customers to avoid the reserve requirement tax and interest rate prohibition on overnight loans.

The Federal funds market today is in many ways a functional equivalent of the call loan market of the 1920s and earlier. The most notable differences are that the nonbank portion of the market is now a net lender rather than a net borrower, and the collateral used is exclusively debt of the United States government and its agencies rather than private stocks and bonds. Like the old call loan market, the Federal funds market of today facilitates the distribution of reserves among

---

[18] Even if collateralized by U.S. government securities, as a legal matter RPs might also be subject to custodial risk due to incompletely specified contracts. See Ringsmuth [1985].

[19] See footnote 2.

banks, and has much wider participation and a more general role as the core of an overnight credit market unencumbered by reserve requirements and legal restrictions on interest rates.

References

Board of Governors of the Federal Reserve System. *Annual Report of the Board of Governors*, various editions.

———. *Banking and Monetary Statistics, 1914-1941*. Washington: FRB, 1943.

———. *Banking and Monetary Statistics, 1941-1970*. Washington: FRB, 1976.

———. *The Federal Funds Market—A Study by a Federal Reserve System Committee*. Washington: FRB, 1959.

———. *Federal Reserve Bulletin*, various issues.

"Federal Funds' Rate Index of Credit Status." *New York Herald Tribune*, April 5, 1928.

Friedman, Milton and Anna J. Schwartz. *A Monetary History of the United States, 1867-1960*. Princeton, NJ: Princeton University Press, 1963.

Goodfriend, Marvin. "A Model of Money Stock Determination with Loan Demand and a Banking System Balance Sheet Constraint." Federal Reserve Bank of Richmond, *Economic Review* 68 (January/February 1982), pp. 3-16.

———. "Interest Rate Smoothing and Price Level Trend-Stationarity." Federal Reserve Bank of Richmond, July 1986.

Goodfriend, Marvin and Monica Hargraves. "A Historical Assessment of the Rationales and Functions of Reserve Requirements." Federal Reserve Bank of Richmond, *Economic Review* 69 (March/April 1983), pp. 3-21.

Myers , Margaret G. *The New York Money Market*, vol. 1. New York: Columbia University Press, 1931.

Ringsmuth, Don. "Custodial Arrangements and Other Contractual Considerations." Federal Reserve Bank of Atlanta, *Economic Review* 70 (September 1985), pp. 40-48.

Turner, Bernice C. *The Federal Fund Market*. New York: Prentice-Hall, Inc., 1931.

Willis, Parker B. *The Federal Funds Market: Its Origin and Development*. Boston: Federal Reserve Bank of Boston, 1970.

3

THE DISCOUNT WINDOW

David L. Mengle

The discount window refers to lending by each of the twelve regional Federal Reserve banks to depository institutions. Discount window loans generally fund only a small part of bank reserves. For example, at the end of 1985 discount window loans were less than three percent of total reserves. Nevertheless, the window is perceived as an important tool both for reserve adjustment and as part of current Federal Reserve monetary control procedures.

MECHANICS OF A DISCOUNT WINDOW TRANSACTION

Discount window lending takes place through the reserve accounts depository institutions are required to maintain at their Federal Reserve Banks. In other words, banks borrow reserves at the discount window. This is illustrated in balance sheet form in Figure 1. Suppose the funding officer at Ralph's Bank finds it has an unanticipated reserve deficiency of $1,000,000 and decides to go to the discount window for an overnight loan in order to cover it. Once the loan is approved, the Ralph's Bank reserve account is credited with $1,000,000. This shows up on the asset side of Ralph's balance sheet as an increase in "Reserves with Federal Reserve Bank," and on the liability side as an increase in "Borrowings from Federal Reserve Bank." The transaction also shows up on the Federal Reserve Bank's balance sheet as an increase in "Loans to Depository Institutions" on the asset side and an increase in bank reserve accounts, listed as "Deposits: Depository Institutions," on the liability side. This set of balance sheet entries takes place in all the examples given in the Box.

The next day, Ralph's Bank could raise the funds to repay the loan by, for example, increasing deposits by $1,000,000 or by selling $1,000,000 of securities. In either case, the proceeds initially increase reserves. Actual repayment occurs when Ralph's Bank's reserve account is debited for $1,000,000, which erases the corresponding entries on Ralph's liability side and on the Reserve Bank's asset side.

Figure 1

BORROWING FROM THE DISCOUNT WINDOW

Ralph's Bank

Assets	Liabilities
Reserves with Federal Reserve Bank	Borrowings from Federal Reserve Bank
+ $1,000,000	+ $1,000,000

Federal Reserve Bank

Assets	Liabilities
Loans to Depository Institutions	Deposits: Depository Institutions
+ $1,000,000	+ $1,000,000

EXAMPLES OF DISCOUNT WINDOW TRANSACTIONS

Example 1—It is Wednesday afternoon at a regional bank, and the bank is required to have enough funds in its reserve account at its Federal Reserve Bank to meet its reserve requirement over the previous two weeks. The bank finds that it must borrow in order to make up its reserve deficiency, but the money center (that is, the major New York, Chicago, and California) banks have apparently been borrowing heavily in the Federal funds market. As a result, the rate on Fed funds on this particular Wednesday afternoon has soared far above its level earlier that day. As far as the funding officer of the regional bank is concerned, the market for funds at a price she considers acceptable has "dried up." She calls the Federal Reserve Bank for a discount window loan.

Example 2—A West Coast regional bank, which generally avoids borrowing at the discount window, expects to receive a wire transfer of $300 million from a New York bank, but by late afternoon the money has not yet shown up. It turns out that the sending bank had, due to an error, accidentally sent only $3,000 instead of the $300 million.

Although the New York bank is legally liable for the correct amount, it is closed by the time the error is discovered. In order to make up the deficiency in its reserve position, the West Coast bank calls the discount window for a loan.

Example 3—It is Wednesday reserve account settlement at another bank, and the funding officer notes that the spread between the discount rate and Fed funds rate has widened slightly. Since his bank is buying Fed funds to make up a reserve deficiency, he decides to borrow part of the reserve deficiency from the discount window in order to take advantage of the spread. Over the next few months, this repeats itself until the bank receives an "informational" call from the discount officer at the Federal Reserve Bank, inquiring as to the reason for the apparent pattern in discount window borrowing. Taking the hint, the bank refrains from continuing the practice on subsequent Wednesday settlements.

Example 4—A money center bank acts as a clearing agent for the government securities market. This means that the bank maintains book-entry securities accounts (see the chapter on Treasury Bills) for market participants, and that it also maintains a reserve account and a book-entry securities account at its Federal Reserve Bank, so that securities transactions can be cleared through this system. One day, an internal computer problem arises that allows the bank to accept securities but not to process them for delivery to dealers, brokers, and other market participants. The bank's reserve account is debited for the amount of these securities, but it is unable to pass them on and collect payment for them, resulting in a growing overdraft in the reserve account. As close of business approaches, it becomes increasingly clear that the problem will not be fixed in time to collect the required payments from the securities buyers. In order to avoid a negative reserve balance at the end of the day, the bank estimates its anticipated reserve account deficiency and goes to the Federal Reserve Bank discount window for a loan for that amount. The computer problem is fixed and the loan is repaid the following day.

Example 5—Due to mismanagement, a privately insured savings and loan association fails. Out of concern about the condition of other privately insured thrift institutions in the state, depositors begin to withdraw their deposits, leading to a run. Because they are not federally insured, some otherwise sound thrifts are not able to borrow from the Federal Home Loan Bank Board in order to meet the demands of the depositors. As a result, the regional Federal Reserve Bank is called upon to lend to these thrifts. After an extensive examination of the collateral the thrifts could offer, the Reserve Bank makes loans to them until they are able to get federal insurance and attract back enough deposits to pay back the discount window loans.

Discount window loans, which are granted to institutions by their district Federal Reserve Banks, can be either advances or discounts. Virtually all loans today are advances, meaning they are simply loans secured by approved collateral and paid back with interest at maturity. When the Federal Reserve System was established in 1914, however, the only loans authorized at the window were discounts, also known as rediscounts. Discounts involve a borrower selling "eligible paper," such as a commercial or agricultural loan made by a bank to one of its customers, to its Federal Reserve Bank. In return, the borrower's reserve account is credited for the discounted value of the paper. Upon repayment, the borrower gets the paper back, while its reserve account is debited for the value of the paper. In the case of either advances or discounts, the price of borrowing is determined by the level of the discount rate prevailing at the time of the loan.

Although discount window borrowing was originally limited to Federal Reserve System member banks, the Monetary Control Act of 1980 opened the window to all depository institutions, except bankers' banks, that maintain transaction accounts (such as checking and NOW accounts) or nonpersonal time deposits. In addition, the Fed may lend to the United States branches and agencies of foreign banks if they hold deposits against which reserves must be kept. Finally, subject to determination by the Board of Governors of the Federal Reserve System that "unusual and exigent circumstances" exist, discount window loans may be made to individuals, partnerships, and corporations that are not depository institutions. Such lending would only take place if the Board and the Reserve Bank were to find that credit from other sources is not available and that failure to lend may have adverse effects on the economy. This last authority has not been used since the 1930s.

Discount window lending takes place under two main programs, adjustment credit and extended credit.[1] Under normal circumstances adjustment credit, which consists of short-term loans extended to cover temporary needs for funds, should account for the larger part of discount window credit. Loans to large banks under this program are generally overnight loans, while small banks may take as long as two weeks to repay. Extended credit provides funds to meet longer-term requirements in one of three forms. First, seasonal credit can be extended to small institutions that depend on seasonal activities such as farming or tourism, and that also lack ready access to national money markets. Second, extended credit can be granted to an institution facing special difficulties if it is believed that the circumstances warrant such aid. Finally, extended credit can go to groups of

---

[1] For more detailed information on discount window administration policies, see Board of Governors of the Federal Reserve System, *The Federal Reserve Discount Window* (Board of Governors, 1980). The federal regulation governing the discount window is Regulation A, 12 C.F.R. 201.

institutions facing deposit outflows due to changes in the financial system, natural disasters, or other problems common to the group (see Box, Example 5). The second and third categories of extended credit may involve a higher rate than the basic discount rate as the term of borrowing grows longer.

In order to borrow from the discount window, the directors of a depository institution first must pass a borrowing resolution authorizing certain officers to borrow from their Federal Reserve Bank. Next, a lending agreement is drawn up between the institution and the Reserve Bank. These two preliminaries out of the way, the bank requests a discount window loan by calling the discount officer of the Reserve Bank and telling the amount desired, the reason for borrowing, and the collateral pledged against the loan. It is then up to the discount officer whether or not to approve it.

Collateral, which consists of securities which could be sold by the Reserve Bank if the borrower fails to pay back the loan, limits the Fed's (and therefore the taxpaying public's) risk exposure. Acceptable collateral includes, among other things, U.S. Treasury securities and government agency securities, municipal securities, mortgages on one-to-four family dwellings, and short-term commercial notes. Usually, collateral is kept at the Reserve Bank, although some Reserve Banks allow institutions with adequate internal controls to retain custody.

The discount rate is established by the Boards of Directors of the Federal Reserve Banks, subject to review and final determination by the Board of Governors. If the discount rate were always set well above the prevailing Fed funds rate, there would be little incentive to borrow from the discount window except in emergencies or if the funds rate for a particular institution were well above that for the rest of the market. Since the 1960s, however, the discount rate has more often than not been set below the funds rate. Chart 1, which portrays both adjustment credit borrowing levels and the spread between the two rates from 1955 to 1985, shows how borrowing tends to rise when the rate spread rises.

The major nonprice tool for rationing discount window credit is the judgment of the Reserve Bank discount officer, whose job is to verify that lending is made only for "appropriate" reasons. Appropriate uses of discount window credit include meeting demands for funds due to unexpected withdrawals of deposits, avoiding overdrafts in reserve accounts, and providing liquidity in case of computer failures (see Box, Example 4), natural disasters, and other forces beyond an institution's control.[2]

---

[2] In order to encourage depository institutions to take measures to reduce the probability of operating problems causing overdrafts, the Board of Governors announced in May 1986 that a surcharge would be added to the discount rate for large borrowings caused by operating problems unless the problems are "clearly beyond the reasonable control of the institution." See "Fed to Assess 2–Point Penalty on Loans for Computer Snafus," *American Banker*, May 21, 1986.

Chart 1

THE SPREAD BETWEEN
THE FEDERAL FUNDS RATE AND DISCOUNT RATE
COMPARED WITH DISCOUNT WINDOW BORROWING

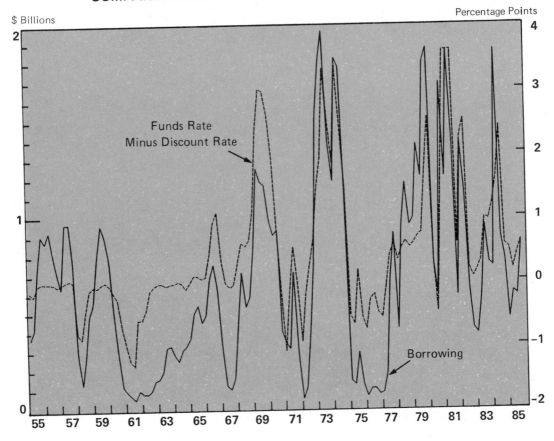

An inappropriate use of the discount window would be borrowing to take advantage of a favorable spread between the Fed funds rate and the discount rate (Example 3). Borrowing to fund a sudden, unexpected surge of demand for bank loans may be considered appropriate, but borrowing to fund a deliberate program of actively seeking to increase loan volume would not. Continuous borrowing at the window is inappropriate. Finally, an institution that is a net seller (lender) of Federal funds should not at the same time borrow at the window, nor should one that is conducting reverse repurchase agreements (that is, buying securities—see the chapter on Repurchase Agreements) with the Fed for its own account.

The discount officer's judgment first comes into play when a borrower calls for a loan and states the reason. The monitoring does not end when (and if) the loan is approved, however. The discount officer watches for patterns in borrowing and may look at such summary measures as discount window loans as a percentage of deposits and of reserves, and duration and frequency of past borrowing. In addition, special circumstances and efforts to obtain credit elsewhere receive attention. Finally, discount window borrowings are compared with Fed funds market activity to make sure banks are not borrowing from the Fed simply to lend at a higher rate in the Fed funds market.

If the discount officer suspects that borrowing by an institution has possibly gone beyond what is appropriate, he or she makes an "informational" call in order to find out the particular problems and circumstances of the case (Example 3), as well as how the institution plans to reduce its reliance on the discount window. If little or nothing changes, it may be time for counseling as well as a more direct effort to help the borrower find new sources of credit. It is conceivable that an institution's credit could be terminated if counseling were to fail, but this is rarely if ever necessary.

THE BORROWING DECISION

When deciding whether and how much to borrow from the discount window, a bank's funding officer can be expected to compare the benefit of using the discount window with the cost. The benefit of an additional dollar of discount window credit is the savings of the rate on Federal funds, which is normally the next best alternative to the window. The marginal cost contains two elements. The first is the price of discount window credit, that is, the discount rate. The second is the cost imposed by nonprice measures used by the Fed to limit the amount of borrowing. An equilibrium level of borrowing would be reached when the marginal benefit of savings of the Fed funds rate is balanced by the marginal cost including both the discount rate and the cost imposed by nonprice measures.[3]

ANTECEDENTS

In the United States in the late nineteenth and early twentieth century, establishment of a central bank was urged in order to provide an "elastic" currency. The central bank's task would be to expand discount window loans as production (and demand for money) expanded over the business cycle. The loans would then be repaid as goods finally went to market. Such a view of the central bank's role was based on the "real bills" or "commercial loan" school, which asserted that expansion of the money supply would not be inflationary so

---

[3] See Goodfriend [1983].

long as it was done to meet the "needs of trade." In other words, loans made by rediscounting commercial loans (which were considered to be made for "productive" purposes) would be self-liquidating since they would be paid back as the goods produced were sold on the market The money supply increase would consequently be extinguished.[4] Reflecting the influence of the real bills doctrine, the Preamble to the Federal Reserve Act of 1913 included as a stated purpose "to furnish an elastic currency." Accordingly, the Act contained provisions for the rediscounting of bank loans "arising out of actual commercial transactions" and defining what paper was eligible for rediscount.

Although the real bills doctrine had the most practical influence on the development of central bank lending, some nineteenth century writers argued that the most important function of a central bank was to act as lender of last resort to the financial system. The first major writer to detail the role of a lender of last resort was Henry Thornton at the beginning of the nineteenth century.[5] In today's terms, Thornton described a lender acting as a "circuit breaker," pumping liquidity into the market in order to prevent problems with particular institutions from spreading to the banking system as a whole. He emphasized that the lender of last resort's role in a panic is precisely opposite that of a private banker in that the former should expand lending in a panic while the latter contracts it. At the same time, Thornton did not advocate lending in order to rescue unsound banks, since that would send the wrong message to bankers, namely, that imprudent management would be rewarded with a bailout. Rather, he urged that loans be made only to banks experiencing liquidity problems due to the panic. In other words, the central bank has a responsibility to protect the banking system as a whole, but not to protect individual banks from their own mistakes.

The other important architect of the lender of last resort idea was Walter Bagehot, who detailed his beliefs in *Lombard Street* in 1873. Generally, Bagehot agreed with Thornton, but developed the lender's role in far greater detail. His contribution is best summed up in the venerable Bagehot Rule: Lend freely at a high rate. This implies three points. First, the public should be confident that lending will take place in a panic, so that there is no question as to the central bank's commitment. Second, lending should go to anyone, not just banks, who presents "good" collateral. In addition, collateral should be judged on what it would be worth in normal times, and not on the basis of its temporarily reduced value due to a panic. Finally, borrowers should be charged a rate higher than

---

[4] For a demonstration of the fallaciousness of this doctrine, see Humphrey [1982].

[5] For a more detailed treatment of the material in this and the following paragraph, see Humphrey and Keleher [1984].

prevailing market rates. The justifications for a high rate are several, namely, ensuring that central bank credit goes to those who value it highest, encouraging borrowers to look first to other sources of credit, giving borrowers incentives to pay back such credit as early as possible, and compensating the lender for affording borrowers the insurance provided by a lender of last resort.

The ideas set forth by both Thornton and Bagehot emphasized emergency lending rather than adjustment credit. In actual practice, the Bank of England did act as lender of last resort several times during the late nineteenth century, but such lending was done in addition to its normal practice of providing adjustment credit at the "bank rate." In the United States, the real bills doctrine was more influential in shaping the central bank than were the ideas of Thornton or Bagehot.[6]

EVOLUTION OF DISCOUNT WINDOW PRACTICES

The only type of lending allowed Federal Reserve Banks by the Federal Reserve Act of 1913 was discounting. In 1916 the Act was amended to add the authority for Federal Reserve Banks to make advances, secured by eligible paper or by Treasury securities, to member banks. Advances replaced discounts in practice during 1932 and 1933, when the volume of banks' eligible paper fell precipitously due to the general banking contraction taking place at the time. Emphasis on lending on the basis of "productive" loans gave way to concern with whether or not collateral offered to secure an advance, be it commercial or government securities, was sound enough to minimize risk to the Fed. Since then, advances have been the predominant form of discount window lending.

Nonprice rationing of Federal Reserve credit became firmly established as a matter of practice during the late 1920s. Use of the discount window to finance "speculative" investments was already discouraged due to the real bills doctrine's stress on "productive" uses of credit, but other reasons for lending also received the Board's disapproval. For example, in 1926 the Board adopted a policy of discouraging continuous borrowing from the discount window. In 1928, it specifically stated that banks should not borrow from the window for profit. Since then, the Federal Reserve has emphasized nonprice measures along with the discount rate to control borrowing.

Because market rates were well below the discount rate, banks used the discount window sparingly between 1933 and 1951. From 1934 to 1943, daily borrowings averaged $11.8 million, and only $253 million from 1944 to 1951. For the most part, banks held large amounts of excess reserves and were under little

---

[6] The lender of last resort idea did surface in the practice of some American clearinghouses acting as emergency lenders during panics. See Gorton [1984].

pressure to borrow. Even after the business recovery of the early 1940s, borrowing remained at low levels. Banks held large quantities of government securities, and the Federal Reserve's practice of pegging the prices of these securities, instituted in 1942, eliminated the market risk of adjusting reserve positions through sales of governments.

The pegged market for government securities ended in 1947, and the subsequent increased fluctuations of these securities' prices made buying and selling them a riskier way for banks to change reserves. As a result, the discount window began to look more attractive as a source of funds. By mid-1952, borrowings exceeded $1.5 billion, a level not seen since the early 1930s. Given the new importance of the window, Regulation A, the Federal Reserve regulation governing discount window credit, was revised in 1955 to incorporate principles that had developed over the past thirty years. In particular, the General Principles at the beginning of Regulation A stated that borrowing at the discount window is a privilege of member banks, and for all practical purposes enshrined nonprice rationing and the discretion of the discount officer regarding the appropriateness of borrowing as primary elements of lending policy.

The new version of Regulation A notwithstanding, the discount rate was for the most part equal to or greater than the Fed funds rate during the late 1950s and early 1960s. As a result, there was not much financial incentive to go to the window. By the mid-1960s, however, the difference between the Fed funds rate and the discount rate began to experience large swings, and the resulting fluctuations in incentives to borrow were reflected in discount window credit levels (see Chart 1).

In 1973, the range of permissible discount window lending was expanded by the creation of the seasonal credit program. More significantly, in 1974 the Fed advanced funds to Franklin National Bank, which had been experiencing deteriorating earnings and massive withdrawals. Such an advance was made to avoid potentially serious strains on the financial system if the bank were allowed to fail and to buy time to find a longer term solution. This particular situation was resolved by takeover of the bulk of the bank's assets and deposits by European American Bank, but the significant event here was the lending to a large, failing bank in order to avert what were perceived to be more serious consequences for the banking system. The action set a precedent for lending a decade later to Continental Illinois until a rescue package could be put together.

Reflecting a discount rate substantially below the Fed funds rate from 1972 through most of 1974, discount window borrowings grew to levels that were high by historical standards. A recession in late 1974 and early 1975 drove loan demand down, and market rates tended to stay below the discount rate until mid-1977. During the late 1970s, the spread was positive again, and borrowing from the window increased. Borrowing then jumped abruptly upon the adoption of a new operating procedure for day-to-day conduct of monetary policy (described in the following section), which deemphasized direct Fed funds rate pegging in favor of targeting certain reserve aggregates. Because this procedure generally requires a positive level of borrowing, the gap between the Fed funds rate and the discount rate has frequently remained relatively high during the first half of the 1980s.

The Monetary Control Act of 1980 extended to all banks, savings and loan associations, savings banks, and credit unions holding transactions accounts and nonpersonal time deposits the same borrowing privileges as Federal Reserve member banks. Among other things, the Act directed the Fed to take into consideration "the special needs of savings and other depository institutions for access to discount and borrowing facilities consistent with their long-term asset portfolios and the sensitivity of such institutions to trends in the national money markets." Although the Fed normally expects thrift institutions to first go to their own special industry lenders for help before coming to the window, private savings and loan insurance system failures in 1985 led to increased use of extended credit.

THE ROLE OF THE DISCOUNT WINDOW IN MONETARY POLICY

As a tool of monetary policy, the discount window today is part of a more complex process than one in which discount rate changes automatically lead to increases or decreases in the money supply. In practice, the Federal Reserve's operating procedures for controlling the money supply involve the discount window and open market operations working together.[7] In the procedures, there is an important distinction between borrowed reserves and nonborrowed reserves. Borrowed reserves come from the discount window, while nonborrowed reserves are supplied by Fed open market operations. While nonborrowed reserves can be directly controlled, borrowed reserves are related to the spread between the funds rate and the discount rate.

During the 1970s, the Fed followed a policy of targeting the Federal funds rate at a level believed consistent with the level of money stock desired. Open market operations were conducted in order to keep the funds rate within a narrow range, which in turn was selected to realize the money growth objective set by the Federal Open Market Committee. Under this practice of in effect pegging the Fed funds rate in the short run, changes in the discount rate only affected the spread between the two rates and therefore the division of total reserves between

---

[7] These are described in more detail by Gilbert [1985] and Broaddus and Cook [1983].

borrowed and nonborrowed reserves. In other words, if the discount rate were, say, increased while the Fed funds rate remained above the discount rate, borrowing reserves from the Fed would become relatively less attractive than going into the Fed funds market.[8] This would decrease quantity demanded of borrowed reserves, but would increase demand for their substitute, nonborrowed reserves, thereby tending to put upward pressure on the funds rate. Given the policy of pegging the funds rate, however, the Fed would increase the supply of nonborrowed reserves by purchasing securities through open market operations. The result would be the same Fed funds rate as before, but more nonborrowed relative to borrowed reserves.[9]

After October 6, 1979, the Federal Reserve moved from Federal funds rate targeting to an operating procedure that involved targeting nonborrowed reserves. Under this procedure, required reserves, since they were at the time determined on the basis of bank deposits held two weeks earlier, were taken as given. The result was that, once the Fed decided on a target for nonborrowed reserves, a level of borrowed reserves was also implied. Again assuming discount rates below the Fed funds rate, raising the discount rate would decrease the Fed funds-discount rate spread. Since this would decrease the incentive to borrow, demand would increase for nonborrowed reserves in the Fed funds market. Under the new procedure the target for nonborrowed reserves was fixed, however, so the Fed would not inject new reserves into the market. Consequently, the demand shift would cause the funds rate to increase until the original spread between it and the discount rate returned. The upshot here is that, since discount rate changes generally affected the Fed funds rate, the direct role of discount rate changes in the operating procedures increased after October 1979.

In October 1982, the Federal Reserve moved to a system of targeting borrowed reserves.[10] Under this procedure, when the Federal Open Market Committee issues its directives at its periodic meetings, it specifies a desired degree of "reserve restraint." More restraint generally means a higher level of borrowing, and vice versa. Open market operations are then conducted over the following period to provide the level of nonborrowed reserves consistent with desired borrowed reserves and demand for total reserves. A discount rate increase under this procedure would, as in nonborrowed reserves targeting, shrink the spread between the Fed funds and discount rates, and shift demand

---

[8] Broaddus and Cook [1983] analyze the effect of discount rate changes if the discount rate is kept above the Fed funds rate.

[9] Although under this procedure discount rate changes did not directly affect the funds rate, many discount rate changes signaled subsequent funds rate changes.

[10] See Wallich [1984]. In addition, since February 1984 required reserves have been determined on an essentially contemporaneous basis.

toward nonborrowed reserves. In order to preserve the targeted borrowing level, the Fed funds rate should change by about the same amount as the discount rate so that the original spread is retained. As a result, discount rate changes under borrowed reserves targeting affect the funds rate the same as under non-borrowed reserves targeting.

References

Broaddus, Alfred, and Timothy Cook. "The Relationship between the Discount Rate and the Federal Funds Rate under the Federal Reserve's Post-October 6, 1979 Operating Procedure." Federal Reserve Bank of Richmond, *Economic Review* 69 (January/February 1983), pp. 12-15.

Gilbert, R. Alton. "Operating Procedures for Conducting Monetary Policy." Federal Reserve Bank of St. Louis, *Review* 67 (February 1985), pp. 13-21.

Goodfiend, Marvin. "Discount Window Borrowing, Monetary Policy, and the Post-October 6, 1979 Federal Reserve Operating Procedure." *Journal of Monetary Economics* 12 (September 1983), pp. 343-56.

Gorton, Gary. "Private Clearinghouses and the Origins of Central Banking." Federal Reserve Bank of Philadelphia, *Business Review* (January/February 1984), pp. 3-12.

Humphrey, Thomas M. "The Real Bills Doctrine." Federal Reserve Bank of Richmond, *Economic Review* 68 (September/October 1982), pp. 3–13. Reprinted in Thomas M. Humphrey, *Essays on Inflation*, 5th Ed. Richmond: Federal Reserve Bank of Richmond, 1986, pp. 80-90.

Humphrey, Thomas M., and Robert E. Keleher. "The Lender of Last Resort: A Historical Perspective." *Cato Journal* 4 (Spring/Summer 1984), pp. 275-318.

Wallich, Henry C. "Recent Techniques of Monetary Policy." Federal Reserve Bank of Kansas City, *Economic Review* (May 1984), pp. 21-30.

4

LARGE CERTIFICATES OF DEPOSIT

Rob J. M. Willemse

Large denomination ($100,000 or more) certificates of deposit (CDs) are important to large banks as a means of managing their liability positions and are also one of the most important assets in the portfolios of many large money-market investors. Large CDs are generally divided into four classes based on the type of issuer because the rates paid, risk, and depth of the market vary considerably among the four types. The oldest of the four groups consists of CDs issued by U.S. banks domestically, which are called domestic CDs. Dollar-denominated CDs issued by banks abroad are known as Eurodollar CDs or Euro CDs. CDs issued by U.S. branches of foreign banks are known as Yankee CDs. Finally, some savings and loan associations issue large CDs, referred to as thrift CDs.

DOMESTIC CDs

A certificate of deposit is a certificate issued by a bank as evidence that a certain amount of money has been deposited for a fixed period of time and will be redeemed with interest at maturity. The certificate specifies the amount of the deposit, the date on which it matures, the interest rate, and the method of calculating the interest on the deposit. Large CDs are usually issued in denominations of $1 million or more.

A CD can be legally negotiable or nonnegotiable, depending on certain legal specifications of the CD. Negotiable CDs assure the buyer of a perfect title to the deposit. Most large CDs are issued in negotiable form because they can be sold more easily before maturity.

A CD can be payable to the bearer or registered in the name of the investor. Most large negotiable CDs are issued in bearer form because investors can resell bearer CDs more easily. Registered large CDs are technically negotiable but are in practice nonnegotiable because of the administrative difficulty involved in changing ownership. Registered CDs are generally issued only to depositors who intend to hold the CDs until maturity.

36

Federal Reserve regulations limit the minimum maturity of a time deposit to 7 days. In practice the shortest maturity of large CDs commonly issued is 14 days. Large domestic CDs typically have initial maturities of 1 to 12 months. The most popular maturities are 1, 2, 3, and 6 months. In early 1986 the average maturity of large CDs outstanding at the forty largest U.S. banks was 5 months.

Interest rates on CDs are generally quoted on an interest-bearing basis with the interest computed on the basis of a 360-day year. A $1 million, 90-day CD with a 7 percent annual interest rate would after 90 days entitle the holder of the CD to:

$$1{,}000{,}000 * (1 + \frac{90}{360} * 0.07) = \$1{,}017{,}500.$$

Banks usually pay interest semiannnually on CDs with maturities longer than one year.

Variable-Rate CDs Variable-rate CDs (VRCDs), also called variable-coupon CDs or floating-rate CDs, accounted for 15 percent of all newly issued large domestic CDs in early 1986. VRCDs have the distinguishing feature that the total maturity of the CD is divided into equally long rollover periods, also called legs or roll periods, in each of which the interest rate is set anew. The interest accrued on a leg is paid at the end of that leg.

The interest rate on each leg is set at some fixed spread to a certain base rate which is usually either the composite secondary market rate for domestic CDs published by the Federal Reserve Bank of New York or the London interbank offered rate (LIBOR); the maturity of the base rate chosen is equal to the length of the leg. For example, a VRCD with a 1-month roll is repriced every month with a fixed spread to the composite 1-month secondary CD rate or 1-month LIBOR. The most popular maturities of VRCDs are 18 months or 2 years with a roll of 1 or 3 months. Banks are willing to pay higher rates on VRCDs than on fixed-rate CDs with maturity equal to the roll period since VRCDs with total maturities of 1 1/2 years or more currently are exempt from reserve requirements. VRCDs also improve banks' liquidity positions by providing funds for relatively long periods. The typical size of the mark-up for a VRCD with a 3-month roll period is 5 to 15 basis points over the 3-month secondary CD rate or 12.5 basis points under 3-month LIBOR. (One basis point equals one-hundredth of a percentage point.) The spread to the base rate depends on market conditions, the creditworthiness of the issuing bank, and the total maturity of the CD.

VRCDs appeal to money market investors who want to invest funds for longer periods because of the protection they offer against a rise in interest rates. Among the largest investors in VRCDs are money market funds because investing in VRCDs enables them to earn a rate above the prevailing CD rate of the roll period,

Chart 1

QUARTERLY CHANGE IN
COMMERCIAL AND INDUSTRIAL LOANS AND LARGE CDs
(Large Weekly Reporting Banks)

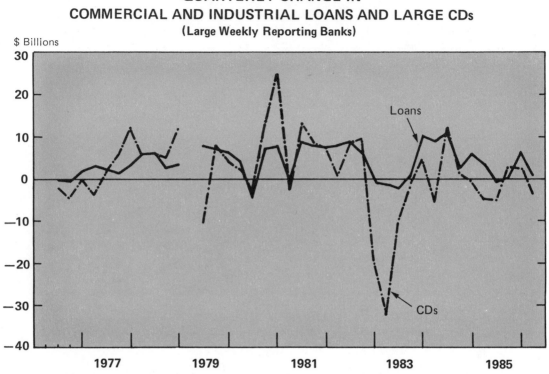

Note: Break in data occurs in first quarter of 1979.

Source: *Federal Reserve Bulletin;* Quarterly Reports of Condition (Call Reports).

without increasing the effective maturity of their portfolios. Investors treat a VRCD as a conventional CD once the rate has been set for the last time and the VRCD is on its last leg.

Issuing Banks   Only the largest banks are able to sell $1 million CDs in the national market. This group of banks comprises both money-center and large regional banks. Large CDs perform two important functions for these banks. First, they can issue large CDs to fund new loans. Chart 1 shows the correspondence between the quarterly changes in large CDs and commercial and industrial loans outstanding at large weekly reporting banks for the period 1976 through early 1986. Other flexible instruments of funding for banks are Federal funds, repurchase agreements, and Eurodollar deposits. Second, large CDs provide a means for these banks to manage their exposure to interest rate risk arising due to the difference between the interest rate sensitivity of their assets relative to that of their liabilities. For example, when the average maturity of their assets is longer than the average maturity of their liabilities, the assets tend to be more rate sensitive than the liabilities. Consequently, a rise in interest rates will cause a decline in net worth.[1] Large CDs offer these banks a flexible instrument to vary the maturity of their liabilities outstanding, and thus manage interest rate risk.

History and Recent Development of Domestic CDs In the late 1950s large New York City banks lost deposits as corporations, spurred by rising interest rates. began to minimize their cash balances and invest their excess cash reserves in money market instruments like Treasury bills and commercial paper. To provide an attractive investment for corporations, First National City Bank of New York (now Citibank) started issuing large CDs in 1961 and a major money market dealer agreed to make a secondary market in the CDs. Other major banks in New York City soon followed and, within a year, domestic CDs outstanding exceeded $1 billion.[2]

During its first decade, the CD market grew rapidly except for two major setbacks. In 1966, and more severely in 1969, domestic CDs outstanding fell dramatically because open market interest rates rose above Regulation Q ceiling rates on large time deposits set by the Federal Reserve. Both times the binding interest rate ceilings reflected the policy of the Federal Reserve to slow the growth in bank loans. Since banks were unable to raise funds by issuing domestic CDs, they turned to the Eurodollar market as an additional source of funds. Businesses also raised money by issuing commercial paper. After the failure of the Penn Central Transportation Company in June 1970, however, businesses found it difficult to issue commercial paper. To prevent a general liquidity crisis, the Federal Reserve eliminated the interest rate ceilings on large CDs with maturities of less than 3 months. In 1973 the Federal Reserve also dropped the ceilings on rates of large CDs with longer maturities. Ceilings on rates of large CDs have not been imposed since then.

Large CDs outstanding grew steadily from the mid-70s until late 1982 (see Chart 2). An important factor behind this growth was the emergence of money market funds (MMFs). Although interest rate ceilings were eliminated in 1973 on large time deposits in amounts of $100,000 or more, they continued to exist for smaller time and savings deposits. In the late 1970s interest rates rose above these ceiling rates and stayed above them for several years. Small investors were able to circumvent the regulatory ceilings and earn a market rate of interest by

---

[1] Interest rate sensitivity is more correctly described by duration than by the average maturity of assets and liabilities. See Kaufman [1984] for a definition of duration and its application in analyzing the interest rate risk of a bank.

[2] A detailed exposition of the origin of the domestic CD market is given in Fieldhouse [1962].

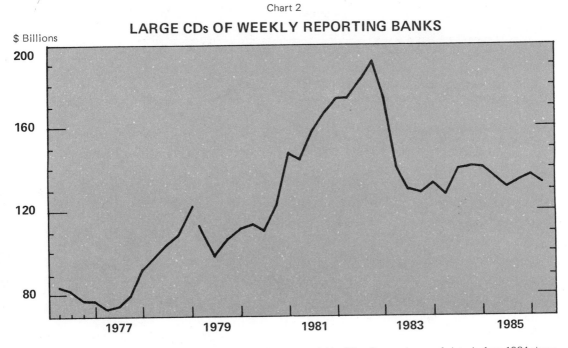

Chart 2

LARGE CDs OF WEEKLY REPORTING BANKS

$ Billions

Note: Large CDs include both negotiable and nonnegotiable CDs. Comparisons of data before 1984 show that nonnegotiable CDs make up about 10 percent of all large CDs at large weekly reporting banks.

Break in data occurs in first quarter of 1979.

Source: Quarterly Reports of Condition (Call Reports)

investing in MMFs, which pooled the savings of many small investors in order to invest in money market instruments. MMFs grew rapidly from only $10 billion in 1978 to $206 billion in 1982 and a large part of their assets were invested in CDs (see Table I).

To counter the outflow of savings balances from banks into MMFs, Congress authorized banks and thrifts to offer two ceiling-free accounts: the Money Market Deposit Account (MMDA) and the Super NOW. The MMDA was introduced in December 1982 and the Super NOW in January 1983. These accounts, especially the MMDA, proved to be very popular and by year-end 1983 they had attracted more than $400 billion to commercial banks and thrifts. Some of this money came from MMFs, the total assets of which fell by $46 billion in 1983. The rapid inflow of funds into MMDAs and Super NOWs led banks to cut back on their issuance of large CDs. Domestic CDs outstanding at large weekly reporting banks fell $60 billion from their peak in late 1982 to $130 billion at year-end 1983. MMFs' holdings of domestic CDs fell in 1983 from $36 billion to $22 billion.

From 1984 to early 1986 the total amount of large CDs outstanding at large

Table I

TOTAL ASSETS AND LARGE CDs of MONEY MARKET FUNDS

(Billions of Dollars; Percentage of Total Assets in Parentheses)

Year -end	Total Assets	Domestic CDs	Yankee and Thrift CDs	Euro CDs	Total CDs
1978	10.9	5.3 (48.8%)			5.3 (48.8%)
1979	45.2	18.1 (40.1%)			18.1 (40.1%)
1980	74.4	19.7 (26.4%)	1.3 (1.8%)	6.8 (9.1%)	27.8 (37.3%)
1981	181.9	39.2 (21.5%)	4.7 (2.6%)	18.8 (10.4%)	62.7 (34.5%)
1982	206.6	35.5 (17.2%)	5.3 (2.6%)	23.8 (11.5%)	64.5 (31.2%)
1983	162.5	21.9 (13.5%)	5.1 (3.1%)	21.9 (13.5%)	48.9 (30.1%)
1984	209.7	18.5 (8.8%)	5.2 (2.5%)	21.2 (10.1%)	44.9 (21.4%)
1985	207.5	13.3 (6.4%)	3.6 (1.7%)	19.0 (9.2%)	35.9 (17.3%)

Note: Euro CDs also include one-day Euro time deposits.
Source: Investment Company Institute.

weekly reporting banks remained relatively constant at about $135 billion.[3] This can be related to several factors. Loan demand was sluggish as many bank borrowers turned to the commercial paper market to raise short-term funds. Borrowers also turned to longer term financing such as bond issuance. Strong inflows into MMDAs reduced banks' needs to raise money by issuing large CDs. Finally, in 1985 banks with access to the Eurodollar market substituted Eurodollar deposits for domestic CDs when Eurodollars became an effectively cheaper source of funds.

Although the total amount of large CDs changed little from 1984 to early 1986, money-center banks actually decreased their issuance of large CDs while regional banks increased their issuance.[4] This difference reflected the stronger growth in loan demand at the regional banks and their more limited access to the Eurodollar market.

EURODOLLAR CDs

Patterned after the domestic CD, a Eurodollar CD is a dollar-denominated negotiable instrument, evidencing a time deposit placed with a bank at an agreed

---

[3] The number of weekly reporting banks—currently about 150 banks—overstates the number of banks which are important for the national CD market. A Federal Reserve release on the maturity distribution of large negotiable CDs shows that in early 1986 the amount of large negotiable CDs outstanding at the 40 largest U.S. banks was about $50 billion.

[4] Based on data from the Quarterly Reports Of Condition (Call Reports), the proportion of CDs outstanding at the 10 largest banks in New York City fell from 20 percent of the total amount of CDs outstanding at large weekly reporting banks at year-end 1983 to 15 percent in early 1986.

upon rate of interest for a fixed period of time. Although denominated in dollars, Eurodollar CDs are issued abroad. Eurodollar CDs are primarily issued in London and therefore frequently termed London dollar CDs.[5]

Most Eurodollar CDs are issued in amounts ranging from $250,000 to $5 million and typically have maturities ranging from one to twelve months with a fixed rate of interest. Eurodollar CDs are also issued in floating-rate form, typically having longer maturities of one-and- one-half to five years and usually yielding a spread below LIBOR. A third type of Eurodollar CD is the so-called tranche CD. Tranche CDs are geared towards the smaller investor and have maturities from three to five years. Tranche CDs are issued in large aggregate amounts ($10 to $30 million) composed of smaller certificates ($10,000 to $25,000), each having the same interest rates, issue dates, payment dates and maturities. Tranche CDs are underwritten by various large brokerage houses, which offer the CDs to private investors.

Eurodollar CDs are mostly sold to institutional investors and large corporations in the United States. Eurodollar CDs are also sold to other banks in the London interbank market. These interbank placements totaled around $15 billion at year-end 1985.

The major issuers of London dollar CDs are the branches of major U.S., Japanese, Canadian and continental banks and the British clearing banks.[6] The U.S. banks issue the most Eurodollar CDs but their dominant position has been challenged recently by the Japanese banks (see Table II).

Banks issue Eurodollar CDs to fund international lending and to raise funds to transfer to their home head offices where they can be used as additional funding for domestic lending. Large U.S. banks continually compare the effective costs of raising funds in the United States and in the Eurodollar markets, and they substitute domestic CDs for Eurodollar CDs when the effective cost is lower in the United States and vice versa. (The effective cost of funds is the interest paid adjusted for the costs of holding noninterest-bearing reserve requirements and paying deposit insurance.) Although Eurodollar CDs are a widely accepted instrument in the Eurodollar market, banks rely more on the non-negotiable Eurodollar time deposit as a source of funds. Eurodollar CDs are about 13 percent of all Eurodollar time deposits in the London market, in contrast to the domestic market where CDs are about 90 percent of all large time deposits.

---

[5] The amount of Eurodollar CDs outstanding at other financial off-shore centers like Nassau and Singapore is small compared to London. *Federal Reserve Bulletin* data show that at year-end 1985 the amount of negotiable Eurodollar CDs outstanding at the foreign branches of U.S. banks was about $31 billion of which $29 billion was outstanding at the London branches.

[6] British clearing banks are a few large banks that are members of the London Clearing system, which is the national payment system.

Table II

LONDON DOLLAR CDs OUTSTANDING

(Billions of U.S. Dollars; Percentage of Total in Parentheses)

Year-end	Total	U.S. Banks	Japanese Banks	British Banks	Other Banks
1980	48.7	26.8 (55.0%)	8.8 (18.1%)	4.6 (9.4%)	8.5 (17.5%)
1981	76.1	43.8 (57.6%)	11.9 (15.6%)	6.6 (8.7%)	13.8 (18.1%)
1982	92.6	50.3 (54.3%)	19.0 (20.5%)	9.3 (10.0%)	14.0 (15.1%)
1983	99.8	46.0 (46.1%)	29.2 (29.3%)	8.6 (8.6%)	16.1 (16.1%)
1984	94.7	34.0 (35.9%)	33.5 (35.4%)	7.6 (8.0%)	19.7 (20.8%)
1985	92.1	32.1 (34.8%)	28.9 (31.4%)	8.9 (9.7%)	22.2 (24.1%)

Source: Bank of England, *Quarterly Bulletin.*

The market in Eurodollar CDs originated in 1966 when a London branch of a U.S. bank started issuing Eurodollar CDs. The size of the Eurodollar CD market peaked in early 1984 at about $100 billion. The amount at branches of American banks reached its highest levels earlier in 1982 at around $50 billion. During 1983 and 1984 Eurodollar CDs outstanding at branches of American banks dropped by almost $20 billion.

The decline in this period in Eurodollar CDs issued by American banks can be attributed to three reasons. The inflow of new retail funds into MMDA and Super NOW accounts in the United States led to a transfer of funds from U.S. banks to their foreign offices, which reduced the need to fund with Eurodollar CDs. U.S. banks also significantly reduced their international lending following the international debt crisis in 1982.[7] And the crisis that surrounded the problems of Continental Illinois in 1984 made international investors wary of large U.S. banks' CDs.

YANKEE CDs

Yankee CDs are negotiable certificates of deposit issued in the United States by branches of foreign banks. Foreign branches located in New York account for 80 percent of all Yankee CDs outstanding. The major issuers of Yankee CDs are well-known international banks headquartered in Japan, Canada, England and Western Europe. The principal business of foreign banks in the United States

---

[7] Statistics published by Morgan Guaranty [1985] indicate that while international lending by U.S. banks in 1983 stayed the same, there was a drop of almost $30 billion in 1984.

consists of wholesale banking. Yankee CDs provide funding for loans made to U.S. corporations and to foreign corporations operating in the United States.

The market in Yankee CDs developed in the early 1970s. In the first stage of the market, U.S. money market investors were wary of the new instrument and Yankee CDs paid a considerable higher yield than domestic CDs. The effect of this difference in yields on the cost of raising funds was partially offset by the exemption of foreign banks from Federal Reserve reserve requirements, which lasted until the International Banking Act of 1978. This exemption probably helped considerably to establish the market in Yankee CDs.

The size of the market in Yankee CDs was relatively constant at about $35 billion from late 1982 through early 1986. One development that contributed to the weakness in the Yankee CD market was the narrowing of the differential between the rates in the Eurodollar and the domestic CD market in 1985 which led foreign banks to raise funds in the Euro market.

THRIFT CDs

At year-end 1985 the amount of large denomination CDs outstanding at all insured thrifts was about $100 billion. A large proportion of these CDs are sold locally. Only a few large savings and loans (mostly in California) are able to sell their large CDs in the national CD market through dealers. This situation is likely to persist because of the small size of even the largest thrifts relative to banks.

Smaller thrifts have also gained access to a nationwide market for their CDs by using brokers as intermediaries. CDs sold through brokers have come to be known as "brokered CDs" or "brokered deposits". To appeal to investors, brokers often offer CDs in $100,000 denominations since Federal insurance coverage for CDs is limited to $100,000. In 1982 a computerized exchange was created where investors can buy large denomination packages of newly issued CDs. These CDs are fully insured by packaging together $100,000 CDs of different depository institutions (both banks and thrifts).

RISK AND RETURN

Large CDs yield a premium over Treasury bills of comparable maturity. This is commonly attributed to three factors. First, unlike investors in Treasury bills, investors in large CDs are subject to credit risk because of the possibility of default by the issuing bank. The Federal Deposit Insurance Company (FDIC) insures only the first $100,000 of a domestic CD whereas the standard denomination of large CDs is $1 million or more. Second, although the secondary market in large CDs is well developed, it does not possess the depth of the market in

Chart 3

SPREADS BETWEEN RATES ON
3-MONTH CDs AND 3-MONTH TREASURY BILLS

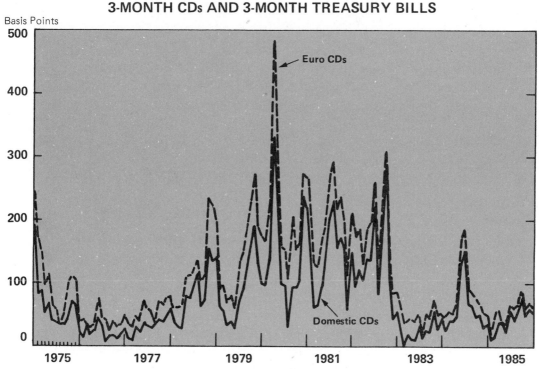

Note: First day of the month, bond equivalent, secondary market rates.

Source: Salomon Brothers, *An Analytical Record of Yields and Yield Spreads.*

Treasury securities. Investors may demand a slightly higher yield to compensate for this smaller liquidity of CDs. Third, interest on Treasury bills is exempt from state and local income taxes. Consequently, many investors have to earn a higher before-tax yield on CDs than on Treasury bills to get the same after-tax yield.

Chart 3 plots the yield spread between the secondary market yields on 3-month domestic CDs and Treasury bills from 1975 through 1985. The yield spread between 3-month Eurodollar CDs and Treasury bills is also plotted for the same period. From 1975 through 1985 domestic CDs yielded on average 75 basis points more than Treasury bills. The highest spreads were reached in the early 1980s when interest rates were high and volatile.

The spread between CD rates and T-bill rates tends to increase when the general level of interest rates rises. One factor underlying this relationship is the fact that Treasury bills are exempt from state and local income taxes. Because these taxes are proportional, spreads between CD and Treasury bill rates have to

45

widen when the general level of interest rises in order to leave an investor with a given state income tax indifferent between Treasury bills and CDs. Another factor might be that higher interest rates tend to increase the probability of defaults on bank loans. This would increase the risk of bank failures which would lead investors to demand a higher risk-premium.

In late 1982 the spread between the domestic CD and Treasury bill rates increased to almost 200 basis points even though interest rates were falling. The cause was a rise in the bank risk premium due to several problems in the banking industry in the second half of 1982. The first important event was the failure of Penn Square Bank in Oklahoma in July 1982. This failure had a negative impact on a number of large banks because of their involvement with Penn Square, especially Chase Manhattan Bank and Continental Illinois National Bank & Trust Co. The second was the emergence in August 1982 of the problems of large U.S. banks related to their international lending activities, especially loans to Latin America. The bank risk premium rose again after Continental Illinois ran into well-publicized troubles in May 1984. The domestic CD/T-bill spread increased from 40 basis points in April to nearly 150 basis points in July of that year.

Rates on Eurodollar CDs have been consistently higher than the rates on their domestic counterparts. The rate differential at the three-month maturity averaged about 40 basis points from 1975 through 1985, although the differential fell sharply in the latter part of the period and in the first half of 1986. The rate differential is heavily influenced by the arbitrage activities of large U.S. banks who continually compare the effective costs of raising funds in the U.S. or through their branches in the Eurodollar markets.[8] The rate differential may also reflect differences in the perceived riskiness of Eurodollar and domestic CDs. The host country of the Eurobank can issue regulations (for example foreign exchange controls) that prevent Eurobanks from redeeming Eurodollar CDs. Eurodollar CDs routinely bear the inscription that the instrument is "construed under and subject to the laws of [the host country]."

Yankee CDs also offer a premium over the rates on domestic CDs. This premium, which was about 10 to 15 basis points in early 1986, can be attributed to two reasons. First, the U.S. investor is less familiar with foreign banks and might have difficulty assessing the credit quality of these banks because of different accounting rules and less available information. Second, Yankee CDs are subject to country risk because the foreign country in which the parent bank is located might prevent the foreign branches from redeeming their deposits.

The rates that are paid on large CDs issued by different banks vary

---

[8] Kreicher [1982] provides a detailed discussion of the links between the Eurodollar market and the U.S. domestic banking system.

considerably. CDs that have lower default risk and are more liquid can be offered at lower rates. The size of a bank also influences the rate of its CDs. Larger banks are more likely to pay lower rates. The amount of a bank's CDs outstanding may also influence the rate on its CDs. When a less well-regarded bank increases its issuance of CDs, it has to offer a higher rate in order to attract funds.

The ten or so largest U.S. money-center banks pay on average the lowest rates on their CDs. There is considerable variation in the spreads between the rates on regional and money-center bank CDs. Currently, well-regarded regional banks are able to issue CDs at about the same rate as the top-quality money-center banks. Some regionals, however, pay as much as 25 basis points more than money-center banks.

A possible additional reason why the nation's largest banks command the lowest rates is that some banks may be too big to be allowed to fail. Some observers feel that the nation's ten largest banks are so important to the banking system that the FDIC effectively fully guarantees their uninsured deposits. These observers cite the FDIC's handling of major bank failures in the 1980s. In 1982 Penn Square, a bank with assets of about $500 million, was allowed to fail and depositors were paid back only up to the $100,000 federal insurance limit. The FDIC's handling of the failure was partly based on a desire to force large uninsured depositors to more closely monitor the creditworthiness of individual banks. In mid-1984 when Continental Illinois, one of the nation's 10 largest banks at that time, was in trouble, the FDIC fully guaranteed all depositors regardless of denomination. Much attention has been focused on whether this decision has led uninsured depositors to perceive that the FDIC's implicit coverage is higher for money center banks than for smaller banks, thereby giving money center bank CDs a preferential status.[9]

RATINGS

Ratings help investors in determining the investment grade of different banks' large CDs. Five rating agencies rate large CDs: Standard & Poor's Corporation; Duff & Phelps, Inc.; Moody's Investor Service, Inc.; McCarthy, Crisanti & Maffei, Inc.; and Keefe, Bruyette and Woods, Inc. Unlike the other four rating agencies, Keefe does not specifically rate short-term bank paper, but gives an overall credit evaluation of the bank. Whereas Duff & Phelps and McCarthy rank only domestic CDs, Moodys, Keefe, and Standard & Poor's rank both domestic and foreign banks' CDs. Moodys, McCarthy and Duff & Phelps make their ratings public. The other two agencies provide the rating as a private subscribers

---

[9] See Gilbert [1985] and Huertas and Strauber [1986].

service. A CD rating is based on the agency's assessment of the ability of the issuer to redeem the CDs at maturity relative to other issuers. The rankings are divided into three (Duff & Phelps, Moodys), four (Standard & Poor's) or six categories (McCarthy, Keefe).

PRIMARY MARKET

Each day, banks actively issuing large CDs post a set of rates for the most popular maturities—1, 2, 3, 6 and 12 months—at which they are willing to issue CDs. The posted rates are dependent on the funding needs of the particular bank. When a bank wants to limit its CDs outstanding, it will post low rates. The rates are also influenced by its interest rate expectations. When a bank expects interest rates to rise, it will post higher rates for long-term CDs than for short-term CDs.

A bank tries to sell as many CDs as possible directly to retail investors in order to reduce the prospect of its CDs reappearing in the secondary market when the bank is issuing new CDs at a later point in time. Because banks have a limited capability to sell all their CDs directly to investors, they often sell part of their CDs to dealers who resell them to investors. Smaller and foreign banks rely more on dealers when selling their CDs. Banks also sell to dealers CDs that are hard to sell directly to retail investors such as longer term CDs and variable-rate CDs.

In a typical transaction in the primary domestic CD market a large U.S. money center bank located in New York City issues a CD to a large domestic investor also headquartered in New York City. After the investor and the bank have agreed on the rate, maturity and amount of the CD, the issuing bank delivers the certificate to the custodian bank specified by the investor.[10] After the custodian has verified the certificate, it debits the investor's account and credits the issuing bank with the amount of the CD. The custodian makes the payment by using the Federal Reserve's wire transfer network to transfer Federal funds from its reserve account at the Fed to the issuing bank's reserve account. Issuing banks require payment in Federal funds because Federal funds are immediately available for use. Custodian banks have deadlines for delivery of incoming paper. If the transaction is executed early in the day, same-day settlement is feasible. At maturity the CD is redeemed by presenting the certificate to the issuing bank and the holder is paid in Federal funds. Since the secondary market in large CDs is centered in New York City, large out-of-town banks that are active in the national

---

[10] Large CDs are sometimes issued in book-entry form where the physical transfer of the security is eliminated.

CD market issue and redeem through a correspondent bank in New York City. Yankee and thrift CDs have similar mechanics.

Transaction mechanics in the London CD market are different from those used for domestically issued CDs. When issuing CDs, the London branches or banks issue and deliver the certificates in London to a specified custodian. The issuing bank receives payment in New York by the crediting of its account at its head office or branch. Payment in New York is usually made through CHIPS and usually takes place two business days after the transaction.[11] Maturing certificates are repaid with interest at the New York office or correspondent upon surrender of the certificate to the London bank. Several Clearing Centres in London facilitate primary and secondary market transactions. The First Chicago Clearing Centre, set up by the First National Bank of Chicago, handles most Eurodollar CD transactions.

SECONDARY MARKET

The organized secondary market in large CDs makes it possible for holders to sell their CDs quite readily and enables investors in CDs to buy outstanding CDs as an alternative to buying new issues. Like the secondary market in other money market instruments, the market in large CDs is an over-the-counter market. The market is made up of a linked network of dealers and brokers and trades are made by telephone.

Dealers make a market in CDs by standing ready to buy and sell large CDs for their own account. To be effective as a marketmaker, a dealer must be willing to position (take into inventory) CDs. There are currently about 35 dealers in large CDs but only about 10 of these are active marketmakers in both good and bad markets.

Dealers quote rates at which they are willing to buy (bid rate) and sell (ask rate) CDs. The quotes vary with the particular issuing bank and the maturity of the CD. All quotes move together, however, in response to changes in the overall money market, thereby keeping secondary market CD rates in line with rates on other money market instruments and with rates on primary CDs. The typical difference between the bid and ask rates for CDs is around 5 basis points. The CDs that are most heavily traded have the lowest bid-ask spreads.

Dealers trade with customers and with other dealers. Trades between dealers in general involve only top-quality CDs with remaining maturities of six

---

[11] CHIPS (Clearing House Interbank Payment System) is an electronic payments system set up by the the New York Clearing House Association. Payment with clearing house funds is different from payment with Federal funds in that they are not "immediately available good funds". Funds paid through CHIPS are not available until the end of the day.

months or less. At the end of 1985 the amount of daily secondary market transactions in the domestic CD market was about $1.5 billion whereas daily trading in Eurodollar CDs was about $2 billion. Trading activity in domestic CDs has declined due to decreased issuance of these CDs by the large money-center banks and greater efforts by banks to sell their CDs directly to retail investors using the banks' own sales staffs.

Dealers take positions in CDs to satisfy customers' demands and to speculate on interest rate movements. Dealers finance CDs held in inventory through overnight repurchase agreements. The rate dealers pay for repurchase agreements with CDs as collateral is slightly higher than the rate on repurchase agreements against Treasury bills.

Brokers intermediate in transactions by bringing together buyers and sellers. They do not hold an inventory of CDs. Brokers are often used by dealers to do trades with other dealers because of the anonymity they provide. Brokers are present in all CD markets—domestic, Eurodollar, Yankee and thrift.

Currently the CDs of about 25 U.S. banks, 15 resident-foreign banks, 20 London banks and about 10 thrifts are traded in the secondary market. The typical size of a CD transaction, called a round lot, varies from 5 to 10 million dollars. Trades between dealers and customers tend to have somewhat lower sizes than trades between dealers.

The secondary market in domestically issued CDs (domestic, Yankee and thrift) is predominantly located in New York City, where most of the large money-center banks and dealers are located. A small proportion of trading takes place in Chicago, San Francisco, and Los Angeles. New York City also serves as the headquarters for many of the investors in large CDs. Eurodollar CDs are traded in both London and New York City. The secondary market in London is made up of the British money market dealers and the London branches of major U.S. dealers. Eurodollar CD dealers who have offices in both London and New York integrate their trading activities in both cities.

The mechanics of secondary market transactions are similar to those for primary market transactions. The certificates have to be physically transported between the participants or, more likely, their custodian banks. The settlement date on secondary market transactions in domestic, Yankee and thrift CDs varies depending on the time of trade. Trades that are executed in the morning are usually settled the same day (cash settlement), whereas trades later in the day are settled the next business day (regular delivery). Trades between dealers are usually settled the next business day regardless of the time of trade. Secondary market trades in Eurodollar CDs are generally made for settlement two business days forward (skip-day settlement). Payments for trades in domestic, Yankee and thrift CDs are made in Federal funds through the dealers' clearing banks whereas payments for Eurodollar CDs are made in clearing house funds.

Secondary market trading in large CDs is complicated by the fact that CDs are more heterogeneous than Treasury bills since CDs differ with respect to the quality of the issuing bank. In the late 1970s a practice was established among dealers that tended to improve secondary market trading of domestic CDs issued by top quality banks. Dealers started quoting rates on domestic CDs of these money-center banks on a no-name basis. CDs of these banks are all traded for the same price (yield). Trading on a no-name basis increased the liquidity of top-quality domestic CDs. Currently the no-name list contains nine banks but the list varies from time to time. For example, when Continental Illinois ran into difficulties in 1982 its CDs were removed from the no-name list. At present it is not unusual for the CDs of certain banks from the no-name list to trade at a slightly lower yield than other no-name banks' CDs. Although no-name trading of top-quality banks' CDs still exists among dealers, retail customers usually specify names when buying money-center banks' CDs.

Eurodollar CDs of certain banks are also traded on a no-name basis. Currently there are three different groups of no-name banks. The five largest U.S. banks form the first group, the five largest Japanese banks are the second group and the four British Clearing banks form the last group.

References

"CDx - a new exchange for fully insured CDs." *American Bankers Association Banking Journal* (February 1983).

Fieldhouse, Richard. *Certificates of Deposit.* Bank Study Series. Boston: The Bankers Publishing Company, 1962.

Gilbert, R. Alton. "Recent Changes in Handling Bank Failures and Their Effects on the Banking Industry." Federal Reserve Bank of St. Louis, *Review* 67 (June/July 1985).

Hung, Tran Q. "U.S. Banks Have Resumed Issuing Eurodollar CDs." *Currency & Bond Market Trends*, vol. 1, no. 18, May 6, 1985. Merrill Lynch Capital Markets, Securities Research Division/International Research.

Huertas, Thomas F., and Rachel L.S. Strauber. "Deposit Insurance: Overhaul or Tune-Up?" *Issues in Bank Regulation* (Winter 86), pp. 3-24.

Kaufman, George G. "Measuring and Managing Interest Rate Risk: A Primer." Federal Reserve Bank of Chicago, *Economic Perspectives* 8 (January/February 1984), pp. 16-29.

Kreicher, Lawrence L. "Eurodollar Arbitrage." Federal Reserve Bank of New York, *Quarterly Review* (Summer 1982), pp. 10-21.

Melton, William C. "The Market for Large Negotiable CDs." Federal Reserve Bank of New York, *Quarterly Review* (Winter 1977-78), pp. 22-34.

Smith, Craig W. *Negotiable Instruments & The Payments Mechanism*. American Bankers Association, 1983.

Stigum, Marcia. *The Money Market*. Rev. ed. Homewood, Illinois: Dow Jones-Irwin, 1983.

Summers, Bruce J. "Negotiable Certificates of Deposit." In *Instruments of The Money Market*, 5th ed. Edited by Timothy Q. Cook and Bruce J. Summers. Richmond: Federal Reserve Bank of Richmond, 1981.

"The London dollar certificate of deposit." *Bank of England Quarterly Bulletin* 13 (December 1973), pp. 446-52.

World Financial Markets. Morgan Guaranty Trust Company of New York, July 1985.

5

EURODOLLARS

Marvin Goodfriend

THE NATURE OF THE EURODOLLAR

Eurodollars are bank deposit liabilities, denominated in United States dollars, not subject to United States banking regulations.[1] For the most part, banks offering Eurodollar deposits are located outside the United States. However, since late 1981 non-United States residents have been able to conduct business free of United States banking regulations at International Banking Facilities (IBFs) in the United States. Eurodollar deposits may be owned by individuals, corporations, or governments from anywhere in the world, with the exception that only non-United States residents can hold deposits at United States IBFs.

The term Eurodollar dates from an earlier period when the market was located primarily in Europe. Although the bulk of Eurodollar deposits is still held in Europe, today Eurodollar deposits are held in such places as the Bahamas, Bahrain, Canada, the Cayman Islands, Hong Kong, Japan, the Netherlands Antillies, Panama, Singapore, and United States IBFs.[2] Nevertheless, dollar-denominated deposits located in United States IBFs and anywhere in the world outside the United States are still referred to as Eurodollars.

Banks in the Eurodollar market including United States IBFs compete with United States banks to attract dollar-denominated funds. Since the Eurodollar market is relatively free of regulation, banks in the Eurodollar market can operate on narrower margins or spreads between dollar borrowing and lending rates than can banks in the United States. This gives Eurodollar deposits an advantage relative to deposits issued by banks operating under United States regulations. In short, the Eurodollar market has grown up as a means of separating the United States dollar from the country of jurisdiction or responsibility for that currency, the

---

[1] Dollar-denominated deposits at a bank located outside the United States or in a United States IBF are Eurodollars, even if the bank if affiliated with a bank whose home office is a non-IBF United States bank. See Terrell and Mills [1983], Key [1982] and Lichtenstein [1982] for discussions of IBFs.

[2] See Ashby [1978] and [1979] for discussions of Europe's declining share of the global Eurocurrency market. The Eurocurrency market includes, along with Eurodollars, foreign currency-denominated deposits held at banks located outside a currency's home country.

United States. It has done so largely to reduce the regulatory costs involved in dollar-denominated financial intermediation.

THE SIZE OF THE EURODOLLAR MARKET

Measuring the size of the Eurodollar market involves looking at the volume of dollar-denominated loans and deposits on the books of banks located outside the United States. However, dollar-denominated loans and deposits may not match. Consequently, a decision must be made whether to measure the volume of Eurodollars from the asset or liability side of the bank balance sheet.

A liability side measure may be too broad, since it may include foreign currency liabilities incurred to fund loans to domestic residents denominated in domestic currency. Strictly speaking, this is a traditional type of international financial intermediation. Measuring Eurodollar market volume from dollar-denominated assets, however, may also overstate the size of Eurodollar volume since these assets may reflect nothing more than traditional foreign lending funded with domestic currency-denominated deposits supplied by domestic residents.

In practice, Eurodollar volume is measured as the dollar-denominated deposit liabilities of banks located outside the United States. For example, the Bank for International Settlements (BIS) defines and measures Eurodollars as dollars that have "been acquired by a bank outside the United States and used directly or after conversion into another currency for lending to a nonbank customer, perhaps after one or more redeposits from one bank to another."[3]

Under a liability side measure such as the one used by the BIS, the sum of all dollar-denominated liabilities of banks outside the United States measures the gross size of the Eurodollar market. For some purposes, it is useful to net part of interbank deposits out of the gross to arrive at an estimate of Eurodollar deposits held by original suppliers to the Eurodollar market. Roughly speaking, to construct the net size measure, deposits owned by banks in the Eurodollar market are netted out. But deposits owned by banks located outside of the Eurodollar market area are not netted out because these banks are considered to be original suppliers of funds to the Eurodollar market. For still other purposes, such as comparing the volume of deposits created in the Eurodollar market with the United States monetary aggregates, it is useful to further net out all bank-owned Eurodollar deposits. Doing so leaves only the nonbank portion of the net size measure, or what might be called the net-net size of the Eurodollar market.

The most readily accessible estimates of the size of the Eurodollar market are compiled by Morgan Guaranty Trust Company of New York and reported in its

---

[3] Bank for International Settlements [1964, p. 127]. In principle, today the definition includes acquisitions of IBFs.

monthly bank letter *World Financial Markets*.[4] Morgan's estimates are based on a liability side measure and include data compiled by the BIS. However, Morgan's estimates are somewhat more comprehensive. Morgan reports estimates of the size of the entire Eurocurrency market based roughly on all foreign-currency liabilities of banks in major European countries, nine other market areas, and United States IBFs.

As of December 1985 Morgan estimated the gross size of the Eurocurrency market at $2,796 billion.[5] The net size was put at $1,668 billion.[6] Morgan also reports that Eurodollars made up 75 percent of gross Eurocurrency liabilities, putting the gross size of the Eurodollar market at $2,097 billion.[7] No net Eurodollar market size is given. However, 75 percent of the net size of the Eurocurrency market yields $1,251 billion as an approximate measure of the net size of the Eurodollar market.

M2 is the narrowest United States monetary aggregate that includes Eurodollar deposits. M2 includes overnight Eurodollar deposits held by United States nonbank non-money market fund residents at branches of Federal Reserve member banks worldwide. As of December 1985, M2 measured $2,567 billion; its Eurodollar component was $17 billion.[8] Eurodollar deposits owned by United States nonbank non-money market fund residents continue to grow, but this comparison shows clearly that such Eurodollar deposits still account for a relatively small portion of United States nonbank non-money market fund resident holdings of monetary assets.

INCENTIVES FOR DEVELOPMENT OF THE EURODOLLAR MARKET[9]

By accepting deposits and making loans denominated in United States dollars outside the United States and in United States IBFs, banks can avoid United States banking regulations. In particular, banks located outside the United

---

[4] See Morgan Guaranty [January 1979, pp. 9-13], for a discussion of Morgan's method of measuring the size of the Eurodollar market. Other informative discussions of issues involved in measuring the Eurodollar market's size are found in Dufey and Giddy [1978, pp. 21-34] and Mayer [1976].

[5] Morgan Guaranty [June/July 1986, p. 11]. Most of the growth of the Eurocurrency market has occurred in the last two decades. For instance, Dufey and Giddy [1978, p. 22] report Morgan's earliest estimate of the gross size of the Eurocurrency market as only $20 billion in 1964. See Dufey and Giddy [1978, Chapter III] for a discussion of the growth of the Eurocurrency market.

[6] Morgan Guaranty [June/July 1986, p. 11].

[7] Ibid.

[8] Board of Governors of the Federal Reserve System [1986, pp. 1, 5]. At present, Eurodollars held by non-United States residents are not included in any of the United States monetary aggregates. As improved data sources become available, the possible inclusion of Eurodollars held by non-United States residents other than banks and official institutions could be reviewed. See Board of Governors of the Federal Reserve System [1980, p. 98].

[9] See Dufey and Giddy [1978, pp. 110-12] for more discussion of the conditions that made large-scale Eurodollar market growth possible.

States and in United States IBFs have no non-interest-bearing reserve requirements against their dollar-denominated deposits. These banks hold balances with United States banks for clearing purposes only. Moreover, there is no required Federal Deposit Insurance Corporation insurance assessment associated with Eurodollar deposits. Virtually no restrictions exist for interest rates payable on Eurodollar deposits or charged on Eurodollar loans, and there are few restrictions on the types of assets allowed in portfolio.

In most Eurodollar financial centers, entry into Eurodollar banking is virtually free of regulatory impediments. In addition, banks intending to do Eurodollar business can set up in locations where tax rates are low. For example, Eurodollar deposits and loans negotiated in London or elsewhere are often booked in locations such as Nassau and the Cayman Islands to obtain more favorable tax treatment. In fact, various states in the United States have amended their tax codes to grant IBFs relief from local taxes.

Foreign monetary authorities are generally reluctant to regulate Eurodollar business because to do so would drive the business away, denying the host country income, tax revenue, and jobs. Even if the United States monetary authorities could induce a group of foreign countries to participate in a plan to regulate their Euromarkets, such a plan would be ineffective unless every country agreed not to host unregulated Eurodollar business. In practice, competition for this business has been fierce, so even if a consensus should develop in the United States to regulate Eurodollar business, it would be extremely difficult to impose regulations on the entire Eurodollar market.

INSTRUMENTS OF THE EURODOLLAR MARKET[10]

The overwhelming majority of money in the Eurodollar market is held in fixed-rate time deposits (TDs). The maturities of Eurodollar TDs range from overnight to several years, although most are from one week to six months. Eurodollar time deposits are intrinsically different from dollar deposits held at banks in the United States only in that the former are liabilities of financial institutions located outside the United States or in United States IBFs. The bulk of Eurodollar time deposits are interbank liabilities. They pay a fixed, competitively determined rate of return.[11]

From their introduction in 1966, the volume of negotiable Eurodollar certificates of deposit (CDs) outstanding reached roughly $50 billion at the beginning

---

[10] Bank for International Settlements [1986, Chapters 1 and 4], Dobbs-Higginson [1980, pp. 55-61], Dufey and Giddy [1978, pp. 228-32], and Stigum [1983, Chapters 15 and 16] contain informative discussions of Eurodollar instruments.

[11] See Stigum [1983, p. 578-80] and Dufey and Giddy [1978, p. 227] for discussions of Eurodollar deposit rate tiering according to perceived issuing bank creditworthiness.

of 1980.[12] By 1985, Eurodollar CD volume was around $100 billion. Essentially, a Eurodollar CD is a negotiable receipt for a dollar deposit at a bank located outside the United States or in a United States IBF.

Recently, fixed-rate three-month Eurodollar CDs have yielded approximately 30 basis points below the three-month time deposit London Interbank Offer Rate (LIBOR).[13] LIBOR is the rate at which major international banks are willing to offer term Eurodollar deposits to each other. An active secondary market allows investors to sell Eurodollar CDs before the deposits mature. Secondary market makers' spreads for short-term fixed-rate CDs have been around 3 basis points.[14]

Eurodollar CDs are issued by banks to "tap" the market for funds. Consequently, they have come to be called Tap CDs. Such Tap CDs are commonly issued in denominations of from $250,000 to $5 million. Some large Eurodollar CD issues are marketed in several portions in order to satisfy investors with preferences for smaller instruments. These are known as Tranche CDs. Tranche CDs are issued in aggregate amounts of $10 million to $30 million and offered by banks to individual investors in $10,000 certificates with each certificate having the same interest rate, issue date, interest payment dates, and maturity.

Since the late 1970s Eurodollar Floating Rate CDs (FRCDs) and Eurodollar Floating Rate Notes (FRNs) have come into use as means of protecting both borrower and lender against interest rate risk. These "floaters" shift the burden of risk from the principal value of the paper to its coupon.

Eurodollar FRCDs and FRNs are both negotiable bearer paper. The coupon or interest rate on these instruments is reset periodically, typically every three or six months, at a small spread above the corresponding LIBOR. Depending on maturity, Eurodollar FRCD yields range from 1/8 percent under the London Interbank Bid Rate (LIBID) up to LIBOR.[15] Eurodollar FRN yields also range from 1/8 percent under LIBID up to LIBOR. To determine LIBOR for Eurodollar FRNs, "the issuer chooses an agent bank who in turn polls three or four Reference Banks—generally, the London offices of major international banks. Rates are those prevailing at 11:00 a.m. London time two business days prior to the commencement of the next coupon period."[16]

Eurodollar FRCDs have been issued in maturities from 1-1/2 to 5 years and are employed as an alternative to short-term money market instruments. Eurodol-

---

[12] Bank of England, Financial Statistics Division, International Banking Group. This data only includes London dollar CDs. But until then, virtually all Eurodollar CDs were issued in London. See *The Economist* [1980, p. 89].

[13] This spread was calculated from data in Salomon Brothers [1986].

[14] Data on interest rate spreads in the Eurodollar market were provided by Robert Smith, First Boston Corporation.

[15] The interbank bid rate is normally 1/8 percent below the interbank offer rate.

[16] Salomon Brothers [1980, p. 7].

lar FRNs have been issued in maturities from 4 to 20 years, with the majority of issues concentrated in the 5- to 7-year range. Eurodollar FRNs tend to be seen as an alternative to straight fixed-interest bonds, but they can in principle be used like FRCDs. Eurodollar FRNs have been issued primarily, but not exclusively, by banks.

A secondary market exists in Eurodollar FRCDs and FRNs. Secondary market makers' spreads for FRCDs are around 5 basis points. The spread quoted on FRNs in the secondary market is generally 10 basis points.

Since 1984, Note Issuance Facilities (NIFs) have become a significant Eurodollar instrument.[17] NIFs are medium-term arrangements between a borrower and a bank, usually 5 to 7 years, under which a borrower can issue short-term paper, usually 3 to 6 months maturity, in its own name. Under this arrangement, underwriting banks are committed either to purchase any notes, known as Euro-notes, which the borrower cannot sell or to provide standby credit at a predetermined spread relative to some reference rate such as LIBOR. Underwriting fees are paid on the full amount of the line of credit, regardless of the amount currently drawn. The fee is 5 basis points for top borrowers and ranges up to 15 basis points for worse credit risks. The notes are generally denominated in United States dollars, with large face amounts of $100,000, $500,000, or more.

Well-regarded borrowers can issue Euro-notes at around LIBID. Top borrowers can issue at yields 1/16 or 1/8 percentage point below LIBID. The latter are comparable investments to Eurodollars CDs.

In 1985, nonbank corporate borrowers accounted for roughly 60 percent of NIFs arranged. Most borrowers were from countries in the Organization of Economic Cooperation and Development. As of April 1986, about $75 billion of NIFs had been arranged, with only an estimated $10 billion to $15 billion having been drawn. Most paper is placed with smaller, non-underwriter, banks. In 1985, about one third or more of placements may have been with nonbank investors, including money market funds, corporations, insurance companies, wealthy individuals, and central banks.

Since mid-1984, some NIFs have been arranged partly or entirely without underwriting commitments. Non-underwritten agreements represented half the total of NIFs arranged in the second half of 1985. Since the middle of 1985, NIFs have become more like United States commercial paper programs. The issuance of notes has been separated from the standby arrangement, notes are issued in shorter odd maturities, and the notes can be marketed quickly. Under this arrangement, the bank is simply a marketing agent. Euro-notes issued under

---

[17] Material on NIFs was taken from Bank for International Settlements [1986, Chapter 1].

such conditions are known as Euro-commercial paper. As of April 1986 about $17 billion of Euro-commercial paper had been issued.

For most United States corporations, the United States commercial paper market probably remains a cheaper source of funds than Euro-commercial paper. Most United States corporate NIFs are maintained for supplementary purposes at present. For some non-United States corporations, however, Euro-commercial paper may be as cheap as U.S commercial paper because of the premium that foreign issuers pay in the United States commercial paper market. The secondary market for Euro-commercial paper is relatively undeveloped compared to the United States commercial paper market. Trading is particularly thin and concentrated in the first few days after notes are issued. The overwhelming majority of notes are apparently held to maturity.

INTEREST RATE RELATIONSHIPS BETWEEN EURODOLLAR DEPOSITS AND DEPOSITS AT BANKS IN THE UNITED STATES

Arbitrage keeps interest rates closely aligned between Eurodollar deposits and deposits with roughly comparable characteristics at banks located in the United States. This is illustrated in Charts 1 and 2. Chart 1 compares yields on Federal funds and overnight Eurodollar deposits. Chart 2 compares yields on Eurodollar CDs and CDs issued by banks located in the United States.[18]

THE RELATIVE RISKINESS OF EURODOLLAR DEPOSITS AND DOLLAR DEPOSITS HELD IN THE UNITED STATES[19]

There are three basic sources of risk associated with holding Eurodollars. The first concerns the chance that authorities where a Eurodollar deposit is held may interfere in the movement or repatriation of interest or principal of the deposit. But this risk factor does not necessarily imply that Eurodollar deposits are riskier than dollar deposits held in the United States. Rather, it can depend on the deposit holder's residence. For United States residents, Eurodollars may appear riskier than domestic deposits because of the possibility that authorities in the foreign country where the deposit is located may interfere in the movement or repatriation of the interest or principal of the deposit. Foreign residents, Iranians for example, may feel that the United States Government is more likely to block their deposits than the British Government. Consequently, they may perceive

---

[18] See Kreicher [1982] for a detailed discussion of Eurodollar arbitrage.
[19] See Dufey and Giddy [1978, pp. 187-90] and Tyson [1980] for more discussion of the riskiness of Eurodollars.

Chart 1

YIELDS ON FEDERAL FUNDS
AND OVERNIGHT EURODOLLAR DEPOSITS

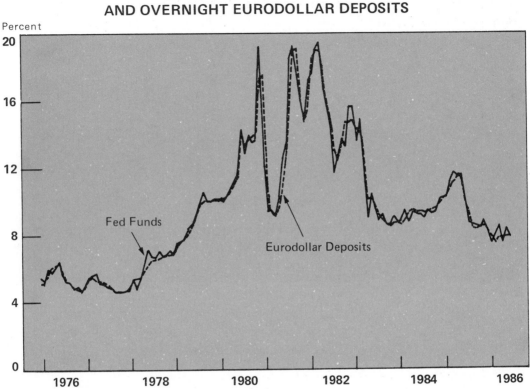

Source: Morgan Guaranty Trust Company of New York, *World Financial Markets.*

greater risk from potential government interference by holding dollar deposits in the United States than by holding Eurodollar deposits in London.

A second element of risk associated with Eurodollars concerns the potential for international jurisdictional legal disputes. For example, uncertainty surrounding interaction between United States and foreign legal systems compounds the difficulty in assessing the likelihood and timing of Eurodollar deposit payment in the event of a Eurodollar issuing bank's failure.

A third type of risk associated with holding Eurodollars concerns the relative soundness per se of foreign banks compared to banks located in the United States. Specifically, it has been argued that Eurodollars are riskier than deposits held in the United States because deposits held in the United States generally carry deposit insurance of some kind while Eurodollar deposits generally do not. In addition, it has been argued that in event of a financial crisis banks located in

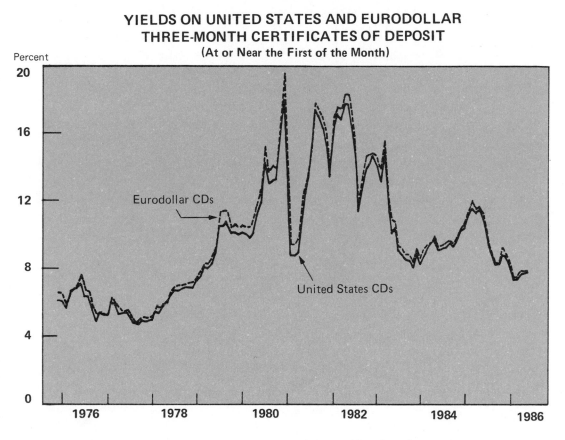

Chart 2

**YIELDS ON UNITED STATES AND EURODOLLAR
THREE-MONTH CERTIFICATES OF DEPOSIT**
(At or Near the First of the Month)

Percent

Eurodollar CDs

United States CDs

1976   1978   1980   1982   1984   1986

Source: Salomon Brothers, *An Analytical Record of Yields and Yield Spreads.*

the United States are more likely to be supported by the Federal Reserve System, whereas neither Federal Reserve support nor the support of foreign central banks for Eurodollar banking activities in their jurisdictions is certain.

A related factor compounding the three basic risk factors identified above is the greater cost of evaluating foreign investments compared with domestic investments. Acquiring information on the soundness of foreign banks is generally more costly than assessing the soundness of more well-known domestic banks. This means that for a given level of expenditure on research, investors must generally accept more ignorance about the soundness of a foreign bank than a domestic bank.

Two comments on this argument are relevant here. First, the fact that it is more costly to evaluate foreign than domestic investments does not imply that Eurodollar deposits are inherently riskier than deposits held in the United States.

61

If a depositor resides in the United States, the argument implies that a given expenditure on research will generally yield more information about the safety of deposits located in the United States than in the Eurodollar market. But if the depositor resides outside the United States, the reverse may be true. Having said this, it must be pointed out that the amount of financial disclosure required by regulatory authorities abroad is generally not as great as in the United States. This fact may make it more difficult to evaluate the soundness of non-United States banks than United States banks for any depositor, regardless of his residence.

Second, to a large extent assessing the safety of Eurodollar deposits relative to deposits in banks located in the United States is made easier by the fact that many banks in the Eurodollar market are affiliated with and bear the name of a bank whose home office is in the United States. For example, a London branch of a United States bank is as closely associated with its home office as a branch located in the United States.

However, in many cases foreign offices bearing the name of a United States bank, usually in a slightly altered form, have been set up as subsidiaries rather than branches. Under most legal systems, a branch cannot fail unless its head office fails; but a subsidiary can fail even if its parent institution remains in business. Technically, a foreign office can bear the name of a United States bank in some form, but the parent institution may not be legally bound to stand fully behind the obligations of its foreign office. This suggests that a foreign office named after a parent United States bank may not be as sound as its namesake, although the parent bank unquestionably has great incentive to aid the foreign office in meeting its obligations in order to preserve confidence in the bank's name.[20]

On the whole, it is difficult to assess the relative riskiness of Eurodollar deposits and dollar deposits held in the United States. Some factors affecting relative risk can be identified, but their importance is difficult to measure. What is more, perceived relative riskiness can depend on the residence of the depositor. The extent to which risk-related factors affect the interest rate relationship between Eurodollar deposits and comparable deposits at banks in the United States remains unclear.

SUMMARY

From the depositor's point of view, Eurodollar deposits including those at United States IBFs are relatively close substitutes for dollar deposits at non-IBF

---

[20] See Mendelsohn [1984] and Stoakes [1985] for discussion of a case where a large United States bank refused to make good deposits of its Philippine branch after they were frozen by Philippine exchange controls. Also see Dufey and Giddy [1984] on this issue.

banks located in the United States. Eurodollar deposits are attractive because they are free of reserve requirements and most other regulatory burdens imposed by United States authorities. In fact, the tremendous growth of the Eurodollar market in the last two decades has largely resulted from efforts to move dollar financial intermediation outside the regulatory jurisdiction of the United States.

Host countries have competed eagerly for Eurodollar business by promising relatively few regulations, low taxes, and other incentives to attract a portion of the Eurodollar banking industry. Even the United States, by introducing IBFs in 1981, has begun competing for Eurodollar business. Financial intermediation in United States dollars is likely to continue to move abroad or to IBFs as long as incentives exist for it to do so. Since these incentives are not likely to disappear soon, the Eurodollar market's share of world dollar financial intermediation is likely to continue growing.

References

Ashby, David F. V. "Challenge from the New Euro-Centres." *The Banker*, January 1978, pp. 53-61.

"Changing Patterns in the $800 Billion Super-Dollar Market." *The Banker*, March 1979, pp. 21-23.

Bank of England, Personal correspondence, Financial Statistics Division, International Banking Group, April 28, 1980.

Bank for International Settlements. *1964 Annual Report.* Basle, Switzerland.

Bank for International Settlements. *Recent Innovations in International Banking.* Basle, Switzerland, April 1986.

Board of Governors of the Federal Reserve System. *Federal Reserve Bulletin* (February 1980).

———. H.6 statistical release, "Money Stock Measures and Liquid Assets." September 11, 1986.

Credit Suisse First Boston Limited. "A Description of the London Dollar Negotiable Certificate of Deposit Market." January 1980.

Dobbs-Higginson, M.S. *Investment Manual for Fixed Income Securities in the International and Major Domestic Capital Markets.* London: Credit Suisse First Boston Limited, 1980.

Dufey, Gunter and Ian H. Giddy. "Eurocurrency Deposit Risk." *Journal of Banking and Finance* 8 (December 1984), pp. 567-89.

———. *The International Money Market.* Englewood Cliffs, New Jersey: Prentice-Hall, 1978.

Key, Sydney J. "International Banking Facilities." *Federal Reserve Bulletin* (October 1982), pp. 565-77.

Kreicher, Lawrence. "Eurodollar Arbitrage." Federal Reserve Bank of New York, *Quarterly Review* (Summer 1982), pp. 10-21.

Lichtenstein, Cynthia C. "United States Banks and the Eurocurrency Markets: The Regulatory Structure." *The Banking Law Journal* 99 (June/July 1982), pp. 484-511.

"The London Dollar Certificate of Deposit." *Bank of England Quarterly Bulletin* 13 (December 1973), pp. 446-52.

Mayer, Helmut W. "The BIS Concept of the Eurocurrency Market." *Euromoney*, May 1976, pp. 60-66.

Mendelsohn, M.S. "Wells Suit Revives Jurisdiction Issue." *American Banker*, March 2, 1984, p. 18 +.

Morgan Guaranty Trust Company of New York. *World Financial Markets*. Various issues.

"Out-of-Towners." *The Economist*, July 12, 1980, p. 89.

Salomon Brothers. *An Analytical Record of Yields and Yield Spreads*. New York: Salomon Brothers, 1986.

————. *Eurodollar Floating Rate Notes: A Guide to the Market*. New York: Salomon Brothers, 1980.

Stigum, Marcia. *The Money Market: Myth, Reality, and Practice*. Homewood, Illinois: Dow Jones-Irwin, 1983.

Stoakes, Christopher. "Eurodollar Deposits on Trial." *Euromoney*, August 1985, p. 25.

Terrell, Henry S., and Rodney H. Mills. "International Banking Facilities and the Eurodollar Market." Staff Study 124. Washington: Board of Governors of the Federal Reserve System, August 1983.

Tyson, David O. "Fund Managers Wary of Risks in Non-Domestic CDs." *The Money Manager*, July 14, 1980, pp. 3-4.

6

REPURCHASE AND REVERSE REPURCHASE AGREEMENTS

Stephen A. Lumpkin

Recent years have witnessed a considerable growth in the market for repurchase agreements (RPs), both in terms of daily activity and in the numbers and types of participants in the market. Many years ago RPs, or "repos" as they are frequently called, were used primarily by large commercial banks and government securities dealers as an alternative means of financing their inventories of government securities, but their use has expanded substantially in recent years. RPs are now used regularly by a variety of institutional investors in addition to banks and dealers, and the Federal Reserve Bank of New York (FRBNY) uses repo transactions to implement monetary policy directives and to make investments for foreign official and monetary authorities. This chapter describes RPs and their principal uses and discusses the factors influencing the growth and development of the RP market over the past few years.

INTRODUCTION

A standard repurchase agreement involves the acquisition of immediately available funds through the sale of securities with a simultaneous commitment to repurchase the same securities on a date certain within one year at a specified price, which includes interest or its equivalent at an agreed upon rate.[1] Repo transactions have many characteristics of secured lending arrangements in which the underlying securities serve as collateral. Under this characterization, the sale of securities under an agreement to repurchase is a type of collateralized borrowing and represents a liability to the "seller" at the purchase price, reflecting the contractual obligation to transfer funds to the "buyer" on the final maturity date of the agreement.

A reverse RP (technically a matched sale-purchase agreement) is the mirror image of an RP. In a reverse repo, securities are acquired with a simultaneous

---

[1] Immediately available funds include deposits in Federal Reserve Banks and certain collected liabilities of commercial banks that may be transferred or withdrawn on a same-day basis.

commitment to resell. Because each party to the transaction has the opposiste perspective, the terms repo and reverse repo can be applied to the same transaction. A given transaction is a repo when viewed from the point of view of the supplier of the securities (the party acquiring funds) and a reverse repo when described from the point of view of the supplier of funds.[2] In general, whether an agreement is termed a repo or a reverse repo depends largely on which party initiated the transaction, but an RP transaction between a dealer and a retail customer usually is described from the dealer's point of view. Thus, a retail investor's purchase of securities and commitment to resell to a dealer is termed a repo, because the dealer has sold the securities under an agreement to repurchase.

There is no central physical marketplace in which RPs are negotiated. Rather, transactions are arranged over-the-counter by telephone, either by direct contact or through a group of market specialists (dealers or repo brokers). The securities most frequently involved in repo transactions are U.S. Treasury and federal agency securities, but repos are also arranged using mortgage-backed securities and various money market instruments, including negotiable bank certificates of deposit, prime bankers acceptances and commercial paper. If executed properly, an RP agreement is a low-risk, flexible, short-term investment vehicle adaptable to a wide range of uses. For instance, dealers use repo and reverse repo transactions not only to finance the securities held in their investment and trading accounts, but also to establish short positions, implement arbitrage activities, and acquire securities for their own purposes or to meet specific customer needs.[3] Investors in the repo market, such as nonfinancial corporations, thrift institutions, state and local government authorities, and pension funds, in turn, are provided with a low cost investment alternative which offers combinations of yields, liquidity, and collateral flexibility not available through outright purchases of the underlying securities.

The key features of RP agreements are described in the following section. Subsequent sections explain the pricing of RP contracts and discuss the various procedures for transferring the different types of collateral between the repo counterparties.

---

[2] For some participants, notably thrift institutions and Federal Reserve, the terminology is reversed. That is, the Federal Reserve arranges RPs when it wants to inject reserves (supply funds) temporarily.

[3] A dealer establishes a short position by selling a security he does not have in his inventory. To make delivery of the securities the dealer either borrows them or reverses them in.

CHARACTERISTICS OF RP AGREEMENTS

In most RP agreements, the purchaser of the repo securities acquires title to the securities for the term of the agreement and thus may use them to arrange another RP agreement, may sell them outright, or may deliver them to another party to fulfill a delivery commitment on a forward or futures contract, a short sale, or a maturing reverse RP. This feature makes RPs particularly useful for securities dealers, who use repos and reverses to implement a wide variety of trading and arbitrage strategies. As suggested previously, a wide range of other institutional participants also derive benefits from the RP market. The principal use of repos by these investors is the short-term investment of surplus cash either for their own accounts or on behalf of others in their fiduciary capacities or as agent. The various yields and maturities offered in RP transactions make them well-suited for this purpose.

Maturities   RP agreements usually are arranged with short terms to maturity. Most RPs in Treasury securities, for example, are overnight transactions. In addition to overnight contracts, longer-term repos are arranged for standard maturities of one, two, and three weeks, and one, two, three, and six months. Other fixed-term multi-day contracts ("term repos") are negotiated occasionally and repos also may be arranged on an "open" or continuing basis. Continuing contracts in essence are a series of overnight repos in that they are renewed each day with the repo rate adjusted to reflect prevailing market conditions. These agreements usually may be terminated on demand by either party.

Yields   In some RP agreements, the agreed upon repurchase price is set above the initial sale price with the difference between the two reflecting the interest expense incurred by the borrower. It is more typical, however, for the repurchase price to be set equal to the initial sale price plus a negotiated rate of interest to be paid on the settlement date by the borrower. Repo interest rates are straight add-on rates calculated using a 360-day "basis" year. The dollar amount of interest earned on funds invested in RPs is determined as follows:

$$\text{Interest earned} = \frac{\text{Dollar amount}}{\text{invested}} \times \frac{\text{Repo}}{\text{rate}} \times \frac{\text{Number of days to maturity}}{360}$$

For example, a $25 million overnight RP investment at a 6-3/4 percent rate would yield an interest return of $4,687.50:

$$(\$25,000,000 \times .0675)/360 \times 1 = \$4,687.50$$

Suppose instead, that the funds were invested in a 10-day term agreement at the same rate of 6-3/4 percent. In this case, the investor's earnings would be $46,875.00:

$$(\$25,000,000 \times .0675)/360 \times 10 = \$46,875.00$$

As a final example, suppose that the investor chose to enter into a continuing contract with the borrower at an initial rate of 6-3/4 percent, but withdrew from the arrangement after a period of five days.

First day:	($25,000,000 x .0675)/360	x 1 = $4,687.50
Second day:	($25,000,000 x .07)/360	x 1 = $4,861.11
Third day:	($25,000,000 x .065)/360	x 1 = $4,513.89
Fourth day:	($25,000,000 x .06375)/360	x 1 = $4,427.08
Fifth day:	($25,000,000 x .0625)/360	x 1 = $4,340.28
Total interest earned:		$22,829.86

If the investor had entered into a term agreement for the same period at the rate of 6-3/4 percent prevailing on the first day, he would have earned $23,437.50 in interest. Thus, in this hypothetical example, the movement in rates worked to the advantage of the borrower.

The purchaser of securities in a repo transaction earns only the agreed upon rate of return. If a coupon payment is made on the underlying securities during the term of the agreement, the purchaser in most cases must account to the seller for the amount of the payment. Securities in registered definitive form generally are left registered in the seller's name so that any coupon payments made during the repo term may be received directly.

Principal Amounts RP transactions are usually arranged in large dollar amounts. Overnight contracts and term repos with maturities of a week or less are often arranged in amounts of $25 million or more, and blocks of $10 million are common for longer maturity term agreements. Although a few repos are negotiated for amounts under $100,000, the smallest customary amount is $1 million.

Valuation of Collateral Typically, the securities used as collateral in repo transactions are valued at current market price plus accrued interest (on coupon-bearing securities) calculated to the maturity date of the agreement less a margin or "haircut" for term RPs.[4] Technically, the haircut may protect either the lender or the borrower depending upon how the transaction is priced. In the usual case, the initial RP purchase price is set lower than the current market value of the collateral (principal plus accrued interest), which reduces the lender's exposure

---

[4] The failure of Drysdale Government Securities in May 1982 and Lombard-Wall in August 1982 uncovered weaknesses in the pricing of RPs. RPs are now priced with accrued interest included in full in the purchase price, but prior to adoption of full accrual pricing in October 1982, it was common for RPs to be priced without accrued interest.

to market risk. A dealer arranging a reverse RP with a nondealer customer frequently takes margin, which covers his exposure on the funds transferred.

In principle, the dollar amount of the haircut should be sufficient to guard against the potential loss from an adverse price movement during the repo term. The sizes of haircuts taken in practice usually vary depending on the term of the RP contract, type of securities involved, and the coupon rate of the underlying securities. For example, discount bonds are more price volatile than premium bonds and thus are given larger haircuts. Similarly, haircuts taken on private money market instruments generally exceed those of comparable-maturity Treasury securities, due to an additional credit risk-induced component of price volatility. In general, haircuts are larger the longer the term to maturity of the repo securities, and larger haircuts are common for less liquid securities as well. Currently, market risk haircuts range from about one to five percent, but may be as low as 1/8 of a point for very short-term securities.

Because both parties in a term repo arrangement are exposed to the risk of adverse fluctuations in the market value of the underlying securities due to changes in interest rates, it is common practice to have the collateral value of the underlying securities adjusted daily ("marked to market") to reflect changes in market prices and to maintain the agreed upon margin. Accordingly, if the market value of the repo securities declines appreciably, the borrower may be asked to provide additional collateral to cover the loan. However, if the market value of the collateral rises substantially, the lender may be required to return the excess collateral to the borrower.

Special Repo Arrangements   The bulk of the activity in the RP market involves standard overnight transactions in Treasury and agency securities, usually negotiated between a dealer and its regular customers. Although standard overnight and term RP arrangements are most prevalent, dealers sometimes alter various provisions of these contracts in order to accommodate specific needs of their customers. Other arrangements are intended to give the dealer flexibility in the designation of collateral, particularly in longer-term agreements. For example, some contracts are negotiated to permit substitution of the securities subject to the repurchase commitment. In a "dollar repo," for instance, the initial seller's commitment is to repurchase securities that are similar to, but not necessarily the same as, the securities originally sold. There are a number of common variants. In a "fixed-coupon repo," the seller agrees to repurchase securities that have the same coupon rate as those sold in the first half of the repo transaction. A "yield maintenance agreement" is a slightly different variant in which the seller agrees to repurchase securities that provide roughly the same overall return as the securities originally sold. In each case, the maturity of the repurchased securities must be within an agreed upon range, but may be only approximately the same as that of the original securities. These agreements are frequently arranged so that the purchaser of the securities receives the final principal payment from the issuer of the securities.

In other repo arrangements, the repo counterparties negotiate flexible terms to maturity. A common example of this type of contract is the repo to maturity (or reverse to maturity for the lender of funds). In a repo to maturity, the initial seller's repurchase commitment in effect is eliminated altogether, because the purchaser agrees to hold the repo securities until they mature. The seller's repurchase commitment depends on the manner in which the final principal payment on the underlying securities is handled. When the purchaser of the repo securities receives the final principal payment directly from the issuer of the securities, he usually retains it and nets it against the seller's repurchase obligation. However, if the seller of the repo securities receives the principal payment, he must pay the purchaser the full amount of the agreed upon repurchase price when the repo is unwound.

Reverses to maturity often involve coupon securities trading at a discount from the price at which the "seller" initially purchased them. Typically, reverses to maturity are initiated by an investor who is reluctant to sell the securities outright, because an outright sale would require taking a capital loss on the securities. A reverse to maturity enables the investor to acquire funds to invest in higher yielding securities without having to sell outright and realize a capital loss. The dealer participating in the transaction usually takes margin on the securities "purchased".

Another example of a flexible-term repo is the so-called "flex repo." Flex repos are arranged between a dealer and a major customer, typically a municipality or similar authority. In a flex repo the customer places funds with a dealer in a collateralized arrangement. Often, the funds are intended for use in financing construction or a similar project to be completed in phases. Flex repos are similar to deposit accounts in that the investor merely "withdraws" the needed amount from the repo arrangement when the funds are required for a part of the project. The balance is automatically recommitted to the repo. These agreements usually are collateralized by government-issued or government-backed securities.

PARTICIPANTS IN THE RP MARKET

The favorable financing rates and variety of terms and collateral arrangements available have led government securities dealers to expand their use of repos in recent years. Many years ago, dealers relied primarily on collateralized loans from their clearing banks ("box loans") to meet their financing needs, but RPs and reverse RPs are now their principal sources of financing. Major dealers and large money center banks in particular finance the bulk of their holdings of Treasury and agency securities by RP transactions. Most of these transactions are arranged on a short-term basis (i.e., overnight or continuing contracts) via direct contact with major customers, typically banks, public entities, pension funds, money market mutual funds, and other institutional investors. The Federal Reserve Bank of New York also arranges repos and reverse repos with dealers to implement monetary policy directives and to make investments for foreign central banks and other official accounts.

Early each morning, a dealer's financing desk arranges repo financing for expected changes in the firm's securities inventory ("long position") and for replacement of maturing RPs, and also arranges reverse RPs to cover known or planned short sales or to meet specific customer needs.[5] The bulk of these arrangements are finalized by 10:00 a.m. ET.

Dealers use reverse RPs to establish or cover short positions and to obtain specific issues for redelivery to customers. Major suppliers of securities to the market include large commercial banks, thrifts, and other financial institutions. Nonfinancial corporations and municipalities also supply collateral to this market. A dealer "reverses in" securities, in effect, by buying them from the holder under an agreement to resell; the term of the agreement usually ranges from a week to a month, but may also run for the remaining term to maturity of the securities (reverse to maturity). The use of reverse repos to cover short positions is similar to securities borrowing arrangements in which the dealer obtains securities in exchange for funds, other securities, or a letter of credit. However, reversing in securities typically is cheaper than borrowing the securities outright and also gives the dealer greater flexibility in his use of the securities. For instance, reverse RPs are arranged for fixed time commitments, but borrowing arrangements usually may be terminated on a day's notice at the option of the lender.

If a dealer has exhausted its regular customer sources but is still in need of funds or specific collateral, it may contact a repo broker. Dealers use repo brokers most often for term RP agreements and in arranging reverse RPs. The repo brokers market is particularly important for obtaining popular issues in short supply ("on special"). Although the use of bank loans as a source of financing has declined considerably, a dealer still may obtain financing from its clearing bank in the form of an overnight box loan if it has a negative balance in its cash account

---

[5] A short sale is the sale of securities not currently owned, usually under the expectation that the market price of the securities will fall before the termination date of the transaction. The seller later purchases the securities at a lower price to cover his short position and earns an arbitrage profit.

at the end of the day.[6] The rate the clearing bank charges is generally 1/8 to 1/4 of a point or more above the Federal funds rate, with slightly higher rates charged for loans arranged late in the day, so dealers acquire box loans only as a last resort. A dealer who is unable to obtain adequate financing using his own customer base, or has an unexpected receipt of securities late in the day, may choose to obtain a "position" loan from another bank rather than a box loan from his own clearing bank. Position loans are often available at more favorable rates than available on box loans. In these circumstances, the lender frequently wires the dealer's clearing bank the amount of the loan. The clearing bank, in turn, segregates the required amount of the dealer's securities as collateral for the loan and acts as custodian for the lender.

In addition to using repos and reverse repos to finance their long and short positions, dealers also use RP agreements in transactions in which they act as intermediaries between suppliers and demanders of funds in the repo market. A dealer acts as principal on each side of the arrangement, borrowing funds from one party (against the sale of securities) and relending the funds to another party (against the receipt of securities). The combination of repo and reverse repo transactions in this fashion is termed a "repo book." A repo book in which an RP and a reverse RP in the same security have equal terms to maturity is referred to as a "matched book." Larger, better capitalized dealers are able to borrow in the RP market at more favorable rates than smaller dealers and non-dealer customers, and thus can profit through arbitrage in matched transactions. Dealers also may profit from a differential in the margin taken on the underlying collateral in the two transactions.

At times, a dealer may choose not to match the maturities of the repo and reverse repo agreements in an effort to increase profits. For example, if interest rates are expected to rise during the term of the agreement, the dealer may arrange an RP with a longer term than the reverse RP in order to "lock in" the more favorable borrowing rates. Conversely, in a declining rate environment, a longer-term reverse RP may be financed through a number of shorter-term RPs arranged at successively lower rates.

Many types of institutional investors derive benefits from RP and reverse RP transactions with dealers, including nonfinancial corporations, state and local government authorities and other public bodies, banks, and thrift institutions. Repos are adaptable to many uses and RP maturities can be tailored precisely to meet the needs of lenders. This enables corporations and municipalities with

---

[6] Securities received by a clearing bank on behalf of a dealer customer generally are delivered first into a central clearing account known as the "box." Any securities that have not been allocated to other uses by the dealer, and have not been financed through other means, may be used to collateralize an overnight loan (box loan) from the clearing bank.

temporary surplus cash balances to earn market rates of return on a timely basis but have their funds available when needed. Thus, in effect, RP agreements convert cash balances into interest-bearing liquid assets. In this fashion, RPs are more attractive investments than alternative money market instruments which do not offer the same combination of liquidity, flexibility, and ease of negotiation. Newly issued negotiable CDs, for example, must have a minimum maturity of at least 14 days and commercial paper is seldom written with maturities as short as a day.

Repos are also attractive investments for investors subject to restrictions on the types of assets in which they may invest. Many public bodies, for example, are required by law to invest their tax receipts and proceeds from note and bond sales in Treasury or federal agency issues until the funds are to be spent. As opposed to buying the securities outright, these entities often invest in repos collateralized by government securities and record the ownership of the securities rather than the repos on their books.

The Federal Reserve also is a major participant in the repo market. When the Manager of the System Open Market Account needs to inject reserves in the banking system overnight or for a few days, the Domestic Trading Desk of the FRBNY arranges RPs with primary dealers in government securities.[7] These agreements are arranged for specified periods of up to 15 days and are collateralized by Treasury and agency securities. Investments on behalf of foreign official and international accounts also involve RPs, either arranged in the market or internally with the System's Account. When the Manager wants to absorb reserves for a few days, the Desk arranges matched sale-purchase transactions with primary dealers, in which specific securities are sold from the System's portfolio for immediate delivery and simultaneously repurchased for settlement on the desired date.

GROWTH AND DEVELOPMENT OF THE RP MARKET

It is difficult to ascertain when the repurchase agreement originated. Some suggest that RPs date back to the 1920s, about the time that the Federal funds market evolved. Other sources state that the use of RPs was initiated by government securities dealers after World War II as a means of financing their positions. There is general agreement, however, that for many years RPs were used almost exclusively by government securities dealers and large money

---

[7] Primary dealers are a group of dealers who have met eligibility criteria established by the Federal Reserve Bank of New York (FRBNY). To be on the FRBNY's primary dealer list, a firm is expected to make markets in the full range of Treasury and agency issues under "good" and "bad" market conditions for a diverse group of nondealer customers, and to maintain certain minimum capital levels. The FRBNY selects appropriate counterparties from this list when it conducts open market operations.

Table I

**ANNUAL AVERAGES OF OUTSTANDING
REPURCHASE AND REVERSE REPURCHASE
AGREEMENTS BY CATEGORY OF PRIMARY
DEALER[1]**

(Millions of Dollars)

Year	Bank Dealers	Nonbank Dealers	Total
1981	19,173	92,565	111,738
1982	22,337	147,890	170,227
1983	24,812	159,319	184,131
1984	26,706	218,282	244,988
1985	34,453	286,365	320,818

[1] Figures are obtained from reports submitted weekly to the Federal Reserve Bank of New York by the U.S. government securities dealers on its published list of primary dealers. Figures include matched agreements.

center banks. Since the late 1960s, however, the number and types of participants in the RP market has grown considerably.

A number of factors have influenced the growth and development of the RP market over this period, including changes in the regulatory environment, inflation, growth in federal debt outstanding, and increased interest rate volatility. The higher levels and greater volatility of interest rates since the 1960s have been particularly important in that they have raised the opportunity cost of holding idle cash balances in demand deposit accounts, on which the explicit payment of interest is prohibited, and have led to an expanded use of active cash management techniques. This has been accompanied by important innovations in telecommunications and computer technology, which have contributed to the development of sophisticated cash management systems for managing and transferring large volumes of funds. As a consequence, a variety of financial institutions, nonfinancial corporations, pension funds, mutual funds, public bodies, and other institutional investors have joined securities dealers and money center banks as active participants in the RP market.

As a result of this growth, the RP market is now considered to be one of the largest and most liquid markets in the world. Although total daily activity in the RP market is not known, as most agreements are negotiated directly between counterparties over the telephone, an indication of the growth in the market over recent years can be seen in the use of RPs and reverse RPs by primary dealers. As shown in Table I, on an annual average basis, repo financing by major dealers

Table II

ANNUAL AVERAGES OF OUTSTANDING MATCHED REPURCHASE AND REVERSE REPURCHASE AGREEMENTS OF PRIMARY DEALERS[1]

(Millions of Dollars)

Year	Bank Dealers	Nonbank Dealers	Total
1981	6,167	51,177	57,344
1982	7,534	88,315	95,849
1983	6,839	84,523	91,362
1984	7,207	121,938	129,145
1985	9,118	152,914	162,032

[1] Figures are obtained from reports submitted weekly to the Federal Reserve Bank of New York by the U.S. government securities dealers on its published list of primary dealers. Figures include repurchase agreements, duebills, and collateralized loans used to finance reverse repurchase agreements, and vice versa.

has nearly tripled since 1981. The same is true for the use of matched book transactions (Table II), which account for about half of all repo transactions. In fact, for some nonbank dealers matched book transactions account for as much as 90 percent of overall repo activity. Bank dealers are subject to capital requirements imposed by bank regulators, which raise the cost of using these transactions relative to alternative investments; thus, they have not participated as much in the use of matched RP agreements.

The rapid growth and development of the RP market over recent years has not occurred without incident. In particular, the failures of a few unregistered non-primary government securities dealers has had a significant effect on the operation of the market. These failures generally had some common characteristics, including the use of pricing techniques which ignored accrued interest in computing the value of repoed securities, and the fraudulent use of customers' collateral. The failures resulted in considerable uncertainty regarding the legal status of repos and the contractual rights of the counterparties when one of them files for protection under federal bankruptcy laws.

Repurchase agreements have never been defined in a strict legal sense either as collateralized loans or as outright purchases and sales of securities. Under recent court rulings involving the bankruptcy proceedings of Bevill, Bresler, and Schulman, Inc., the court has determined that the appropriate characterization of a repo for legal purposes depends upon the manner in which the transaction was arranged. For instance, if the repo counterparties arranged the transaction as a consummated sale and contract to repurchase, then the court would adopt the same characterization in the event of a default and subsequent bankruptcy of one party.

Market participants have long operated under the assumption that the purchaser of repo securities is entitled to liquidate them if the seller is unable to fulfill the terms of the agreement at settlement, but the validity of this assumption relies importantly on the court's interpretation. For instance, in September 1982, in the bankruptcy proceedings involving Lombard-Wall, Inc., Federal Bankruptcy Judge Edward J. Ryan ruled that certain repos involved in that case were to be considered secured loan transactions for purposes of the proceedings.[8] As a consequence, under the existing law, RPs became subject to the "automatic stay" provisions of the Bankruptcy Code. The automatic stay provisions block any efforts of a creditor to make collections or to enforce a lien against the property of a bankrupt estate. Consequently, Lombard-Wall's repo counterparties could neither use the funds obtained nor sell the underlying repo securities without the court's permission, because to do so would constitute the enforcement of a lien and thus would violate the automatic stay provision.

As a result of the developments in the Lombard-Wall case, the perceived risks of lending in the RP market were raised, resulting in a contraction in the volume of repo transactions entered into by non-dealer entities, including mutual funds and state and local government authorities. With the reduction in a major source of repo funds, the financing costs for some non-primary dealers rose, as other participants regarded them as higher credit risks. At the same time, RP rates paid by some well-capitalized firms declined somewhat. Similar movements in repo financing rates have occurred in the wake of failures of other government securities dealers, including the recent failures of E.S.M. Government Securities, Inc. and Bevill, Bresler, and Schulman Asset Management Corp. in 1985.

In response to the repurchase agreement issue, Congress, in June 1984, enacted the Bankruptcy Amendments Act of 1984, which amended title 11 of the U.S. Code covering bankruptcy. The legislation exempts repurchase agreements in Treasury and agency securities, certain CDs, and bankers acceptances from the automatic stay provision of the Bankruptcy Code. Although the legislation does not resolve the question of whether an RP agreement is a secured lending arrangement or a purchase and sale transaction, it enables lenders to liquidate

---

[3] Lombard-Wall failed in August 1982 when it was unable to return funds it had obtained in overvalued long-term RPs. The failure of Lombard-Wall occurred shortly after the collapse of Drysdale Government Securities, Inc. Drysdale failed in May 1982 when it was unable to make payments on accrued interest on securities it had acquired under RP agreements and could not return the securities it had obtained through over-collateralized reverse RPs.

the underlying securities under either interpretation and resolves a major question about the status of RP collateral in bankruptcy proceedings.[9]

With the encouragement of the Federal Reserve Bank of New York (FRBNY), primary dealers began to include the value of accrued interest in the pricing of RPs and related transactions in October 1982. At that time, the FRBNY also recommended that dealers follow uniform procedures in establishing repo contract value for purposes of maintaining margin. These actions helped to correct certain inadequacies in standard repo pricing practices.

However, recent dealer failures have demonstrated that proper pricing of repo transactions alone is insufficient to ensure the safety of a repo investment. Investors must also concern themselves with the creditworthiness of their repo counterparties. For instance, many of the investors dealing with E.S.M. and Bevill, Bresler, and Schulman lost their money because they did not protect their ownership interest in the repo securities pledged to them as collateral. Investors can best establish their ownership claim to repo securities by taking delivery of the securities, either directly or through a clearing bank-custodian.

REPO COLLATERAL ARRANGEMENTS

As mentioned previously, most RPs involve Treasury and federal agency securities, the bulk of which are maintained in book-entry form. Usually, when an RP is arranged, the underlying securities are transferred against payment over the Federal Reserve's securities wire ("Fedwire") to the lender/purchaser, resulting in a simultaneous transfer of funds to the borrower. At maturity, the RP collateral is returned over the wire against payment and the transfers are reversed. Direct access to the Federal Reserve's securities and payments transfer systems is restricted, so transfers of the repo securities usually are processed by means of Reserve Bank credits and debits to the securities and clearing accounts of depository institutions acting as clearing agents for their customers. Transfers of physical securities also frequently involve clearing agents.

The transaction costs associated with the payment and delivery of repo securities include some combination of securities clearance fees, wire transfer charges for securities in book-entry form, custodial fees, and account maintenance fees. The exact charges can vary considerably from case to case depending on the type of securities involved and the actual method of delivery. For example, Fedwire charges for securities transfers are higher for off-line originations than for transfers initiated on-line, and the fees for transfers of agency

---

[9] Note that the automatic stay provision is irrelevant if an RP is considered to be an outright purchase and sale of securities.

securities are slightly higher than those for Treasury securities. In any event, the total transaction costs to process transfers of securities from the seller/borrower to the buyer/lender are higher the greater the number of intermediate transactions. Although these costs are often inconsequential for longer-maturity transactions in large dollar amounts, they may add significantly to the overall costs of others. As a result, a number of repo collateral arrangements have been developed that do not involve the actual delivery of collateral to the lender. Not surprisingly, the rates available to investors in such nondelivery repos are higher than rates offered on standard two-party RPs with collateral delivery. Of course, the risks may be greater as well.

At one end of the spectrum of nondelivery repos is the "duebill" or letter repo. A duebill in essence is an unsecured loan similar in form to commercial paper; the borrower merely sends a transaction confirmation to the lender. Although specific securities might be named as collateral, the lender does not have control of the securities. Thus, the lender relies for the most part on the integrity and creditworthiness of the borrower. Duebills are used primarily in overnight arrangements that involve small par amounts of non-wireable securities.

A similar arrangement is the "hold-in-custody" repo in which the borrower retains possession of the repo securities but either transfers them internally to a customer account or delivers them to a bulk segregation account at its clearing bank; the securities are left in the dealer's name and not that of the individual customers. The extent to which the investor's ownership interest in the pledged securities is protected depends on the type of custody arrangement. If the borrower acts as both custodian and principal in the transaction, the investor relies on the borrower's integrity and creditworthiness.[10]

A lender can protect his ownership claim to repo securities by using "safekeeping" arrangements involving a clearing bank-custodian acting solely in its behalf or jointly as agent for both repo counterparties. The most popular of these arrangements is the "tri-party repo" in which a custodian, typically the borrower's clearing bank, becomes a direct participant in the repo transaction with the borrower and lender. The clearer-custodian ensures that exchanges of collateral and funds occur simultaneously and that appropriate operational controls are in place to safeguard the investor's ownership interest in the underlying collateral during the term of the agreement. When the repo is unwound at maturity, the clearer makes an entry in its internal records transferring the securities from the segregation account to the borrower's clearing account and wires the loan repayment to the lender.

---

[10] Under the Uniform Commercial Code, an investor can establish an ownership interest in securities it has left with a dealer for a period of up to 21 days if it obtains a proper written agreement and "gives value" for the securities.

The rates available to investors in tri-party repos are lower than those available on nonsegregated RPs without collateral delivery, but higher than the rates offered on standard two-party RPs with delivery. Thus, safekeeping arrangements of this type are attractive both to investors, who earn a higher risk-adjusted return than available on standard RPs, and to borrowers, whose total financing costs are lowered through the avoidance of clearance costs and wire transfer fees.

DETERMINANTS OF RP RATES

The interest rate paid on RP funds, the repo rate of return, is negotiated by the repo counterparties and is set independently of the coupon rate or rates on the underlying securities. In addition to factors related to the terms and conditions of individual repo arrangements, repo interest rates are influenced by overall money market conditions, the competitive rates paid for comparable funds, and the availability of eligible collateral. As mentioned previously, changes in the perceived risks associated with RP investments also affect the level of RP rates and the spreads between RP rates and comparable money market rates.

Because repurchase agreements are close substitutes for Federal funds borrowings, overnight RP rates to a large extent are determined by conditions in the market for reserve balances and thus are closely tied to the Federal funds rate. For example, when the demand for reserves is high relative to the existing supply, depository institutions bid more aggressively for Federal funds, thereby putting upward pressure on the Federal funds rate. As the funds rate rises, some institutions will enter into repurchase agreements, which also puts upward pressure on the RP rate. Both rates will continue to rise until the demand and supply for reserves in the banking system is again in balance.[11] Federal Reserve policy actions have a major influence on overnight financing rates through their effect on the supply of reserves via open market operations and discount window policy.

Repo rates for overnight RPs in Treasury securities usually lie about 25 to 30 basis points below the Federal funds rate. Properly executed RP agreements are less risky than sales of Federal funds because they are fully backed by high-quality collateral. Thus, the rate spread generally reflects a risk premium paid to compensate investors for lending unsecured in the Federal funds market rather than investing in a collateralized RP agreement. The spread between the Federal funds rate and RP rate has narrowed when the perceived risks associ-

---

[11] See Garbade [1982, Chapter 5].

ated with RP investments have increased, e.g., when the legal status of the repo securities backing an RP agreement has come under question.

The spread between the funds rate and the RP rate can also depend on the supply of collateral held by government securities dealers. Dealers reduce their demand for RP financing when the dollar volume of securities they hold in their investment and trading accounts is low.[12] Other things the same, this also puts downward pressure on the RP rate relative to the Federal funds rate. Conversely, the RP rate rises, and the rate spread narrows, when the volume of securities to be financed is high relative to the availability of overnight financing. This sometimes occurs after Treasury mid-quarter refundings, particularly when the new issues are not well distributed to investors.

References

Garbade, Kenneth D. *Securities Markets*. New York: McGraw-Hill, 1982.

Lucas, Charles, Marcos Jones, and Thomas Thurston. "Federal Funds and Repurchase Agreements." *Quarterly Review*, Federal Reserve Bank of New York (Summer 1977), pp. 33-48.

Simpson, Thomas D. "The Market for Federal Funds and Repurchase Agreements." Staff Studies 106. Washington, D.C.: Board of Governors of the Federal Reserve System, 1979.

Smith, Wayne J. "Repurchase Agreements and Federal Funds." *Federal Reserve Bulletin* (May 1978), pp. 353-60.

Stigum, Marcia. *The Money Market: Myth, Reality, and Practice*. Rev. ed. Homewood: Dow Jones-Irwin, 1983

---

[12] This sometimes occurs after major tax payments when incoming tax receipts exceed the capacity of Treasury Tax and Loan (TT&L) accounts at commercial banks and are transferred to the Treasury's account at Federal Reserve Banks. Because the transfer of funds from the public to the Federal Reserve (Fed) drains reserves from the banking system, the Fed often arranges RPs to inject reserves to offset the effect of the movement. These RPs must be collateralized, of course, and funds held in TT&L accounts also must be collateralized. Both actions tend to remove a large quantity of eligible collateral from the market.

7

TREASURY BILLS

Timothy Q. Cook

Treasury bills are short-term obligations of the United States Government. Bills are generally considered to be totally free of default risk and are the most marketable of all money market instruments. They are held by a wide range of investors including individuals, financial institutions, corporations and foreigners. Treasury bills are also an important tool in federal debt management and in the execution of monetary policy. Persistent federal deficits have resulted in rapid growth in Treasury bills in recent years. At the end of 1985 the outstanding volume was $400 billion, the largest for any money market instrument.

TREASURY BILL AUCTIONS

The Treasury sells bills at regularly scheduled auctions to refinance maturing issues and, if necessary, to help finance current federal deficits. The Treasury also sells bills on an irregular basis to smooth out the uneven flow of revenues from corporate and individual tax receipts.

Regularly Scheduled Issues   Treasury bills were first authorized by Congress in 1929. After experimenting with a number of bill maturities the Treasury in 1937 settled on the exclusive issue of three-month bills. In December 1958 these were supplemented with six-month bills in the regular weekly auctions. In 1959 the Treasury began to auction one-year bills on a quarterly basis. The quarterly auction of one-year bills was replaced by an auction occurring every four weeks in August 1963. The Treasury added a nine-month maturity to the monthly auction in September 1966 but the sale of this maturity was discontinued in late 1972. Since then, the only regular bill offerings have been the offerings of three- and six-month bills every week and the offerings of one-year bills every four weeks. The Treasury has increased the size of its weekly and monthly bill auctions as new money has been needed to meet enlarged federal borrowing requirements. In 1985 monthly sales of one-year bills averaged $8.6 billion, while the weekly auctions of three- and six-month bills both ranged from $6.5 to $7.5 billion.

Irregularly Scheduled Issues   Prior to the mid-1970s the Treasury sold bills on an irregular basis through the use of tax anticipation bills.[1] Introduced in October 1951, tax anticipation bills were designed specifically to help smooth out the Treasury's uneven flow of tax receipts while providing corporations with an investment vehicle for funds accumulated for tax payments. These bills were accepted at par on the tax date in payment for taxes due—hence the name, tax anticipation bills. They actually matured a week later, usually on the 22nd of the month. Tax anticipation bills did not have to be used for tax payments, and some investors chose to hold them to maturity.

No tax anticipation bills have been issued since 1974. In their place the Treasury has raised money on an irregular basis through the sale of "cash management" bills, which are typically "reopenings" or sales of bills that mature on the same date as an outstanding issue of bills. Cash management bills are designed to bridge low points in the Treasury's cash balances. Like tax anticipation bills, many cash management bills help finance the Treasury's requirements until tax payments are received. For this reason they frequently have maturities that fall after one of the five major federal tax dates. Thirty-eight issues of cash management bills were sold in the period from 1981 through 1985. The maturities of these issues ranged from 3 to 168 days and averaged 56 days.

Auctioning New Bills   The Treasury sells bills at a discount through competitive auctions; the return to the investor is the difference between the purchase price of the bill and its face or par value. Treasury bills are currently sold in minimum amounts of $10,000 and multiples of $5,000 above the minimum. Treasury bills are issued only in book-entry form. Under this arrangement ownership is recorded in a book-entry account established at the Treasury and investors receive only a receipt as evidence of purchase.

Weekly offerings of three- and six-month bills are typically announced on Tuesday and the amount of the offering is set at that time. The auction is usually conducted on the following Monday, with delivery and payment on the following Thursday. Bids, or tenders, in the weekly auctions must be presented at Federal Reserve Banks or their branches, which act as agents for the Treasury, by 1:00 p.m. New York time on the day of the auction.[2]

Bids may be made on a competitive or noncompetitive basis. In making a competitive bid the investor states the quantity of bills desired and the price he is willing to pay. A subscriber may enter more than one bid indicating the various quantities he is willing to take at different prices. Competitive bids, which are

---

[1] Tax anticipation bills are described in more detail in Nelson [1977].

[2] For a detailed description of the mechanics of purchasing Treasury bills see Tucker [1987].

usually made by large investors who are in close contact with the market, comprise the largest portion of subscriptions on a dollar basis. In making a noncompetitive bid the investor indicates the quantity of bills desired and agrees to pay the weighted-average price of accepted competitive bids. Individuals and other small investors usually enter noncompetitive bids, which are limited to $1,000,000 for each new offering of three- and six-month bills. In recent years the dollar amount of noncompetitive awards as a percent of total awards has generally ranged from 10 to 25 percent of the total auction amount. As shown in Chart 1, the percent awarded to noncompetitive bids typically rises in periods of high interest rates.

After subscription books at the various Federal Reserve Banks and branches are closed at 1:00 p.m., the bids are tabulated and submitted to the Treasury for allocation. The Treasury first allocates whatever part of the total offering is needed to fill all the noncompetitive bids. The remainder is then allocated to those competitive bidders submitting the highest offers, ranging downward from the highest bid until the total amount offered is allocated. The "stop-out price" is the lowest price, or highest yield, at which bills are awarded. Usually only a portion of

Chart 1

NONCOMPETITIVE BIDS AT WEEKLY AUCTION
COMPARED TO LEVEL OF RATES

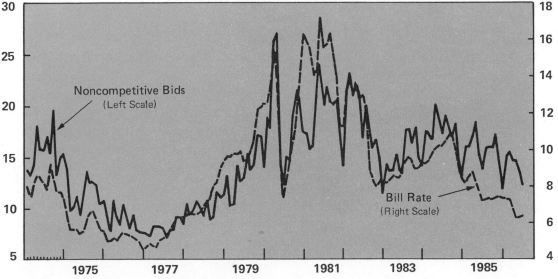

Note: Monthly data are averages of weekly figures.

Source: *Treasury Bulletin; Federal Reserve Bulletin.*

the total bids made at this price is accepted. The average issuing price is then computed as a weighted-average of the competitive bids accepted.

In the weekly auction of July 14, 1986, for example, accepted bids for the three-month bills ranged from a high of $98.547 per $100 of face amount (equivalent to an annual discount rate of 5.75 percent) to a stop-out price of $98.536 (5.79 percent). A total of $7,412 million of bids was accepted, $1,067 million of which was for noncompetitive tenders accepted at the average issuing price of $98.539 (5.78 percent). The relatively small proportion (14 percent) of bills purchased on a noncompetitive basis was typical given the low level of interest rates prevailing at the time of the auction.

In addition to the regular weekly auction, one-year bills are auctioned every fourth Thursday for issue the following Thursday and special auctions are held for cash management bills. The procedure for these auctions is similar to the weekly auctions.

INVESTMENT CHARACTERISTICS

Four investment characteristics of Treasury bills distinguish them from other money market instruments and consequently influence investor decisions to purchase bills. These include (1) lack of default risk, (2) liquidity, (3) favorable tax status, and (4) a low minimum denomination.

Default Risk   Treasury bills are generally considered to be free of default risk because they are obligations of the federal government. In contrast, even the highest grade of other money market instruments, such as commercial paper or CDs, is perceived to have some degree of default risk. Concern over default risk typically increases in times of weak economic conditions. In such periods the risk-free feature of bills becomes more valuable to some investors.

Because Treasury bills are free of default risk, various regulations permit them to be used for purposes that often cannot be served by other money market instruments. For example, banks use bills to make repurchase agreements free of reserve requirements with businesses and state and local governments, and banks use bills to satisfy pledging requirements on state and local and federal deposits. Treasury bills are widely accepted as collateral for selling short various financial securities and can be used instead of cash to satisfy initial margin requirements against futures market positions. And Treasury bills are always a permissible investment for state and local governments, while many other types of money market instruments frequently are not.

Liquidity   A second characteristic of bills is their high degree of liquidity. Liquidity refers mainly to the ability of investors to convert an asset into cash quickly at a low transactions cost. Investors in Treasury bills have this ability because bills are a homogeneous instrument and the bill market is highly organized and efficient. A measure of the liquidity of a financial asset is the spread between the price at which securities dealers buy it (the bid price) and the price at which they sell it (the asked price). In recent years the "bid-asked" spread on actively traded bills has been only two to four basis points, which is lower than for any other money market instrument.

Taxes Unlike other money market instruments, the income earned on Treasury bills is exempt from all state and local income taxes. Given a state income tax rate (t), the relationship between, say, the CD rate (RCD) and the bill rate (RTB) that leaves an investor indifferent between the two, other considerations aside, is

$$RCD(1 - t) = RTB.$$

From this formula it can be seen that the advantage of the tax-exempt feature for a particular investor depends on (1) the investor's state and local tax rate and (2) the current level of interest rates. For a given before-tax yield differential between bill rates and CD rates, the higher the state and local income tax rate and the higher the level of interest rates, the more attractive bills become. The interest rate differential at which an investor subject to a marginal state income tax rate of 6 percent is indifferent between bills and CDs rises from 32 basis points when the Treasury bill rate is 5 percent to 64 basis points when the Treasury bill rate is 10 percent.

This characteristic of bills is relevant only for some investors. Other investors, such as state and local governments, are not subject to state income taxes. Still other investors, such as commercial banks in most states, pay a "franchise" or "excise" tax that in fact requires them to pay state taxes on interest income from Treasury bills.[3]

Minimum Denomination A fourth investment characteristic of Treasury bills is their relatively low minimum denomination. Prior to 1970, the minimum denomination of bills was $1,000. In early 1970 the minimum denomination was raised from $1,000 to $10,000. The stated purposes of this change were to discourage noncompetitive bids by small investors, reduce the costs of processing many small subscriptions yielding only a small volume of funds, and discourage the exodus of funds from financial intermediaries and the mortgage market. Despite the increase in the minimum denomination of bills, investors continued to shift substantial amounts of funds out of deposit institutions into the bill market in

---

[3] Details on the taxation of Treasury bill interest income for different investors are provided in Cook and Lawler [1983].

periods of high interest rates such as 1973 and 1974. This activity was generally referred to as "disintermediation."

Even at $10,000 the minimum denomination of Treasury bills is far below the minimum denomination required to purchase other short-term securities, with the exception of some federally sponsored agency and municipal securities. Typically, it takes at least $100,000 to purchase money market instruments such as CDs or commercial paper.

INVESTORS

Because of their unique investment characteristics Treasury bills are held by a wide variety of investors. Comprehensive data on Treasury bill holdings are not available. Available information suggests that individuals, money market mutual funds, commercial banks, the Federal Reserve and foreigners are among the largest investors in bills.

Individuals Because Treasury bills have a relatively low minimum denomination and can be purchased at Federal Reserve Banks and branches without any service charge, the direct investment by individuals in bills has been greater than in any other money market instrument. (Since the late 1970s individuals have been heavy indirect investors in all money market instruments through their investment in money market funds.) The percentage of bills awarded to noncompetitive bidders at the weekly Treasury bill auctions is a widely used barometer of individual investment activity in the bill market. Chart 1 shows that this percentage moves closely with the level of interest rates. In recent years the major reason for this relationship appears to be that individuals as a group benefit most from the exemption of Treasury bill interest income from state and local income taxes. For a given spread between Treasury bill and other money market rates this exemption makes bills more attractive—relative to other short-term investments— the higher the level of interest rates. Hence, investment in bills by individuals rises with the level of interest rates.

Money Market Funds Money market funds held $20.4 billion of Treasury bills at year-end 1985, representing 9.8% of their total assets. Several money market funds buy only Treasury bills in order to appeal to the most risk-averse investors. The relatively small investment by money market funds in bills partly reflects the fact that the tax-exemption on bill interest income generally cannot be passed through to the money fund shareholder.

Commercial Banks At the end of 1985 commercial banks held about $140 billion of U.S. Treasury securities. A very rough estimate is that about $40 billion of this was Treasury bills. Banks' holding of bills tends to vary inversely with the demand for business loans. When loan demand is slack, banks increase their holdings of Treasury securities. Conversely, when loan demand is increasing, banks reduce their holdings of Treasury securities in order to expand loans. Of course, banks finance increases in business loans not only through the sale of securities but also through the issuance of liabilities such as CDs. Further, as noted above, banks also use Treasury bills to satisfy various collateral requirements and to make repurchase agreements with businesses and state and local governments.

Federal Reserve System   The Federal Reserve System's holdings of Treasury bills at year-end 1985 was $85.4 billion, which represented about half its total holdings of Treasury securities. Treasury bills perform an important role in the implementation of monetary policy. The Federal Reserve System pursues its monetary policy objectives by altering the level of reserves available to depository institutions in order to influence short-term interest rates and the money supply. (See the Federal funds chapter for a discussion of Federal Reserve operating procedures.) The Federal Reserve changes the level of reserves primarily through the purchase and sale of Treasury bills, either outright in the bill market or on a temporary basis in the market for repurchase agreements (RPs). RPs are the purchase or sale of bills under an agreement to reverse the transaction one or more days later. RPs have a temporary effect on the supply of bank reserves and are typically used to offset temporary fluctuations in reserves arising from other sources, such as changes in Treasury deposits at the Federal Reserve Banks. On a day-to-day basis most Federal Reserve operations are RPs. The increase in the Fed's outright holdings of bills over long periods of time reflects permanent increases in the level of reserves and money.

Foreign and Other Investors   Data on total foreign holdings of Treasury bills are not available, but foreign official institutions held $53 billion of bills (including some nonmarketable certificates of indebtedness) at the end of 1985. Other investors in Treasury bills are nonbank financial institutions, nonfinancial corporations, and state and local governments. The share of bills held by state and local governments has fallen in recent years, reflecting the increased investment flexibility available to many of these governments.

YIELDS

Treasury bill yields are generally quoted on a discount basis using a 360-day year. Under this procedure the stated rate of return on a bill of a given maturity is calculated by dividing the discount by par and expressing this percentage at an annual rate, using a 360-day year. For example, in the weekly auction of July 14, 1986, discussed above, an average price of $98.539 per $100 of face amount for a three-month (91-day) bill produced an annual rate of return on a discount basis of

$$\frac{100 - 98.539}{100} \times \frac{360}{91} = 5.78\%.$$

To calculate the true investment yield of a Treasury bill for comparison with other yields, the discount must be divided by the price and a 365-day year used. In the above example the true yield is

$$\frac{100 - 98.539}{98.539} \times \frac{365}{91} = 5.95\%.$$

As this example illustrates, the yield calculated on a discount basis understates the true yield of a Treasury bill.[4] The difference between the true yield of a bill and the discount yield is greater the longer the maturity of the bill and the higher the level of interest rates. For example, at an interest rate level of 12 percent the difference between the true yield and the yield calculated on a discount basis is 55 basis points at the three-month maturity and 95 basis points at the six-month maturity.

Yield Spreads Most money market rates move together closely over time. Perhaps more than any other money market rate, however, the rate on Treasury bills has at times diverged substantially from other short-term rates. Chart 2 shows that the differential between the three-month prime CD rate and the three-month Treasury bill rate varies greatly over time. In attempting to understand the highly variable spread between bill rates and other money market rates, it is useful to focus on three factors: default risk, taxes, and disintermediation.

The most common explanation of the spread between Treasury bill and other money market rates focuses on default risk. According to this explanation, the spreads between other short-term rates and bill rates vary over time due to a cyclical risk premium pushing up the yields on private sector money market instruments relative to the yields on Treasury bills in periods of weak economic activity. Throughout the money market, spreads between yields of securities that differ in their degree of default risk typically rise in recessions and this effect has

---

[4] For a three- or six-month Treasury bill the formula to convert a discount yield (rd) to a true investment yield (r) is:

$$r = \frac{365 \times rd}{360 - (rd \times t)},$$

where t is days to maturity and the interest rates are expressed in decimal form.

Chart 2

THE SPREAD BETWEEN
THE THREE-MONTH CD AND TREASURY BILL RATES

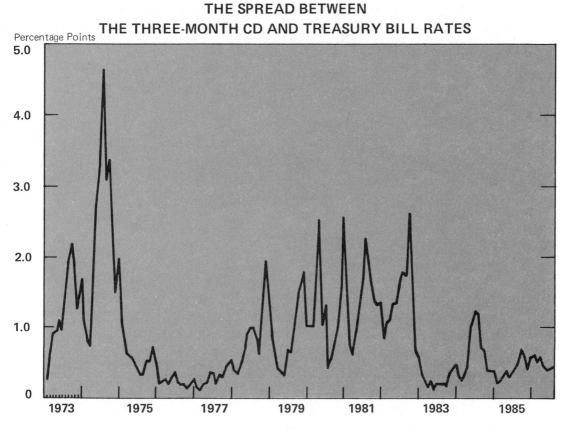

Percentage Points

Source: *Federal Reserve Bulletin.*

clearly been evident in the spread between Treasury bill and other money market rates. (See, for example, the spread between the prime and medium-grade commercial paper rates shown in the commercial paper chapter of this book.) Default risk can also cause the spread to rise in periods of concern over the fragility of the financial system. One major such episode occurred in August 1982 when the failure of a securities dealer along with heightened concern over the ability of some foreign countries to pay off loans to U.S. commercial banks increased investor worries over the soundness of the nation's financial system and resulted in a sharp increase of almost a full percentage point in the spread between CD and bill rates.

Another possible factor influencing the spread between the bill rate and other short-term rates is the exemption of Treasury bills from state and local income tax.

As noted above, the higher the level of interest rates the wider the spread between bill rates and other short-term rates that is necessary to leave an investor with a given state income tax rate indifferent between bills and other money market instruments. Consequently, as interest rates rise, this tax feature of bills induces some investors to increase their purchases of bills, thereby putting upward pressure on the spread between bill rates and other rates. Evidence in favor of this effect is that the spread typically rises in high interest rates periods and falls in low interest rate periods.

This is not to say that the tax-exempt feature of bills must cause the spread to rise with the level of interest rates. As noted above, many investors in the bill market are not subject to state and local income taxes. If, however, investors subject to state income tax rate (t) dominated the bill market, then the observed relationship between the CD rate (RCD) and the bill rate (RTB)—taking default risk into account—would be:

$$RCD(1 - t) = RTB + \text{Default Risk Premium.}$$

One study [Cook and Lawler, 1983] using data from 1979 through mid-1983, when the spread between the CD and Treasury bill rates was particularly volatile, found that the simple model represented by the equation above did a good job of explaining the spread in that period. This study estimated that the average value of (t) over that period was in the neighborhood of 8 percent, which is well within the range of state individual income tax rates on interest income.

A third factor that prior to the late 1970s may have affected the spread in periods of high interest rates such as 1969, 1973 and 1974 is disintermediation. In these periods the large differential between market interest rates and Regulation Q ceiling rates at the depository institutions induced many individuals to move their funds out of these institutions and into the bill market. The large purchases of Treasury bills by individuals in these periods may have driven bill rates down relative to the rates on other money market instruments.[5] Ceilings on savings type deposits at depository institutions were partially eliminated in 1978 with the introduction of $10,000 money market certificates and then totally eliminated in late 1982 with the introduction of money market deposit accounts (MMDAs).

Yield Curves Money market yield curves show the relationship between maturity and yield on money market instruments. An interesting aspect of the Treasury bill yield curve is that it generally has shown greater upward slope than the yield

---

[5] This explanation is given in more detail in Cook [1981].

curves of private money market instruments such as CDs. Thus, the spread between the one-month CD and Treasury bill yields has usually exceeded the spread between the three-month CD and Treasury bill yields. Similarly, the three-month spread has usually exceeded the spread between the six-month CD and Treasury bill yields. The reasons underlying the differential behavior of the Treasury bill and CD yield curves are not entirely clear. According to one study [Rowe, Lawler and Cook, 1986] a key factor is the dominant role of the Treasury in the bill market.

SECONDARY MARKET[6]

The market for Treasury bills is the largest and most efficient for any money market instrument. At the heart of this market is a group of securities dealers known as primary dealers, who purchase a large portion of the Treasury bills sold at auction and make an active secondary market for these securities. Dealers earn the designation of primary dealer from the Federal Reserve after a period of observation of their customer base, business volume, participation in Treasury auctions, ability and commitment to make markets, and the financial strength of the firm. With this designation comes a number of advantages including market recognition and the possibility of daily contact with the Federal Reserve's trading desk since the Fed selects its trading partners for the conduct of monetary policy from the list of primary dealers. In mid-1986 there were 37 primary dealers. Of these, 14 were operated as departments of commercial banks and 23 were nonbank dealers. In addition to the primary dealers, there are a large number of bank and nonbank "secondary" dealers in Government securities. The number of these dealers is unknown, but estimates range from 300 to 500.

The primary dealers make markets by buying and selling securities for their own account. The marketplace is decentralized with most trading transacted over the telephone. As shown in the table, daily average trading in Treasury securities by the primary dealers in 1985 was $75.3 billion, $32.9 billion of which was in Treasury bills. About half of the trading in Treasury securities was with the dealers' customers, including depository institutions, insurance companies, pension funds, nonfinancial corporations, and state and local governments. Dealers also trade actively with each other, mostly through brokers who match buyers and sellers for a commission. Brokers display bid and asked prices via closed circuit television screens located in the trading rooms of the primary dealers, thereby providing them with rapid access to this information, yet maintaining anonymity in their trades.

---

[6] The chapter on repurchase agreements contains more detail on the secondary market for Treasury securities. Also, see McCurdy [1977-78] and General Accounting Office [1985].

TRANSACTIONS IN UNITED STATES GOVERNMENT SECURITIES BY DEALERS REPORTING TO THE FEDERAL RESERVE BANK OF NEW YORK

	By Maturity (in billions of dollars, daily averages)			By Trading Participant (as a percentage of total)		
Year	Due within one year	Due in one year or more	Total	Dealers	Brokers	All others
1981	14.8	10.0	24.7	6.6	47.5	45.9
1982	18.4	13.9	32.3	5.5	49.0	45.5
1983	22.4	19.7	42.1	5.4	49.9	44.7
1984	26.0	26.7	52.8	5.5	48.5	46.0
1985	32.9	42.4	75.3	4.4	48.1	47.5

Source: *Federal Reserve Bulletin.*

As noted above, an indication of the efficiency of the bill market is the narrow bid-asked spread on bills. The bid-asked spread varies over time, largely depending on the volatility of interest rates. The more volatile are interest rates, the greater the spread required by dealers in compensation for the risk of taking a position. Hence, bid-asked spreads tend to rise in periods of increased interest rate volatility. Prior to October 1979 the bid-asked spread on the most actively traded three-month bills was generally only two basis points—i.e., $50 per $1 million. On October 6, 1979 the Federal Reserve announced a change in operating procedures that resulted in much greater volatility in short-term interest rates. (See the chapter on Federal funds for a discussion of these procedures.) Subsequently, the bid-asked spread on Treasury bills rose to as high as eight to ten basis points. In 1982 the Fed reverted to a procedure similar to its pre-October 1979 procedure and since then the bid-asked spread has been in a range of two to four basis points.

References

Cook, Timothy Q. "Determinants of the Spread Between Treasury Bill and Private Sector Money Market Rates." *Journal of Economics and Business* 33 (Spring 1981), pp. 177-87.

———— and Thomas A. Lawler. "The Behavior of the Spread Between Treasury Bill Rates and Private Money Market Rates Since 1978." Federal Reserve Bank of Richmond, *Economic Review* 69 (November/December 1983), pp. 3-15.

General Accounting Office. *Survey of the Federal Reserve System's Supervision of the Treasury Securities Market.* Report prepared for the Subcommittee on Domestic Monetary Policy of the House Committee on Banking Finance and Urban Affairs. 99th Cong., 1st sess., May 1985.

McCurdy, Christopher J. "The Dealer Market for United States Government Securities." Federal Reserve Bank of New York, *Quarterly Review* 2 (Winter 1977-78), pp. 35-47.

Monhollon, Jimmie R. "Treasury Bills." In *Instruments of the Money Market*, 4th ed. Edited by Timothy Q. Cook. Richmond: Federal Reserve Bank of Richmond, 1977.

Nelson, Jane F. "Tax Anticipation Bills." In *Instruments of the Money Market*, 4th ed. Edited by Timothy Q. Cook. Richmond: Federal Reserve Bank of Richmond, 1977.

Rowe, Timothy D., Thomas A. Lawler, and Timothy Q. Cook. "Treasury Bill Versus Private Money Market Yield Curves." Federal Reserve Bank of Richmond, *Economic Review* 72 (July/August 1986), pp. 3-12.

Tucker, James F. "Buying Treasury Securities at Federal Reserve Banks." Federal Reserve Bank of Richmond, 1987.

8

SHORT-TERM MUNICIPAL SECURITIES

John R. Walter

INTRODUCTION

Short-term municipal securities are defined by two characteristics. First, they are issued by state and local governments and the special districts and statutory authorities they establish. Second, they either have original maturities of less than three years or have longer final maturities but include features which, from the investor's point of view, shorten their effective maturities to less than three years.[1] During 1985 approximately $82 billion in short-term municipal securities were issued.

The interest income received by holders of municipal securities is generally exempt from federal income tax. The federal tax-free status of municipal debt was firmly established in the 1895 Supreme Court case Pollock v. Farmers' Loan and Trust Company and was reaffirmed by the first federal income tax law, passed in 1913 following the ratification of the Sixteenth Amendment. Since 1913, each new tax law has included a clause exempting interest income on most municipal securities from federal income taxes. As federal income tax rates increased, the importance of this exemption to investors and to municipal issuers grew. Because the interest income received by holders of most municipal securities is tax-exempt, the securities carry a lower rate of interest which in turn considerably lowers the borrowing costs of states and municipalities.[2,3]

States and municipalities borrow to finance their own expenditures, to provide funds to be used by private firms and individuals (although changes to

---

[1] Municipal market participants generally call securities short-term if they have maturities less than three years, or if they have features shortening their effective maturities to less than three years. Most major data-collecting firms, however, consider municipal securities short-term if they have maturities of no more than 12 or 13 months, or have features making their effective maturities no more than 12 or 13 months. As a result, the figures quoted throughout the article are based upon this criterion.

[2] Because tax law prohibitions or limitations have eliminated or restricted the ability of certain municipal issuers to issue tax-exempt debt, or may do so in the future, some municipal issuers have recently issued taxable securities.

[3] In this article the term municipality refers to local governments and the special districts and authorities created by state and local governments. Some writers also use the term to refer to state governments.

the Tax Code in 1986 will significantly limit this borrowing), and to provide funds to some tax-exempt entities such as private nonprofit hospitals, colleges, and universities. Because municipal security issuers vary greatly in size and motivation for borrowing, the methods and instruments chosen to meet funding demands vary considerably. While a small city may sell a fixed-rate note directly to a local bank to finance the purchase of a snowplow until bonds are issued, a waste management agency may sell, through a municipal underwriter, numerous large denomination variable-rate securities to mutual funds and corporations to raise funds to build a solid waste disposal project.

Until 1980 almost all short-term tax-exempt securities had fixed interest rates and maturities of less than three years. Since then two new instruments have emerged and grown rapidly: tax-exempt commercial paper and variable-rate demand obligations. These instruments have enabled state and municipal issuers to fund long-term projects at short-term rates. Issuers have had the incentive to raise funds at short-term rates because historically the yield curve in the tax-exempt market has been upward sloping.

In the past, state and local governments, school districts, public power and water authorities, and transportation authorities were the major issuers of short-term tax-exempt debt. In recent years agencies and authorities of municipal governments, such as housing, pollution control, and economic and industrial development authorities, have been growing in importance. Since the newer districts and authorities are more frequent users of the new instruments, the increase in the importance of these types of borrowers in the municipal market accounts for some of the growth in these instruments.

CHARACTERISTICS OF SHORT-TERM MUNICIPAL SECURITIES

Definition and Features   Municipal securities are promises made by state and local governments and the districts and authorities they create to pay either one interest and principal payment on a particular date or a stream of interest payments up to maturity and a principal payment at maturity. They are backed by the issuer's ability to tax and borrow, by certain sources of funds, or by collateral. Municipal securities with original maturities of greater than three years are generally called bonds, and those with maturities of three years or less are called short-term securities or notes.

Short-term municipal securities are issued in coupon or discount form. Coupon securities, the most prevalent by far, pay a stated tax-exempt interest rate, called the coupon rate, at maturity or on specified dates. This rate varies over the life of the issue in the case of variable-rate instruments. Discount securities are issued at a price less than their face value. The difference between the issue price and face value is tax-exempt interest income.

Short-term municipal securities are issued in either bearer or registered form. The 1982 tax law included a provision requiring all municipal securities issued after January 1, 1983 with maturities of greater than one year to be issued in registered form.

Short-term municipal securities are normally issued in denominations of $5,000 or more. The denomination chosen depends upon the issuer's assessment of who the purchasers are likely to be. If the issuer is trying to sell to individuals, it will use a smaller denomination than if the issue is intended for institutional investors. Smaller denominations increase the average cost of marketing a new issue.

Short-term municipal securities can be either general obligation securities or revenue securities. General obligation securities are backed by the full faith and credit of the issuer, which uses its ability to tax and any other possible source of income to meet debt payments. The ability to tax may be limited by statute or constitution, in which case the general obligation security is called a limited tax security. Revenue securities are backed by revenues generated by the project the securities finance and not by the full faith and credit of the issuer. The revenues are usually future earnings on projects such as tolls from roads or rental income from a facility leased to a business. In some cases, however, the revenues can be funds from specific taxes, receipts from bond sales, or transfers from the federal government.

Most of the securities issued by special districts and statutory authorities are revenue securities backed by revenues from the projects the securities finance. Many districts and authorities cannot tax, so they do not have the ability to make a general obligation pledge. At times, however, the securities of such a district or authority are backed by a general obligation pledge from the state or local government that founded it. Table I lists the major issuers of municipal debt and the types of securities they normally issue.

Traditional Instruments Traditionally, short-term municipal securities have been issued to meet short-term demands for cash and have paid fixed interest rates. The popular traditional issues are revenue anticipation notes (commonly called RANs), tax anticipation notes (TANs), grant anticipation notes (GANs), tax and revenue anticipation notes (TRANs), and bond anticipation notes (BANs). Each receives its name from its source of repayment. These issues have minimum denominations of $5,000 and their maturities are fixed with repayment coming from funds available at or before the maturity date. Traditional notes remain significant in the short-term municipal market (Chart 1).

96

Table I

**ISSUERS OF SHORT-TERM MUNICIPAL SECURITIES
AND TYPES OF DEBT ISSUED**

Issuer	Types of Debt Generally Issued
State government	G.O. and revenue
Local government:	G.O. and revenue
City	G.O. and revenue
County	G.O. and revenue
Authorities, districts, and agencies created by state and local governments:	
Public school	G.O. and revenue
Higher education	G.O. and revenue
Public power	Revenue
Water or sewer	Revenue
Transportation	Revenue
Health facilities	Revenue
Student loan	Revenue
Housing finance	Revenue
Pollution control	Revenue
Industrial development	Revenue
Waste management	Revenue

Note: G.O. denotes general obligation.

Funds from such sources as taxes, grants, and project revenues are often received as large payments a few times a year, while expenditures must be made continually. In order to make expenditures before funds are received, states and municipalities issue notes that are paid back by future receipts. Funds from future bond issues are used to repay bond anticipation notes. Here, states and municipalities construct projects to be financed with bonds but require immediate funds for payrolls and purchases. Rather than issuing bonds before a project is finished and the final costs are certain, states and municipalities may first sell notes that are retired with the proceeds of bonds issued upon completion of the project. For example, a county recently issued $32 million of one-year fixed-rate bond anticipation notes to finance part of the construction of a waste water treatment facility. The notes were revenue securities, backed by funds to be received from future bond sales.

There are other uses for bond anticipation notes. For example, at certain times states and municipalities may expect to be able to sell long-term securities in the future at lower rates than are available currently, so they issue notes and

Chart 1

SHORT-TERM MUNICIPAL SECURITIES
Volume Issued During Year

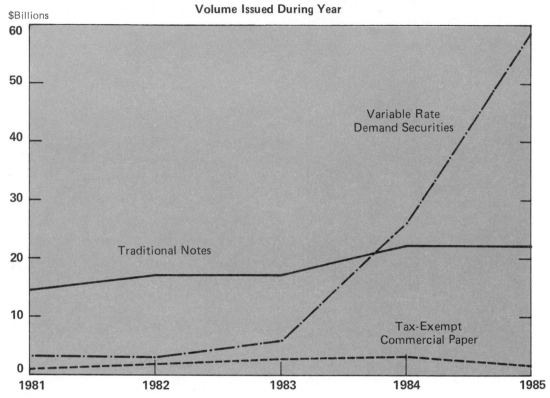

Source: Securities Data Company, Inc.; Standard & Poor's.

retire them with future bond proceeds. Also, municipalities frequently finance several projects with one bond issue. Short-term notes can be issued to pay for the completion of the individual projects, after which the notes are retired with one long-term bond issue. Despite the various uses to which bond anticipation notes may be put, they have become fairly uncommon in recent years as frequent tax law changes have made issuers wary that changes in the law could eliminate their ability to issue bonds needed to repay these notes.

New Instruments   Since 1980 two new instruments have become prominent: tax-exempt commercial paper and variable-rate demand or put obligations. A number of factors contributed to the development of these instruments. The volatile interest rates of the late 1970s and early 1980s lead to greater demand by investors for short-term and variable-rate investments. Issuers were also inter-

98

ested in relying more on short-term debt to meet their demand for longer-term funds because the tax-exempt yield curve was strongly and persistently upward sloping. Issuers were unwilling, however, to use the traditional short-term instruments to raise long-term funds because of the high legal, administrative, and marketing costs of issuing and reissuing these securities for an extended period. Finally, the ability of issuers to sell the new instruments was greatly facilitated by the rapid growth of tax-exempt money market mutual funds which expanded the market for these instruments considerably by increasing the ability of investors to purchase them.

Tax-exempt commercial paper, which began to grow in late 1979, is short-term fixed-rate paper, normally issued with the intention of redeeming maturing paper with funds from newly issued paper. Almost all maturities are between 1 and 270 days and are determined by negotiation with investors. Tax-exempt commercial paper is used to fund both short- and long-term projects. When funding long-term projects, maturing paper is replaced with new issues at current market rates.

The tax-exempt commercial paper market is a highly sophisticated market requiring the issuer to maintain daily contact with the market and good communication with its marketing agent. This is necessary because tax-exempt commercial paper issuers generally allow investors to choose from a span of maturities so that some paper is maturing almost every day and therefore must be replaced with new paper on a daily basis. The frequent involvement of issuers and their agents in the market imposes a significant cost on issuers. Because of this cost states and municipalities do not find it attractive to issue commercial paper unless they are borrowing $15 to $25 million or more.

Minimum denominations range from $50,000 to $100,000. Money market funds are the major investor in tax-exempt commercial paper. Some tax-exempt commercial paper also is purchased directly by corporations, bank trust departments, and wealthy individuals. While there is no developed secondary market in commercial paper because of its extreme short-term nature and its individualized maturities, dealers will as a rule buy back paper they have sold.

As an example of a commercial paper issue, one state has been using a tax-exempt commercial paper program for four or five years to finance its capital projects. The amount outstanding in the program varies with funding demands and is authorized by the state government to be as much as $90 million. Denominations range between $50,000 and $5,000,000 with the securities typically sold in $1,000,000 lots. Maturities are between 3 days and 210 days depending upon investors' desires. Most of the commercial paper has been purchased by money market funds. This program will be continued unless the state decides that bonds can provide lower cost funds.

Variable-rate demand obligations began to grow in 1981.[4] They can be either general obligation or revenue securities, but the majority are revenue securities. Minimum denominations range from $5,000 to $100,000. Variable-rate demand obligations now come in many forms with almost as many variations as there are dealers in the tax-exempt money market. They share certain characteristics, however. First, while these instruments may have final maturities from short-term up to forty years, they all include features which allow for periodic interest rate adjustments. Second, they include a feature known as a demand option which gives the investor the right to tender the instrument to the issuer or a designated party on a specified number of days' notice at a price equal to the face amount (par value) plus accrued interest. The length of the notice period normally corresponds with the frequency of interest rate adjustment. For example, if the interest rate is adjusted on a weekly basis, the variable-rate security will generally have a seven-day notice period. If in the investor's judgement the new rate is too low or if the investor wants his money back for some other reason, he exercises his demand option. In this case the instrument is resold to another investor. Third, many of these securities contain a provision allowing the issuer, after properly notifying all holders and allowing them the opportunity to tender their holdings, to convert the variable-rate security into a fixed-rate security with no demand feature. For example, a higher education authority issued $9 million of variable-rate revenue bonds, in $100,000 minimum denominations, to finance campus construction and renovation. These securities have a 25-year final maturity but include a weekly demand feature. Most of the securities are in the portfolios of tax-exempt money market funds.

Variable-rate demand obligations have one important advantage for states and municipalities over tax-exempt commercial paper. When commercial paper matures and is replaced with new commercial paper, the new security is legally defined as a new debt issue and is subject to regulations in place at the time of its issue. Since Congress has been imposing and shrinking limits on certain types of issues in recent years, issuers wishing to borrow for an extended period by using commercial paper face the danger of having a newly imposed or tightened limit eliminate their source of funds. In contrast, because new debt is not issued when an investor exercises his demand option, variable-rate demand obligation issuers are not faced with this danger. This advantage of variable-rate demand obligations over tax-exempt commercial paper may explain their rapid growth compared with commercial paper (Chart 1).

The length of the notice period on a variable-rate demand obligation

---

[4] The terms "demand" and "put" are used interchangeably in the municipal security market. In this paper "demand" is used.

determines its effective maturity from the investor's point of view and therefore strongly affects the interest rate which must be paid on the instrument. The most common notice periods are one day, seven days, and thirty days. As a result of a fairly consistently upward sloping yield curve in the municipal market, it is generally true that the shorter the notice period the lower the rate paid.[5]

Information on each of the commonly used short-term municipal instruments is summarized in Table II.

DEALERS

Most large banks and securities firms, along with some firms specializing only in municipal securities trading, act as dealers in the short-term municipal market. Municipal securities dealers underwrite and market new security issues and provide a secondary market for outstanding securities. With a few exceptions, banks are limited by the Glass-Steagall Act of 1933 to underwriting only general obligation securities.

Underwriting is the purchase of securities from the issuer with the intention of reselling them to investors. Once the underwriter has purchased the securities it bears the risks of marketing them. Security issues may be underwritten by one dealer if the issue is small or by a group of dealers, called a syndicate, if the issue is larger than one dealer would like to handle. In a syndicate one dealer acts as the lead dealer in the group, taking the largest proportion of securities and managing the sale of the issue. Syndicates are used to spread the market risk among more dealers and to enlarge the number of possible investors. As compensation the underwriter receives the spread between the price paid the issuer for the securities and the price received from investors. The risk faced by the underwriter is that the security issue will not sell at a price that will earn a profit. A major source of this risk occurs when interest rates unexpectedly rise before the underwriter has sold the issue to the public.

Municipalities that choose a public offering must decide whether to sell their securities by competitive bidding or by a negotiated sale. In competitive bidding the issue is advertised for sale and then sold to the underwriting dealer or syndicate of dealers offering the highest price. In a negotiated sale an issuer chooses one dealer or syndicate without soliciting bids from other firms. Variable-rate municipal securities are most frequently sold through negotiated deals, while tax-exempt commercial paper is always sold in this manner.

In a traditional note issue the dealer's responsibility to the issuer is limited to the initial sale of the securities. For variable-rate and commercial paper issues

---

[5] For a more detailed discussion of tax-exempt commercial paper and variable-rate demand obligations see Smith Barney, Harris Upham and Company, Incorporated [1986, pp. 10-14].

TABLE II

INSTRUMENTS COMMONLY USED IN THE SHORT-TERM MUNICIPAL MARKET

Security Name	Types of Pledge	Features
TRADITIONAL NOTES		
Revenue Anticipation Note	G.O. or revenue	Fixed maturity of a few weeks to one year, fixed interest rates
Tax Anticipation Note	G.O. or revenue	Fixed maturity of a few weeks to one year, fixed interest rates
Grant Anticipation Note	G.O. or revenue	Fixed maturity of a few weeks to three years, fixed interest rates
Tax and Revenue Anticipation Note	G.O. or revenue	Fixed maturity of a few weeks to one year, fixed interest rates
Bond Anticipation Note	G.O. or revenue	Fixed maturity of a few weeks to three years, fixed interest rates
NEW SECURITIES		
Variable-Rate Demand Obligation	G.O. or revenue; Liquidity facility, Credit Facility	May be tendered to issuer or designated party on a specified number of days' notice; floating or variable interest rate. Many include features which allow conversion to a fixed-rate long-term maturity.
Tax-Exempt Commmercial Paper	G.O. or revenue; Liquidity facility, Credit facility	Maturities of a few days to one year depending on investor and issuer preference; interest rate fixed to maturity; continuously offered.

Note: G.O. denotes general obligation.

the lead dealer's responsibility is more extensive. When variable-rate obligations are used, the lead dealer generally becomes the remarketing agent and has the responsibility of resetting the interest rate on interest rate adjustment dates and reselling any securities which are tendered by investors. When commercial paper is issued, the dealer is involved in the daily setting of rates and in selling new paper to replace maturing paper.

Dealers generally will make a secondary market in the short-term securities they have sold, which means they will stand ready to buy and sell these securities at any time. Dealers are kept informed of securities being offered and rates being paid through several electronic services and daily publications. Due to the heterogeneous nature of municipal issues, the secondary market in municipal securities is not nearly as developed as that for corporate and government debt issues.

Brokers in the municipal market match dealers selling particular issues with dealers who are interested in buying these issues. Brokers deal only with large volumes and charge a small fee for their middleman services.

PROVIDERS OF CREDIT AND LIQUIDITY ENHANCEMENTS

In order to improve the credit ratings and marketability of their securities, municipal issuers frequently get credit or liquidity enhancing agreements. Under these agreements banks, corporations, and insurance companies promise, for a fee, to provide funds if an issuer is unable or unwilling to make payment to the holders of the issuer's debt. Such an agreement substitutes the credit or liquidity of the bank, corporation, or insurance company for that of the municipal security issuer.

These agreements fall into one of two categories. The first is the credit substitution agreement. This is simply a contract made with the municipal security issuer to make payment if the issuer does not. Under this contract the security holder has a claim against the promising party if the issuer defaults. The second category is the liquidity substitution agreement. This is a promise, generally made by a bank, to provide a loan to the municipal issuer or its agent to redeem maturing or tendered securities, or to itself purchase such securities outright. The liquidity agreement is activated when the remarketing agent cannot resell the maturing or tendered securities at an interest rate below some maximum set by the issuer or when it cannot resell them at all.

Banks are the most common providers of credit substitution agreements in the short-term municipal market. Banks provide the agreement, for a fee, by means of an irrevocable letter of credit. Insurance companies provide the same type of promise through municipal bond insurance. Also, a corporation that benefits from a project often guarantees payment of principal and interest for the related securities. Since only municipal issues with top ratings are purchased by the money market mutual funds, issuers wishing to sell less than top rated securities to these funds must obtain a credit substitution promise.

Most liquidity substitution agreements are provided by large U.S. and foreign banks. The agreements come in the form of either a bank line, a standby letter of credit, or a standby purchase agreement. The liquidity substitution promise provides the investor with the assurance that funds will be immediately available when he redeems his security.

The traditional short-term municipal securities typically do not require liquidity promises, while variable-rate demand obligations and commercial paper issues almost always require such promises. Variable-rate obligations require liquidity substitution backing because of the danger that the security holders will exercise their demand option at a time and in sufficient numbers that the remarketing agent will not be able to resell the securities and the issuer will not have sufficient funds to redeem them. Institutional investors, the biggest purchasers of such securities, require that this risk be covered. Similarly, there is some danger that when existing paper matures the commercial paper issuer's marketing agent will be unable to sell new paper and that the issuer will not have sufficient funds to redeem them. Issuers of commercial paper must back their issues with liquidity facilities to assure investors that funds will be immediately available at maturity.

INVESTORS

An investor's decision whether to purchase a taxable or tax-exempt security depends largely on his marginal tax rate and the rates being paid on tax-exempts and taxables. The after-tax return on a taxable security is $r(1 - t)$ where r is the before-tax rate of return on the taxable security and t is the investor's marginal tax rate. Yields on tax-exempt securities are frequently stated in taxable equivalent terms, or in terms of what taxable interest rate would be necessary to provide the same after-tax interest rate. The taxable equivalent formula is

$$r_T = \frac{r_{TF}}{1 - t},$$

where r_{TF} is the rate paid on the tax-free instrument and r_T is the equivalent yield of a taxable instrument for investors with a marginal tax rate of t. For example, if an investor in the 33 percent marginal federal tax bracket purchases a tax-exempt security paying 6.7 percent, then a taxable security paying 10 percent would yield this investor the same after-tax rate as the tax exempt security. If the investor's taxable equivalent yield on municipal securities is greater than the yields he can earn on taxable securities of comparable risk he will profit by investing in tax-exempt securities.

The value of the tax exemption to the investor is increased when the income earned also is exempt from state income tax. This is true for investors purchasing securities issued by their home state or by municipalities located in their home state. In this case the security is "double tax-exempt" for the investor and the relevant taxable equivalent formula is

$$r_T = \frac{r_{TF}}{1 - [t_F + t_S(1 - t_F)]},$$

where t_F is the marginal federal tax rate of the investor and t_S is the marginal state tax rate of the investor. This formula takes into account the deductability of state income taxes on the federal return. Suppose the above investor in the 33 percent federal tax bracket has a 10 percent state income tax rate. The total tax rate faced by the individual is $.33 + .10(1 - .33) = .40$. If the municipal security being considered is exempt from state income taxes and is paying a 6.7 percent rate of return, then the taxable equivalent yield for this investor is 11.1 percent.

Chart 2 graphs the implicit marginal tax rate that equated the after-tax yields on six-month maturity Treasury securities and six-month maturity prime tax-exempt notes from 1978 through mid-1986. This tax rate averaged 49.4 percent from January 1978 through September 1981, fell to an average 45.4 percent from October 1981 through April 1985, and then fell further to an average 33.6 percent from May 1985 through June 1986. The reasons for the decline in the period after September 1981 are not entirely clear. The 1985 decline probably resulted from the massive issue of new short-term debt brought on by municipal issuers' fears of tax law changes taking affect after the end of 1985.

Individuals   Most individuals investing in short-term municipal securities do so through tax-exempt money market funds, which held approximately 50 percent of all short-term municipal debt at the end of 1985 (Chart 3). Tax-exempt money funds allow smaller investors to diversify their portfolios of municipal securities, which would not otherwise be possible for most of these investors because minimum denominations of short-term tax-exempts start at $5,000. Some individuals do invest in short-term securities directly, either through a securities dealer or through a bank with a dealer department. Chart 3 shows that approximately 7 percent of outstanding short-term municipal debt was held by individuals investing directly.

Individuals can invest in short-term tax-exempt securities through a bank trust department. Bank trust departments held 15 percent of short-term municipal debt outstanding at the end of 1985. Bank trust departments also often invest their

Chart 2

TAX RATE EQUATING AFTER-TAX YIELDS ON TREASURY BILLS
AND PRIME TAX-EXEMPT HOUSING NOTES
(Six-Month Maturities)

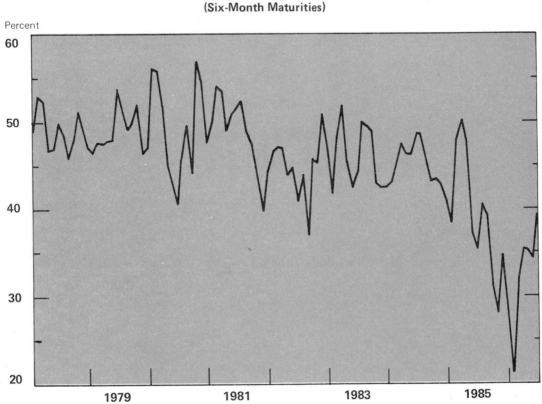

Percent

Source: Yield series are from Salomon Brothers, *An Analytical Record of Yields and Yield Spreads.*

customers' funds in tax-exempt money funds, an item which appears in Chart 3 as investment by money funds.

Corporations At the end of 1985, corporations directly held about 23 percent of the outstanding short-term municipal securities. In addition they indirectly held some short-term municipal securities through money market funds. Corporations invest in these securities because their corporate federal and state tax rates together generally have been high enough to make tax-exempts profitable. Corporations invest in short-term municipal debt mostly as a repository for their short-term operating reserves or seasonal reserves.

Commercial Banks At the end of 1985 banks held about 5 percent of all short-term municipal debt. Banks' holdings of municipal debt as a percentage of

Chart 3

HOLDINGS OF SHORT-TERM TAX-EXEMPT SECURITIES

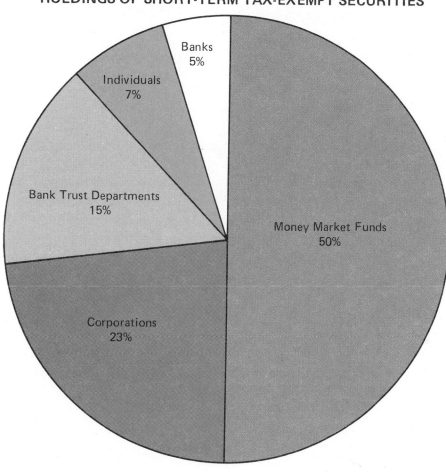

Banks
5%

Individuals
7%

Bank Trust Departments
15%

Money Market Funds
50%

Corporations
23%

Source: *Smith Barney, Harris Upham & Co. Incorporated, Public Finance Division.*

their total assets declined from 1980 through 1984. This decline can be explained by two factors. First, aggregate bank profits consistently fell over those years, and this fall consequently diminished banks' incentive to protect income from taxes. Second, the Tax Equity and Fiscal Responsibility Act (TEFRA) of 1982, eliminated part of the interest deduction of municipal security carrying costs, and therefore lowered the effective return banks could earn on tax-exempts beginning in 1983.[6] In 1985, however, banks' holdings of municipal securities as a percent of total assets grew to slightly more than it was in 1980. This growth was the result of two

---

[6] Proctor and Donahoo [1983-84, pp. 31-32].

factors, namely (1) banks' concern over the possibility of enactment of legislation in 1986 that would render municipal securities purchased after 1985 less attractive and (2) somewhat higher income in 1985.

As it turned out, banks' concern about the 1986 tax law was well-founded. The new tax law will in most cases eliminate banks' ability to deduct the interest expense of funds used to carry municipal securities purchased after August 7, 1986. Before the change, banks were allowed to deduct from their taxable income an amount equal to 80 percent of the interest expense of funds used to carry municipal securities. The elimination of this tax deduction has already caused banks to reduce their investments in municipal securities and will significantly diminish their importance as purchasers of municipal securities.

Banks will be allowed to continue to deduct 80 percent of the interest expense for funds used to carry municipal securities financing traditional governmental projects or hospital and university projects if the issuer expects to issue less than $10 million in debt per year. This will enable these small issuers to continue to sell securities to some banks, but will largely eliminate banks as purchasers of other issuers' securities.

REGULATORY AND LEGISLATIVE EFFECTS

Regulation has only a limited direct effect on the municipal securities market. Issuers' debt offerings are not regulated except by general financial regulations. For instance, conditions under which tax-exempt commercial paper can be issued are set by the Securities and Exchange Commission (SEC). The Municipal Securities Rulemaking Board (MSRB) was established in 1975 to develop and update regulations by which dealers, dealer banks, and brokers in the municipal market are to operate. These regulations are enforced by the SEC, the federal bank regulators, and the National Association of Securities Dealers.

The regulation of money funds by the SEC indirectly affects the short-term municipal market significantly since municipal money funds are such important purchasers in the market. SEC regulations governing money market funds' purchases and holdings have been important in promoting certain types of short-term municipal securities. (See the chapter on money market funds.)

Federal tax legislation can result in significant changes in the municipal market. In particular, the repeal or proposed repeal of the tax-exempt status of certain types of issues can drive the market to extreme reactions. Such a reaction was seen at the end of 1985 when Congress' proposed restrictions on tax-exempt borrowing produced a record volume of municipal issues. The Tax Reform Act of 1986 should have a number of effects on the municipal market. Banks should become less active investors in municipals because of the loss, in most cases, of their interest cost deduction. The ratio of tax-exempt to taxable yields may rise because the act lowers marginal tax rates for many individuals and corporations. And many private use issuers will lose their ability to issue tax-exempt debt, while others will have caps imposed on the amount of tax-exempt debt they are allowed to issue.

State legislation can also cause changes in the municipal market by limiting the amount or type of tax-exempt debt that may be issued. For example, following California's Proposition 13 the volume of general obligation debt issued by California municipalities fell significantly.

CONCLUSION

Short-term municipal securities have become important instruments of the money market. Traditional notes, such as revenue anticipation notes, tax anticipation notes and bond anticipation notes, although remaining important to issuers wishing to borrow funds for short-term purposes, have been responsible for only a small portion of the recent growth of the short-term municipal market. Most of the growth in this market has resulted from states' and municipalities' use of variable-rate securities and tax-exempt commercial paper. The new instruments offer the investor the characteristics of short-term investments, while enabling issuers to gather funds for long-term projects at short-term rates.

References

Conery, Kevin. "Short-term Municipals: An Often Misunderstood Market," in "The Yield Curve." Shearson Lehman Brothers, January 20, 1986.

Feldstein, Sylvan G., and Frank J. Fabozzi. "Option Tender or Put Bonds." *The Municipal Bond Handbook*, Vol. 1. Edited by Frank J. Fabozzi et al. Homewood, Illinois: Dow Jones-Irwin, 1983.

Feldstein, Sylvan G., and Frank J. Fabozzi. "Tax, Revenue, Grant, and Bond Anticipation Notes." *The Municipal Bond Handbook*, Vol. 2. Edited by Sylvan G. Feldstein, Frank J. Fabozzi, and Irving M. Pollack. Homewood, Illinois: Dow Jones-Irwin, 1983.

Goodwin, James J. "Tax-exempt Commercial Paper." *The Municipal Bond Handbook*, Vol. 2. Edited by Sylvan G. Feldstein, Frank J. Fabozzi, and Irving M. Pollack. Homewood, Illinois: Dow Jones-Irwin, 1983.

Hicks , Cadmus M. "Letters-of-Credit Backed Bonds." *The Municipal Bond Handbook*, Vol. 1. Edited by Frank J. Fabozzi et al. Homewood, Illinois: Dow Jones-Irwin, 1983.

Lamb, Robert and Stephen P. Rappaport. *Municipal Bonds: The Comprehensive Review of Tax-Exempt Securities and Public Finance*. New York: McGraw-Hill, 1980.

Laufenberg, Daniel E. "Industrial Development Bonds: Some Aspects of the Current Controversy." *Federal Reserve Bulletin* 68 (March 1982), pp. 135-41.

Longley, Alan. "Variable Rate Bonds and Zero-Coupon Bonds." *The Municipal Bond Handbook*, Vol. 1. Edited by Frank J. Fabozzi et al. Homewood, Illinois: Dow Jones-Irwin, 1983.

Peterson, John E. "Recent Developments in Tax-Exempt Bond Markets." Government Finance Research Center, Government Finance Officers Association, Washington, D. C., April 15, 1985. Photocopy.

Proctor, Allen J., and Kathleene K. Donahoo. "Commercial Bank Investment in Municipal Securities." Federal Reserve Bank of New York, *Quarterly Review* (Winter 1983-84).

Public Securities Association. *Fundamentals of Municipal Bonds*. New York: Public Securities Association, 1981.

Schrager, Steven D. "Special Report: Investor's Guide to Municipal Bond Insurance." L. F. Rothschild, Unterberg, Towbin, Inc., Municipal Bond Research, 1986.

Smith Barney, Harris Upham and Company, Incorporated, Short-Term Finance Group. "An Introduction to Short-Term Tax-Exempt Financing, Innovations and Techniques." Smith Barney, Harris Upham and Company, Incorporated, 1986.

Standard and Poor's. *Credit Overview, Municipal Ratings*. New York: Standard and Poor's Corporation, 1983.

U.S. Congress. Joint Committee on Taxation. *Tax Reform Proposals: Tax Treatment of State and Local Government Bonds*. Report prepared for the Committee on Ways and Means and the Committee on Finance. 99th Cong., 1st sess., 1985. Joint Committee Print.

9

COMMERCIAL PAPER

Timothy D. Rowe

Commercial paper is the oldest and one of the most important money market instruments in the United States. The volume of commercial paper outstanding exceeds that of every other money market instrument except Treasury bills. Commercial paper is a short-term promissory note issued by a company to raise short-term cash. Although companies can raise short-term cash by borrowing from banks, companies with strong credit ratings usually can borrow money more cheaply by issuing commercial paper. Companies issuing commercial paper borrow from investors directly, bypassing the intermediary services of banks. Since the notes are usually unsecured, the market is dominated by large corporations with the highest credit ratings.

MARKET PARTICIPANTS

Issuers of commercial paper are divided into financial companies and nonfinancial companies. Financial companies such as bank holding companies, sales and personal finance companies, insurance companies, and leasing and factoring companies issue the majority of commercial paper (see the table). Financial companies tend to raise funds in the commercial paper market on a more-or-less continuous basis to support their consumer and business lending. Nonfinancial businesses such as public utilities, manufacturers, retailers and wholesalers, and transportation companies issue commercial paper at less frequent intervals to meet seasonal or other short-term needs for funds.

Institutional investors buy nearly all commercial paper issued. Money market funds are the largest investors, buying one third of all commercial paper. Other groups that buy substantial amounts include bank trust departments, pension funds, insurance companies, state and local governments, and nonfinancial corporations.

CHARACTERISTICS OF COMMERCIAL PAPER

Companies generally issue commercial paper in bearer form (payable to the bearer of the note) but at the request of the investor will register the paper in his

COMMERCIAL PAPER OUTSTANDING, MAY 1986

Seasonally Adjusted, Billions of Dollars

	Amount	Percent of Total
All issuers	309.8	100.0
Financial companies	229.7	74.1
Directly placed	142.3	45.9
Dealer-placed	87.4	28.2
Nonfinancial companies	80.1	25.8

Source: *Federal Reserve Bulletin.*

name. Registered paper protects the investor against loss or theft of the note, but bearer paper can be more easily resold if necessary. Although investors can occasionally purchase commercial paper in units as small as $25,000, a realistic minimum investment is $100,000. The denomination of an individual note is determined by the amount the investor has to invest. Because institutional investors dominate the market the most common denomination is $1 million. One of the advantages of commercial paper is that the maturity can be tailored to meet the needs of issuers and investors within a range of one to 270 days. Companies rarely issue commercial paper with longer maturities since a public offering of paper with a maturity greater than 270 days must be registered with the Securities and Exchange Commission; such a registration involves time and expense. Most commercial paper is issued with an original maturity of between 5 and 45 days; 30 days is the most popular maturity.

Yields As is the case with Treasury bills and bankers acceptances, commercial paper is typically issued at a discount from face value. The investor pays less than the face amount for the paper and receives the face amount at maturity. Investors can request, however, to purchase paper as an interest-bearing note, in which case the investor pays the face amount for the paper and receives the face amount plus accrued interest at maturity. Rates on all commercial paper, however, are quoted on a discount basis. When a company issues interest-bearing paper it converts the quoted discount rate to an equivalent add-on rate so that the investor gets the same effective rate of return whether he buys discount or interest-bearing paper. (See the chapter on Treasury bills for the formula for converting a discount rate to an add-on rate.) Average daily interest rates on commercial paper with one, three, and six months to maturity are

Chart 1

YIELDS ON 30-DAY COMMERCIAL PAPER AND TREASURY BILLS

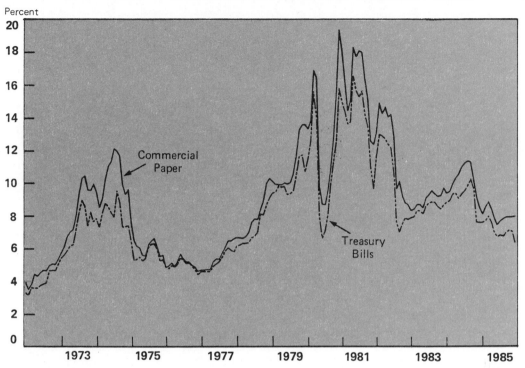

Percent

Source: Board of Governors of the Federal Reserve System.

published weekly by the Federal Reserve's Board of Governors in the "Selected Interest Rates" statistical release.

Yields on commercial paper tend to track the yields on other money market instruments. Rates on commercial paper are always higher than the rates on Treasury bills of the same maturity (Chart 1). One reason for the higher rate on commercial paper is that, unlike the Treasury, an issuer of commercial paper might default on his obligations. Investors demand a higher promised rate of return on commercial paper to offset the risk of default. Additionally, because interest earned on Treasury bills is generally exempt from state and local taxation but interest earned on commercial paper is fully taxable, for many investors commercial paper has to offer a higher interest rate in order to provide the same after-tax return. The rate on commercial paper is more closely related to the rates on negotiable certificates of deposit (CDs) and bankers acceptances. The commercial paper rate is usually a few basis points higher than the rate on CDs, presumably because an investment in commercial paper is somewhat less liquid and possibly slightly riskier than an investment in a CD.

Quality Ratings Since 1970, when the Penn Central Transportation Co. defaulted with $82 million of commercial paper outstanding, most commercial paper has carried ratings. The ratings provide investors with opinions on the ability of the issuers to repay the paper on time and they allow investors to compare the riskiness of commercial paper issued by different companies. Five services currently evaluate commercial paper: Moody's Investors Service, Inc., Standard & Poor's Corporation, Fitch Investors Service, Duff and Phelps, Inc., and McCarthy, Crisanti & Maffei, Inc. The first four charge a fee to the issuing company of around $5,000 for the initial rating plus an annual maintenance fee ranging from $5,000 to $25,000 per year. McCarthy charges the investors that subscribe to its service rather than the issuer. Almost all companies that issue commercial paper obtain ratings from at least one of these services and most obtain two ratings. The rating services classify an issuer into one of three or four basic categories based on the probability of repayment at maturity relative to other issuers. From highest to lowest quality, paper ratings run: Prime-1 (P-1), Prime-2 (P-2), Prime-3 (P-3) for Moody's; A-1+, A-1, A-2, A-3 for Standard and Poor's; F-1, F-2, F-3 for Fitch; Duff-1+, Duff-1, Duff-1-, Duff-2, Duff-3 for Duff and Phelps; and MCM 1 through MCM 6 for McCarthy. Approximately four-fifths of the rated issuers fall into the top-grade category (P-1 or A-1), and most of the others fall into the second grade. Only about 1 percent of the rated issuers fall into the lowest category (P-3 or A-3). Since few investors will purchase grade 3 paper, companies with poor credit ratings typically rely on bank loans for financing.

Companies that are not in the top rating category must pay higher rates to borrow in the commercial paper market since investors demand an interest rate premium for taking on the additional risk of default. The spread between the interest rate on medium-grade (P-2 or A-2) commercial paper and the interest rate on prime-grade (P-1 or A-1) commercial paper has averaged around 40 basis points, except during recessions and other periods of financial stress when it has been considerably higher (see Chart 2).

Backup Lines of Credit Most issuers back their paper with lines of credit from banks. Even though the average maturity of commercial paper is very short, there is still the risk that an issuer might not be able to pay off or roll over maturing paper. For example, the failure of a big issuer might make it impossible or at least extremely expensive for other issuers to sell new paper to pay off maturing paper. Issuers therefore obtain backup lines of credit as liquidity insurance against periods of financial stress. Generally a nonfinancial company must have unused lines of credit equal to 100 percent of its commercial paper outstanding in order to obtain a high rating. A large, well-regarded issuer with excellent liquidity,

Chart 2

SPREAD BETWEEN THE RATES ON
PRIME- AND MEDIUM-GRADE COMMERCIAL PAPER

Basis Points

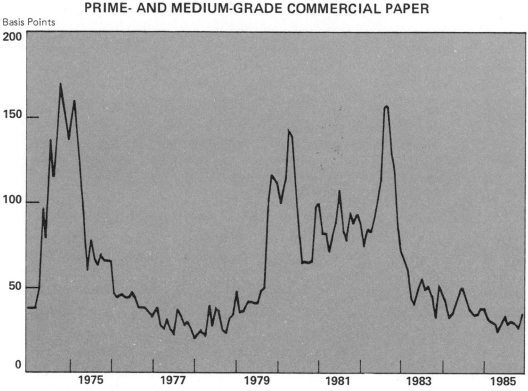

Source: Board of Governors of the Federal Reserve System.

particularly a large finance company or bank holding company, may obtain a high rating with less complete backing, sometimes less than 50 percent.

Lines of credit come in several forms. A standard credit line agreement allows a commercial paper issuer to borrow for up to 270 days. In return for such a line, the issuer either holds compensating balances at the bank or pays an annual fee of about 1/8 percent of the line of credit. A standard line of credit can be withdrawn by the bank at any time in response to a change in the company's finances. A revolving line of credit is more secure because, in return for an initial setup fee and an annual fee of about 1/4 percent of the unused line, the bank guarantees that it will honor the line of credit for some number of years. A swing line of credit is used to borrow funds for very short periods, often to cover a shortfall in the actual proceeds of paper issued on a particular day.

Smaller and less well-known companies are able to borrow in the commercial paper market by issuing commercial paper backed by the financial support of a firm with a high credit rating. One common support arrangement is a letter of credit from a bank. The letter of credit guarantees that the bank will repay the issuer's commercial paper at maturity if the issuer cannot do so. When paper is backed by a letter of credit the rating agencies assign the rating of the bank to the paper rather than the lower rating of the issuer. The bank in effect rents its credit standing to the lower-rated borrower by guaranteeing that principal and interest will be repaid. The bank earns a fee of 1/2 percent to 1-1/2 percent of the outstanding guarantee for issuing such backing. The issuer avoids payment of a very high premium in interest rates and in some instances gains entrance to the market that might otherwise have been denied. A second form of support arrangement is a guarantee or endorsement from an insurance company. The most common form of support is a guarantee by a parent company of its subsidiary's paper. As of May 1986, 7.7 percent of commercial paper outstanding was backed by letters of credit or other guarantees.[1]

THE MARKET

Placement   Issuers sell their paper to investors either directly using their own sales forces or indirectly through dealers. The method of placement used depends primarily on the transactions costs of these alternatives. To place paper, dealers charge a commission of roughly one-tenth to one-eighth of a percentage point at an annual rate, which works out to around $2.75 to $3.50 per $1 million per day. Most dealers are located in New York City and also deal in other instruments.

When a company issues commercial paper through a dealer, early in the day the treasurer of the company tells its dealer how much paper the company wants to sell and in what maturities. The dealer contacts prospective customers to determine the rate at which he will be able to sell the paper. On the basis of this information the dealer determines the rate at which he will buy the paper from the issuer. He also relays to the issuer any special requests for paper in specific quantities and maturities, but the issuer makes the final decision on these matters. The trade is usually settled the afternoon of the same day. The dealer resells the paper to investors as quickly as possible; only 5 to 10 percent of paper bought is taken into inventory. The dealer finances any paper held in inventory either with overnight repurchase agreements or with secured call loans from banks.

---

[1] Federal Reserve Bank of New York, "Commercial Paper" release, June 24, 1986. The figures on commercial paper backed by support arrangements include only nonbank commercial paper issued through dealers. The figures do not significantly understate the total, however, because most direct issuers have no need for support arrangements and bank-related issuers usually do not have them.

A company that consistently has several hundred million dollars or more of paper outstanding and that issues paper on a steady basis usually finds it less costly to set up its own sales force and sell its paper directly to investors. By issuing paper directly the company saves the dealer fees and may be able to issue at slightly better rates by tailoring the maturity of its paper to investor demand. Currently there are about 70 direct issuers. Most direct issuers are large finance companies or bank holding companies and their nonbank affiliates; these companies issue such large volumes of paper that they account for almost half of the commercial paper outstanding (see the table).

Each day the direct issuer determines how much he wants to borrow and in what maturities. He then posts offering rates based on his estimate of investor demand at each maturity. The issuer monitors the flow of money during the day and adjusts his rates as necessary: raising rates if the volume of sales is unsatisfactory and lowering rates if a given day's issue proves too popular.

Some direct issuers offer investors the option of purchasing commercial paper in book-entry form. Under this procedure, ownership is recorded on a computer and the investor receives only a receipt as evidence of purchase. Book-entry paper saves issuers the cost of printing certificates and protects investors against loss, theft, and counterfeiting of the certificates. All market participants save the expense and time involved in transferring and inspecting the certificates. Currently, large volume direct issuers issue about half of their paper in book-entry form, but probably within a few years all commercial paper will be issued in book-entry form.

Approximately 10 percent of direct issue paper is sold under master note agreements. A master note is a type of open-ended commercial paper that allows the investment and withdrawal of funds on a daily basis up to a predetermined amount and pays a daily interest rate tied to the current commercial paper rate. The typical investor is a bank trust department, for whom a master note provides a convenient way to invest for short periods small sums of money from various trust accounts. Some regional bank holding companies offer master notes to their corporate customers. Corporations can invest their excess cash balances in the master note agreements, which offer a slightly higher return than overnight repurchase agreements. Each day the issuer tells the investor the rate on the master note and the investor tells the issuer the amount of paper it will take under the master note.

Secondary Market The secondary market for commercial paper is much less active than the secondary markets for other money market instruments such as Treasury bills, certificates of deposit and bankers acceptances. Virtually no commercial paper is traded between dealers. Commercial paper is very heterogeneous in terms of the mix of issues and maturities which makes it difficult to assemble large blocks of identical paper for trading. In recent years, however, some money market dealers have begun trading the paper issued by large finance companies and large bank holding companies. These companies often have large blocks of paper outstanding which mature on a given day, making it possible to assemble tradeable round lots.

Despite the lack of an active secondary market, an investment in commercial paper is somewhat liquid. If an investor has an urgent demand for funds before the paper he has purchased matures, he can usually sell the paper back to the issuing dealer or the direct issuer. Market participants estimate that less than one percent of commercial paper is bought back, however. Investors rarely request to sell paper back because they can tailor the maturity to coincide with their anticipated cash needs.

HISTORY OF COMMERCIAL PAPER

Commercial paper has been issued since the early 1800s, when business firms began using the sale of open market paper as a substitute for bank loans. A major factor behind the early growth of the commercial paper market was the decentralized banking system in the United States. Since banks were restricted to single states and even localities, it was difficult for the banking system to meet a strong demand for credit in one region of the country by transferring funds from other regions. A strong seasonal demand for credit in one region would therefore cause interest rates in the region to rise relative to interest rates in other regions. Firms within the high interest rate region would obtain funds more cheaply by selling commercial paper to banks in low interest rate regions.

During the 1800s commercial paper borrowers were primarily nonfinancial firms such as manufacturers, wholesalers and retailers. Virtually all paper was sold through dealers and purchased by banks. In the early 1900s, finance companies emerged as major commercial paper borrowers as the automobile industry, sales finance, and small-loan companies grew in importance. In 1920, the largest sales-finance company, General Motors Acceptance Corporation, began to place its paper directly with investors and to tailor maturities to investors' specifications.

Despite strong growth in commercial paper issued by finance companies, the total amount of commercial paper outstanding grew very little on net in the first half of the 20th century. Growth in commercial paper was checked by the sharp fall in business credit demand during the depression of the 1930s and the sharp fall in consumer credit demand during the Second World War. The one major development in the market was that business firms replaced banks as the largest

118

investors in commercial paper. After banks were prohibited from paying interest on demand deposits by the Banking Act of 1933, companies began more closely monitoring their demand deposit balances and investing their excess funds in commercial paper in order to obtain some yield.

The commercial paper market grew rapidly following World War II as strong growth in consumer and business use of credit led to strong growth in finance company paper. At the same time, nonfinancial corporations bought more commercial paper as they became more adept in managing their cash balances.

Developments Since the Mid-1960s Two events stimulated growth in commercial paper in the 1960s. During the last three quarters of 1966, money market interest rates rose above Regulation Q ceilings on negotiable bank certificates of deposit (CDs), making it difficult for banks to raise funds to meet the strong corporate loan demand existing at the time. Many potential commercial paper borrowers who formerly relied exclusively on bank short-term credit were forced to turn to the commercial paper market. Consequently, the annual growth rate of commercial paper outstanding rose from 7.8 percent in 1965 to 46.6 percent in 1966.

In 1969, interest rates in the money market again rose above the Regulation Q ceilings on CDs, and commercial paper outstanding surged 54.7 percent (see Chart 3). Financial innovation by banks contributed to this growth. Since banks could not raise funds by issuing CDs, the banking system sold commercial paper through bank holding companies, which used the funds to purchase part of their subsidiary banks' loan portfolios. This method of financing new loans resulted in strong growth in bank-related commercial paper in late 1969 and early 1970. In August 1970, the Federal Reserve removed the interest-rate ceiling on short-term CDs and imposed a reserve requirement on funds raised in the commercial paper market and channeled to a member bank, effectively putting an end to the practice.

The commercial paper market was rocked in June 1970 by Penn Central's default with $82 million of commercial paper outstanding. Investors became more concerned about the creditworthiness of issuers and many companies experienced difficulty refinancing their maturing paper. Financial disruption was lessened after the Federal Reserve removed the Regulation Q ceilings on 30- to 89-day CDs and temporarily liberalized the discount policy for member banks. These actions insured that funds were available from commercial banks to provide alternative financing for corporations having difficulty rolling over commercial paper.

Wage and price controls imposed during the early 1970s dampened growth of the commercial paper market. On October 15, 1971, the Committee on Interest

Chart 3

COMMERCIAL PAPER OUTSTANDING

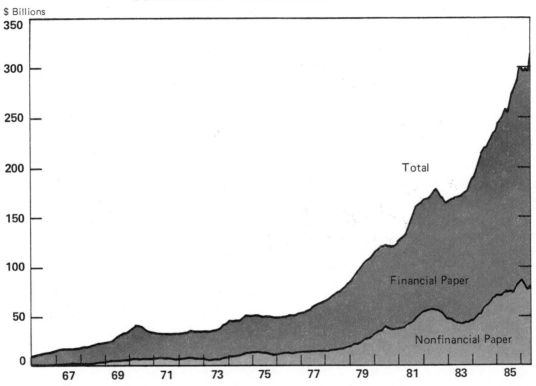

Source: Board of Governors of the Federal Reserve System.

and Dividends established voluntary restraints on "administered" interest rates such as the prime rate. No restraints were placed on open market rates, however. The policy triggered flows of funds between controlled and uncontrolled credit markets as the relationship between administered rates and market rates changed. As interest rates rose in 1972, banks came under pressure from the Committee to moderate their prime rate increases, and by early 1973 the prime rate was held artificially below the commercial paper rate. Nonfinancial firms substituted short-term bank loans for funds raised through commercial paper issues. Consequently the volume of nonfinancial commercial paper outstanding fell sharply during the first half of 1973. In April of 1973, the Committee tried to stem the exodus from the commercial paper market by establishing a dual prime rate: one rate for large firms moved with open market rates and the other rate for smaller firms was controlled. During the next few months, however, the commercial paper rate rose faster than the prime rate for large firms and substitution out

Chart 4

NONFINANCIAL COMMERCIAL PAPER AS A
PERCENTAGE OF SHORT-TERM BUSINESS CREDIT

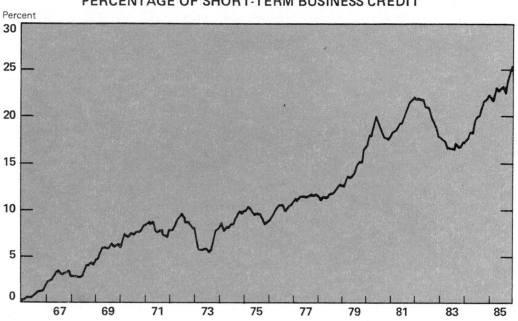

Note: Short-term business credit equals nonfinancial commercial paper plus commercial and industrial loans outstanding.

Sources: *Federal Reserve Bulletin; Business Conditions Digest*

of paper continued. In the fourth quarter of 1973 the controls were removed and the commercial paper rate dropped below the prime rate, causing nonfinancial firms to return to the commercial paper market.

The commercial paper market grew rapidly in the latter part of the 1970s. As market interest rates rose above the Regulation Q ceiling rates on savings and time deposits, many individuals transferred their savings balances into money market funds. Money market funds in turn bought substantial amounts of commercial paper and other money market instruments. At the same time more nonfinancial companies began issuing commercial paper as the cost of commercial paper remained low relative to the cost of bank loans. Nonfinancial commercial paper rose from 10 percent of all short-term business borrowings (nonfinancial commercial paper plus commercial and industrial loans) in the mid-1970s to 20 percent in the early 1980s (Chart 4).

Banks reacted to the loss of market share by becoming more aggressive in pricing loans—offering their large customers short-term loans at rates of interest tied closely to open market rates, which are generally below the prime rate. Banks

121

also began providing services to support their customers' issuance of commercial paper. In particular, banks offered flexible short-term borrowing arrangements to allow commercial paper issuers to adjust the timing of their paper sales. Some banks began placing commercial paper as agents for their customers, although this practice has been challenged in court.

Commercial paper became a more attractive source of financing for companies as interest rates rose in the late 1970s because the effect of reserve requirements on a bank's cost of funds increases as interest rates rise. Large commercial banks fund loans at the margin primarily by issuing certificates of deposit, which pay rates roughly equal to commercial paper rates. Since the cost of funds to banks includes reserve requirements, bank lending rates are higher than open market rates.[2] Since reserve requirements are proportional, higher interest rates increase the cost of reserve requirements in basis points and increase the spread between bank lending rates and open market rates. As bank lending rates rise relative to open market rates, more companies substitute the issuance of commercial paper for bank loans.[3]

In the early 1980s, the commercial paper market continued to grow rapidly. Many medium-sized firms used letter-of-credit backing to obtain high ratings for their commercial paper and access to the commercial paper market. On the investor side of the market, volatile interest rates made investors wary of long-term fixed-rate securities. On the issuer side, high rates in the bond markets prompted many issuers to seek short-term credit while awaiting a decline in long-term rates. Funds therefore tended to flow away from the capital markets and into the money markets. A large share of these funds were channeled into commercial paper. As rates retreated from their 1982 peaks, however, many corporations were encouraged to issue long-term bonds. In 1983 and early 1986 in particular, the flow reversed and outstanding commercial paper of nonfinancial corporations contracted.

NEW DIRECTIONS FOR THE COMMERCIAL PAPER MARKET

Interest Rate Swaps   Part of the strong growth in commercial paper in recent years has been caused by the use of commercial paper to finance the floating-

---

[2] The following example illustrates how reserve requirements against CDs increase the cost of funds to banks. Suppose the reserve requirement against CDs is 3 percent. Then for every dollar obtained through a CD, only 97 cents are available to lend. The funds idled as reserves increase the effective cost of funds raised by issuing a CD. If a bank's CD offers a 10 percent yield, the additional cost imposed by the reserve requirement is 31 basis points (10 / .97 = 10.31).

[3] Since 1980 the cost of reserve requirements has been reduced. The Monetary Control Act of 1980 lowered the basic reserve requirement on short-term nonpersonal time deposits from six percent to three percent.

rate side of many interest rate swap programs. An interest rate swap is a transaction in which two parties, one with fixed-rate debt and the other with floating-rate debt, agree to exchange interest-payment obligations, thereby converting their type of payment from fixed-rate to floating-rate and vice versa. They exchange only interest payments; no principal changes hands.

In one use of interest rate swaps, companies have combined interest rate swaps with commercial paper issuance to obtain long-term fixed-rate financing at lower rates than they could obtain by issuing fixed-rate bonds. In such a transaction, a company first enters into an interest rate swap agreement under which for a number of years it makes payments at a fixed rate of interest and receives floating-rate payments tied to the commercial paper rate.[4] The company then issues commercial paper and rolls over the paper as it matures. The company offsets the interest payments on its commercial paper with the floating-rate payments it receives under the swap agreement, and it is left making fixed-rate payments. The company thus raises money in the commercial paper market but, because of the swap agreement, pays a fixed rate of interest for a number of years.[5]

Collateralized Commercial Paper Some small firms have been able to obtain higher ratings for their commercial paper and gain access to the commercial paper market by backing their paper with collateral. In 1984 Merrill Lynch introduced a program for savings and loan associations that allowed them to sell commercial paper backed by Treasury or agency securities. Because of the strength of the underlying collateral, the issues have generally received top credit ratings, which allow the savings and loan associations to issue paper at a lower rate. This program has been recently adapted to nonfinancial businesses: several retailers have issued commercial paper backed by accounts receivable.

Internationalization The market for commercial paper, formerly exclusively American, is becoming an international market. An increasing number of foreign companies are issuing commercial paper in the United States and companies from the United States and other nations are issuing commercial paper in the Euromarket.

Commercial paper issued by foreign companies in the United States is known as Yankee paper. As of May 1986, foreign issuers collectively had about $34 billion in commercial paper outstanding, which was 11 percent of the total

---

[4] This is only one type of interest rate swap agreement. The floating-rate side of the majority of swaps is priced off the London interbank offered rate on Eurodollar deposits.

[5] For more detail see Bank for International Settlements [1986, Chapter 2].

commercial paper market.[6] Foreign banks and bank holding companies issued about one-half of all Yankee paper outstanding. In addition, foreign utilities, finance companies, multinational corporations, and even foreign governments have tapped the U.S. market. By tapping the large investor base in the United States, foreign companies often can borrow more cheaply than in the Eurodollar market.

Some foreign companies use dollars raised by issuing paper in the United States to finance the activities of subsidiaries in the United States or to support other activities that require dollar payments for goods and services, such as oil imports. Others exchange the dollars for the currency of their home country. Companies have used this procedure because they are prohibited from issuing commercial paper denominated in their currencies. The procedure may become less common, however, because several foreign governments recently have relaxed their prohibitions against paper issuance.

Dollar-denominated commercial paper issued abroad is known as Euro-commercial paper. Euro-commercial paper evolved out of the Eurodollar note issuance facility, in which a group of underwriting banks guarantees the availability of funds for the medium-term (five to seven years) by purchasing any unsold notes at each rollover date or by providing a standby credit. The majority of Euro-notes are now issued without a bank backup facility explicitly attached.[7] Such notes are known as Euro-commercial paper because they closely resemble commercial paper issued in the United States. At present the market is fairly small. As of mid-1986 there was roughly $20 to $25 billion of Euro-commercial paper and Euro-notes outstanding, of which U.S. issuers accounted for perhaps $3 to $4 billion. Companies have issued Euro-commercial paper in order to tap the European investor base and to diversify the maturities of their short-term debt. The Euro-commercial paper market is generally more receptive to firms with well-known names that want to issue paper in longer maturities.

CONCLUSION

Commercial paper is an important source of financing for many companies, both domestic and foreign, and a popular short-term investment for many institutions. The commercial paper market grew substantially over the past decade for several reasons: (1) many new investors obtained indirect access to the market through money market funds, (2) many companies substituted commercial paper issuance for short-term bank credit, (3) new firms gained access to the market through support arrangements, and (4) until recently, many

---

[6] Federal Reserve Bank of New York, "Commercial Paper" release, June 24, 1986.
[7] Most issuers do, however, have a separate backup line of credit.

124

companies substituted short- for long-term financing. Commercial paper will no doubt remain an important source of short-term financing for companies with strong credit ratings given its cost advantage relative to bank loans.

References

Abken, Peter. "Commercial Paper." In *Instruments of the Money Market.* 5th ed. Edited by Timothy Q. Cook and Bruce J. Summers. Richmond: Federal Reserve Bank of Richmond, 1981.

Bank for International Settlements. *Recent Innovations in International Banking.* Basle: Bank for International Settlements, 1986.

Baxter, Nevins D. *The Commercial Paper Market.* Boston: The Bankers Publishing Company, 1966.

Foulke, Roy A. *The Commercial Paper Market.* Boston: The Bankers Publishing Company, 1931.

Hurley, Evelyn. "The Commercial Paper Market." *Federal Reserve Bulletin* 63 (June 1977), pp. 525-36.

———. "The Commercial Paper Market since the Mid-Seventies." *Federal Reserve Bulletin* 68 (June 1982), pp. 327-34.

Puglisi, Donald J. "Commercial Paper: A Primer." *Federal Home Loan Bank Board Journal* 13 (December 1980), pp. 5-10.

Stigum, Marcia. *The Money Market.* Rev. ed. Homewood, Illinois: Dow Jones-Irwin, 1983.

10

BANKERS ACCEPTANCES

Eric Hill

The bankers acceptance is one of the oldest money market instruments, yet it continues to be one of the least familiar. Stripped of procedural details, a bankers acceptance is simply a vehicle that facilitates short-term loans particularly between importers and investors. It is called a "bankers acceptance" because a bank "accepts" the responsibility of repaying the loan, thereby shielding the investor from default risk.

THE CREATION OF A BANKERS ACCEPTANCE

The following example of the life of a bankers acceptance is illustrated in Chart 1.

Mr. Smith, an automobile dealer and customer of American Bank, wants to import cars from Mr. Sato, a Japanese automobile manufacturer and customer of Japan Bank. Smith would like to pay for the cars after they arrive in the United States, but Sato, who is unfamiliar with the creditworthiness of Smith, prefers immediate payment. Bankers acceptances alleviate this commonly occurring problem in international trade.

After suggesting acceptance financing, Smith offers $100,000 payable 60 days after shipment for a certain quantity of cars. Sato considers the discounted present value of the offer, since that is how much he will collect upon shipment, and accepts. Smith then asks American Bank to issue a commercial letter of credit on his behalf in favor of Mr. Sato. The letter of credit contains the terms of the proposed transaction and represents American Bank's promise to stand behind Mr. Smith's ability to pay Mr. Sato's $100,000 invoice in 60 days. The letter also informs Sato that his invoice for $100,000 payable in 60 days (called a "time draft") is eligible for "acceptance" if presented along with shipping documents giving American Bank temporary title to the cars. With the letter of credit in hand, Mr. Sato will be willing to ship the cars before receiving payment.

American Bank sends the letter of credit to Japan Bank, which informs Mr. Sato of its arrival. Sato then ships the cars, blank-endorses the shipping

THE LIFE OF A TYPICAL BANKERS ACCEPTANCE

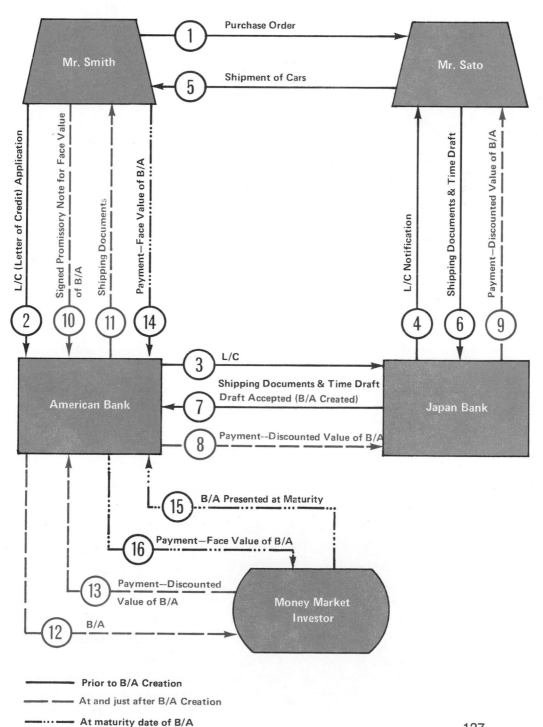

Chart 1

Prior to B/A Creation

At and just after B/A Creation

At maturity date of B/A

127

documents so that title is transferred to the holder, and presents these documents and his $100,000 time draft to Japan Bank. In return, Japan Bank pays him the discounted value of the time draft. As far as Mr. Sato is concerned, the transaction is now over. Japan Bank takes the draft and shipping documents to American Bank, which stamps the draft "Accepted," thereby creating a bankers acceptance and indicating its unconditional obligation to pay $100,000 to whoever presents the accepted draft on its maturity date in 60 days. American Bank informs Mr. Smith of the arrival of the shipping documents, and after he signs a note or makes some other arrangement to pay $100,000 in 60 days, the shipping documents are released to him so that he can claim his cars at the dock when they arrive.

Japan Bank can either take back the newly created bankers acceptance to hold as an investment, or it can request that American Bank discount the acceptance. If the latter occurs, American Bank then faces a similar set of options. It can either hold the acceptance, entering the discounted value of the acceptance onto its books as a loan, or it can sell the acceptance to an investor, thereby replenishing the funds that it paid out when it discounted the acceptance for Japan Bank. Whoever ends up holding the acceptance serves to finance Mr. Smith's import of Japanese cars.

Finally, at some point on or before the maturity date of the acceptance, Mr. Smith pays American Bank $100,000 which it uses to redeem the acceptance when the investor presents it at maturity.

In the above example, the bankers acceptance financed the import of goods into the United States. The vast majority of acceptances created by U.S. banks finance one of three types of transactions: 1) U.S. imports, 2) U.S. exports, and 3) the storage of goods in or shipment of goods between two foreign countries (third-country acceptances). Acceptances are also used to finance the shipment of goods within the United States (domestic shipment), to finance the storage of commodities in the United States (domestic storage), and to provide dollars temporarily to countries that experience seasonal shortages of dollars when their imports are much greater than exports (dollar exchange). Chart 2 depicts the volume of outstanding U.S. bankers acceptances classified according to the nature of the underlying transaction. The total volume of acceptances outstanding grew rapidly during the late 1970s and early 1980s but has levelled off and even fallen somewhat in the past two years. This fall in volume is partly attributable to declines in commodity prices, which have depressed the dollar-volume of world trade, and declines in interest rates, which have diminished the attractiveness to the borrower of acceptances relative to conventional loans. Also, financial deregulation in the United States has led banks to introduce other forms of

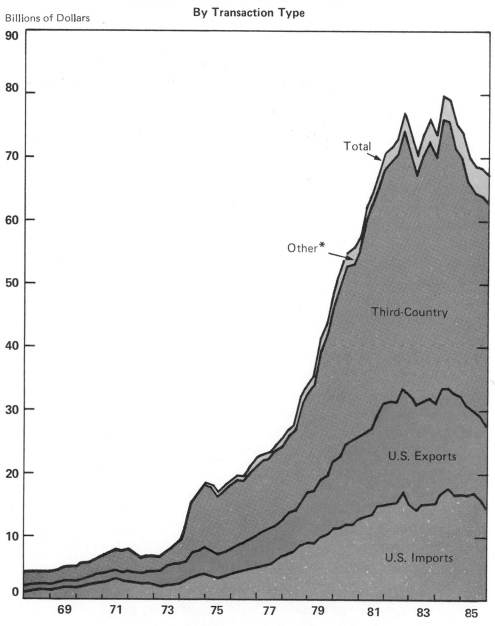

Chart 2

BANKERS ACCEPTANCE VOLUME
By Transaction Type

Billions of Dollars

Total

Other*

Third-Country

U.S. Exports

U.S. Imports

69   71   73   75   77   79   81   83   85

*Includes domestic shipment, domestic storage, and dollar exchange acceptances.

Source: Federal Reserve Bank of New York

below-prime-rate financing that compete with acceptances to fill short-term credit demand.[1]

Whatever the nature of the underlying transaction, the resulting bankers acceptance is a safe, highly marketable short-term money market instrument. The original maturity of acceptances generally ranges from 30 to 270 days, with 90 days being the most common, and it can be tailored to closely match the period needed to ship and dispose of the goods being traded. The market yield on bankers acceptances has historically moved very closely with the yield on negotiable certificates of deposit (CDs). Investors view bankers acceptances as being nearly identical to negotiable CDs because both are short-term unconditional obligations of a bank to pay the holder a specified amount on a specified date in the future. The slightly lower interest rate at which bankers acceptances have historically traded relative to comparable negotiable CDs probably stems from the slight safety advantage of acceptances. While both instruments are primary liabilities of a bank, the face value of an acceptance is also the secondary liability of the drawer of the acceptance (Mr. Sato in our example). Thus, should a bank fail, its CD holders can collect FDIC insurance, but only up to $100,000, whereas holders of acceptances created by the bank have recourse to the drawer for full face value. Because both the accepting bank and the acceptance drawer are liable, bankers acceptances are referred to as "two-name paper."

The market yield of an acceptance does not fully account for the cost of acceptance financing to the borrower, however. In our example, American Bank would have charged Mr. Smith a percentage commission for the service of making his letter of credit eligible for payment acceptance. Commissions currently average about 50 basis points (50 one-hundredths of a percentage point) per year applied to the face value of the acceptance but can vary depending on the perceived soundness of the borrower. Nevertheless, bankers acceptance financing can be an attractive alternative to other forms of financing, especially for firms that are unable to issue prime-quality commercial paper. Even firms that can issue prime commercial paper may find that for certain kinds of transactions, particularly those that can be financed with acceptances that are "eligible for discount" (see below), the "all-in" cost of bankers acceptance financing is less than the commercial paper rate plus associated fees.

THE ACCEPTANCE MARKET

The participants in the bankers acceptance market fall into three categories: 1) the accepting banks, which create the instruments, 2) the dealers, who serve

---

[1] Jensen and Parkinson [1986, pp. 5, 10].

as middle-men between accepting banks and investors, and 3) the investors, who purchase acceptances from both accepting banks and dealers.

Accepting Banks   The accepting bank (American Bank in the example above) serves as an intermediary between an importer seeking a short-term loan and an investor looking for a safe, short-term investment. It guarantees repayment of the loan in exchange for a commission paid by the importer. If the accepting bank sells the acceptance after creating and discounting it (Step 12 in Chart 1), it earns the commission without tying up any of its own funds. If the accepting bank holds the acceptance, it takes on the role of investor for the transaction and adds a highly liquid short-term loan to its portfolio. Most accepting banks hold a portion of the acceptances that they create because if the bank needs to raise cash quickly, its acceptance holdings can be sold much more easily than its conventional loans.

The creation of bankers acceptances is administratively complex, requiring a specialized staff and good foreign connections. In addition, the acceptances of smaller banks trade at higher rates of discount than those of top-name banks. Consequently, smaller banks are rarely in a position to issue acceptances directly. Smaller banks can nevertheless earn bankers acceptance commissions by "participating" in acceptances of the top-name banks. When one bank participates in an acceptance of another, it takes on a portion of the acceptance liability in exchange for a proportionate share of the commission. A top-name bank allows smaller banks to participate in its acceptances mainly to avoid having to turn away preferred customers when it reaches the legal limit on the volume of acceptances that it can create (see below).

Dealers   Although accepting banks often sell their acceptances directly to investors, they commonly sell a portion through bankers acceptance dealers. There are approximately twenty such dealers, and they serve essentially as middlemen. Investors seeking to purchase acceptances place orders with dealers, who then call accepting banks to submit bids. Banks with acceptances to sell might also call dealers to solicit bids. Dealers make money by collecting a spread between their buying price to banks and their selling price to investors. The dealer spread is generally around 5 basis points but can be less depending on the state of the market. Some dealers also try to make money by taking positions in acceptances and speculating on interest rate movements. The presence of dealers greatly enhances the marketability of the bankers acceptance and therefore its attractiveness as an investment.

Investors Bankers acceptances are considered to be safe, liquid investments. Basically, any investor who would consider purchasing a negotiable certificate of deposit would also consider a bankers acceptance. Because the smallest typical denomination is $100,000, the market is dominated by institutional rather than individual investors. At the end of 1985, commercial banks held about 7 percent of all bankers acceptances, with a given bank holding primarily its own acceptances. Money market mutual funds, whose acceptance holdings peaked at 26 percent of the total outstanding in 1984, reduced their holdings somewhat in 1985 and held 17 percent of the total by year end.[2] The remaining 76 percent are held by a variety of other investors including savings banks, bank trust departments, foreign banks, municipalities, and Federal agencies.

BANKERS ACCEPTANCES AND THE FEDERAL RESERVE SYSTEM

Prior to World War I, the bankers acceptance market in the United States was extremely small, partly because national banks were prohibited from accepting time drafts, but also because business conditions favored other forms of short-term trade credit. In London, on the other hand, the Sterling bankers acceptance market was comparatively large. Hoping to steer some of London's acceptance business toward New York, the authors of the Federal Reserve Act included provisions permitting member banks to accept time drafts and authorizing Federal Reserve Banks to discount acceptances. Less than two years after the Act passed, the Board of Governors instructed the Federal Reserve Banks to post preferential rates of discount for bankers acceptances and to purchase all acceptances offered at those rates. In doing so, the Board sought to guarantee a market for dollar-denominated bankers acceptances and to encourage their use. This practice, which continued for roughly two decades, fostered growth in the volume of outstanding acceptances but resulted in an inordinate proportion accumulating at the Federal Reserve Banks. During the late 1920s, the Federal Reserve held between 45 percent and 60 percent of all outstanding acceptances.[3]

The Federal Reserve stopped buying acceptances at preferential rates of discount after the onset of the Great Depression, and the acceptance market floundered until the late 1940s. After World War II, increasing world stability brought about growth in international trade, and consequently bankers acceptance financing began to pick up without Federal Reserve encouragement. In response to the increase in the use of acceptances, the Federal Open Market Committee instructed the New York Federal Reserve in 1955 to begin using

---

[2] Data for money market mutual funds is from the Investment Company Institute.
[3] Hardy [1932, p. 258].

132

acceptance purchases as part of open market operations. In contrast to the purchases of the 1920s, however, these were made at market rates of discount, and in the thirty years since, Federal Reserve acceptance holdings have never accounted for more than 10 percent of the total outstanding.

The Federal Reserve continued to use bankers acceptance purchases and repurchase agreements in open market operations until the mid-1970s, at which time System acceptance activity was re-evaluated in light of the boom in international trade and bankers acceptance financing that had occurred in the preceding few years. Convinced that the acceptance market no longer needed assistance, the Board of Governors of the Federal Reserve System instructed Federal Reserve Banks in 1977 to stop making outright acceptance purchases for their own account. The New York Federal Reserve Bank continued to use repurchase agreements in acceptances as part of open market operations until 1984. Today, the Federal Reserve System only purchases bankers acceptances for the account of foreign central banks.

Although the Federal Reserve is no longer active in the acceptance market, it still plays a significant regulatory role. The most important aspect of its regulation is eligibilty criteria. When the Federal Reserve was active in the acceptance market, it set up criteria to which a bankers acceptance had to conform in order to be "eligible for purchase" or "eligible for discount." An acceptance that was eligible for purchase could be bought from an acceptance dealer by the New York Federal Reserve as part of open market operations, and it could also be used by a member bank as collateral for a loan at the discount window. An acceptance that was eligible for discount was for the most part also eligible for purchase, plus it could be discounted at a Federal Reserve Bank at the request of a member bank.

A bankers acceptance is eligible for purchase if it has a maturity of nine months or less and if it

(1) arises out of the current shipment of goods between countries or within the United States, or
(2) arises out of the storage within the United States of goods under contract of sale or expected to move into the channel of trade within a reasonable time and that are secured throughout their life by a warehouse receipt or similar document conveying title to the underlying goods.

Eligibility-for-discount criteria are with few exceptions the same except that maturity must be six months or less.[4]

Even though the Federal Reserve no longer purchases or discounts accep-

---

[4] For more detailed information concerning eligibility criteria, see Helfrich [1976, p. 54].

tances, these eligibility criteria have enduring significance. Eligibility for purchase is still necessary if an acceptance is to be used as collateral at the discount window. Eligibility for discount is perhaps more important because in 1973 the Federal Reserve imposed a reserve requirement on funds raised through the sale of acceptances that do not conform to the eligibility-for-discount criteria. The extra cost to the bank of having to hold non-interest-bearing reserves is passed on to the importer in the form of a higher interest rate. Importers are thus discouraged from seeking acceptance financing when the underlying transaction is such that it will not give rise to an eligible-for-discount acceptance. Consequently, most of the acceptances that trade in the acceptance market are eligible for discount.

In addition to setting eligibility requirements, the Federal Reserve also limits the dollar amount of eligible acceptances that any one bank can create to 150 percent of the bank's paid-in capital and surplus, which can be raised to 200 percent by special permission.

CONCLUSION

Bankers acceptances will no doubt continue to be an important short-term financing instrument for the foreseeable future. It seems unlikely, however, that the acceptance market will soon rebound from its two-year slump in volume. Financial deregulation abroad, which promotes trade in currencies other than dollars, and the recent appearance of short-term Eurodollar securities such as Euro-commercial paper that can serve as financing alternatives to acceptances, have both been cited as factors mitigating against such a rebound.[5]

References

Duffield, Jeremy G., and Bruce J. Summers. "Bankers' Acceptances." In *Instruments of The Money Market*. 5th ed. Edited by Timothy Q. Cook and Bruce J. Summers. Richmond: Federal Reserve Bank of Richmond, 1981.

Goldberg, Michael A. "Economic Analysis of Commercial Letters of Credit and Bankers Acceptances." Unpublished memorandum, Board of Governors of the Federal Reserve System, November 1979.

Hardy, Charles O. *Credit Policies of the Federal Reserve System*. Washington, D.C.: The Brookings Institution, 1932.

---

[5] Jensen and Parkinson [1986, p. 12].

Helfrich, Ralph T. "Trading in Bankers' Acceptances: A View from the Acceptance Desk of the Federal Reserve Bank of New York." Federal Reserve Bank of New York, *Monthly Review* 58 (February 1976), pp. 51-57.

Hervey, Jack L. "Bankers' Acceptances." Federal Reserve Bank of Chicago, *Business Conditions* (May 1976), pp. 3-11.

Jensen, Frederick H., and Patrick M. Parkinson. "Recent Developments in the Bankers Acceptance Market." *Federal Reserve Bulletin* 72 (January 1986), pp. 1-12.

Madden, Carl H. *The Money Side of "The Street."* New York: Federal Reserve Bank of New York, 1959.

Rothbard, Murray N. *America's Great Depression*. New York: Richardson & Snyder, 1972.

Stigum, Marcia. *The Money Market*. Rev. ed. Homewood, Illinois: Dow Jones-Irwin, 1983.

11

THE FEDERALLY SPONSORED CREDIT AGENCIES

Michael J. Moran

One of the hallmarks of a sophisticated financial system is a well-developed set of financial intermediaries. In the United States such institutions as commercial banks, savings and loans, insurance companies, pension funds and investment companies promote the efficient allocation of capital by offering investors financial instruments with features they could not obtain by investing directly with the ultimate users of the funds. The advantages of investing through a financial intermediary include a better combination of risk and return, greater liquidity, lower transaction costs, smaller denominations for initial savings balances, and greater flexibility for subsequent additions to these balances. Borrowers and equity issuers in turn, find a larger and more readily available pool of funds to support their spending plans. In the U.S. economy, about 75 percent of all newly raised funds are transferred from savers to borrowers through financial intermediaries.

The federal government has established five privately owned intermediaries to channel funds to particular sectors of the economy that are deemed worthy of special support. These institutions are known collectively as the federally sponsored credit agencies:

- Federal Home Loan Banks
- Federal Home Loan Mortgage Corporation
- Federal National Mortgage Association
- Farm Credit Banks
- Student Loan Marketing Association.

The Congress established the first three intermediaries to broaden the flow of credit to the mortgage and housing markets, and the last two intermediaries to provide funds to support agriculture and higher education respectively.

Rather than lending directly to the ultimate borrowers, most of the federally sponsored credit agencies provide funds that private institutions make available to individuals and businesses. The sponsored agencies obtain funds by selling either debt or pass-through securities in the money and capital markets. They channel these funds to private lending institutions either through loan agreements or by buying the assets of the private lenders and thus providing them with funds to make new loans. With these methods, the sponsored credit agencies represent a second layer of intermediation that is built upon the financial structure in the private sector.[1]

Many programs under the direction of the federal government serve an intermediary function, but two features of the federally sponsored credit agencies set them apart. First, the sponsored agencies are wholly owned by the private sector. Although they have certain unique ties with the federal government—such as board members appointed by the President and borrowing privileges from the Treasury Department—ultimately it is the stockholders or the borrowers (all private) that stand to benefit or lose from their activities. As private entities, these institutions are not subject to the appropriations process of the federal budget, nor does the Congress control their financing activity or rate of growth. Second, these intermediaries borrow directly in the financial markets to raise funds, whereas other lenders under the direction of the federal government obtain their funds from the Federal Financing Bank, which, in turn, borrows from the Treasury Department. Because the sponsored agencies are privately owned, their debt securities are not guaranteed by the federal government.

One organization that frequently is associated with the federally sponsored credit agencies, but is quite different, is the Government National Mortgage Association—often referred to as GNMA, or Ginnie Mae. This organization is part of the Department of Housing and Urban Development and currently does not issue debt in the money and capital markets. The popular Ginnie Mae securities that trade in the market place are actually mortgage pass-through certificates issued by mortgage originators, but Ginnie Mae guarantees the timely payment of interest and principal. This institution is not discussed further in this chapter.

A GENERAL DESCRIPTION OF THE FEDERALLY SPONSORED CREDIT AGENCIES

The simplified balance sheet for each federally sponsored agency presented in Table I helps focus on the size and nature of their activities. In general, the sponsored agencies are large participants in the U.S. financial system. The Federal Home Loan Banks (FHLBs), the Federal National Mortgage Association (FNMA, or Fannie Mae), and the Farm Credit Banks (FCBs), taken alone, have assets much larger than those of the largest thrift institution and about the same size as those of the third or fourth largest commercial banks. The Federal Home

---

[1] The Farm Credit Banks are an exception to this method of operation. They either lend directly to farmers and ranchers or lend through associations that are part of the Farm Credit System.

Table I

BALANCE SHEETS OF THE FEDERALLY SPONSORED CREDIT AGENCIES

June 1986

(Millions of Dollars)

	Assets				Liabilities		
	Loans purchased from private lenders	Loans made to private lenders	Other assets	Total Assets, or Total Liabilities plus Equity	Credit market debt	Other liabilities	Equity
Federal Home Loan Banks	. . .	94,840	25,215	120,055	81,558	27,533	10,964
Federal National Mortgage Association	93,941	. . .	4,581	98,522	92,562	4,465	1,495
Federal Home Loan Mortgage Corporation	13,690	. . .	6,022	19,712	13,220	5,641	851
Farm Credit Banks[1]	. . .	61,536	11,189	72,725	63,585	2,136	7,004
Student Loan Marketing Association	7,509	6,268	2,788	16,565	15,419	416	730

[1] The consolidated balance sheet of the Farm Credit Banks, the Federal Land Bank Associations, and Production Credit Associations.

Loan Mortgage Corporation (FHLMC, or Freddie Mac) holds a much smaller volume of total assets than does each of the three largest sponsored agencies, but, as explained more fully below, the balance sheet understates its role in the financial markets. Because the market for student loans is much smaller than either the mortgage or agricultural credit market, the Student Loan Marketing Association (SLMA, or Sallie Mae) is the smallest of the federally sponsored credit agencies, but is still a substantial factor in the credit markets.

The federally sponsored credit agencies hold primarily two types of assets: loans granted to private lending institutions and loans to individuals or businesses that were purchased from private lending institutions or originated directly. The Federal Home Loan Banks issue loans (called advances) to member savings and loan associations and mutual savings banks. These advances, which can have maturities of up to 20 years, are used by the depository institutions to meet short-term liquidity needs and to expand their asset portfolios. The Student Loan Marketing Association grants loans (called warehousing advances) to many types of lenders, including commercial banks, thrift institutions, educational institutions, and state lending agencies. Warehousing advances must be used to maintain or expand the size of a lender's student loan portfolio. The Farm Credit Banks lend directly to individuals and businesses as well as to farm associations and cooperatives. The latter groups, in turn, either lend to farmers or provide services to the agricultural sector.

The Federal National Mortgage Association and the Federal Home Loan Mortgage Corporation provide secondary markets for mortgage loans; that is, they purchase mortgage loans from originating institutions. In addition to providing funds for new loan originations, these programs have served to standardize the terms on conventional mortgage loans. Fannie Mae holds a large portion of the purchased mortgages in its portfolio, while Freddie Mac usually packages them into pass-through certificates and in effect sells them to other investors in the financial markets. Because the issuance of these pass-through securities represents the sale of the underlying mortgages, the total assets of Freddie Mac are not large relative to those of the other sponsored agencies, and its balance sheet greatly understates its role in transferring funds from the money and capital markets to mortgage lenders. Fannie Mae also sells pass-through certificates to investors.

The following paragraphs describe each sponsored agency in more detail and provide some historical background. Table II summarizes some of the major characteristics of the sponsored agencies.

The Federal Home Loan Banks   The Congress established the Federal Home Loan Bank System in 1932 to supervise federally chartered savings and loan

TABLE II

CHARACTERISTICS OF FEDERALLY SPONSORED CREDIT AGENCIES

Agency	Stockholders	Influence of the Administration	Line of Credit with Treasury	Federal Tax on Income of Sponsored Agency[1]	State and Local Tax on Interest Income of Investors
Federal Home Loan Banks	Owned by member thrift institutions but operated by the Federal Home Loan Bank Board	President selects all 3 members of the FHLBB	$4.0 billion	No	No
Federal National Mortgage Association	Owned entirely by private stockholders	President selects 5 of 18 board members; subject to general supervision by HUD	$2.25 billion	Yes	Yes
Federal Home Loan Mortgage Corporation	Nonvoting common stock owned by 12 FHLBs; participating preferred stock issued to member thrift institutions	Same as FHLBs	Indirect line of credit through the FHLBs	Yes[2]	Yes
Farm Credit Banks	Owned by farm cooperatives and credit associations	President selects all 3 members of the Farm Credit Administration	Available at the discretion of the Secretary[3]	No	No
Student Loan Marketing Association	Lenders under the Guaranteed Student Loan Program may hold voting common stock; individual investors may hold nonvoting common and preferred stock	President selects 7 of 21 Board members including the chairman	$1.0 billion[4]	Yes	No

[1] Interest on all debt of the sponsored agencies is subject to federal taxation.
[2] Effective January 1, 1985.
[3] Made available by The Farm Credit Assistance Act of 1985. The funds advanced by the Secretary of the Treasury also must be appropriated by the Congress.

associations and to provide a credit facility for thrift institutions. The system originally comprised only the Federal Home Loan Bank Board, which serves primarily as a regulatory agency, and 12 regional Federal Home Loan Banks, which carry out the policies of the Board and provide the credit facilities and other services for member institutions. The Federal Savings and Loan Insurance Corporation and the Federal Home Loan Mortgage Corporation were added to the system later, in 1934 and 1970 respectively.

The Federal Home Loan Banks are wholly owned by the financial institutions that join the system. The 12 banks operate individually, but they must observe guidelines established by the Board. The most important activity of the banks is to provide credit to members in the form of loans (called advances). The Federal Home Loan Banks finance their advances primarily by selling debt securities in the money and capital markets and by accepting deposits from member institutions. The debt securities are sold on a consolidated basis—that is, they are the joint obligations of all 12 banks. The Federal Home Loan Banks are the only sponsored agency that issues deposit liabilities. Overnight accounts are the largest category of deposit liability at the banks. These accounts are used by member institutions to invest temporarily funds that otherwise might lie idle. The banks also issue demand and time deposits to their members.

Federal Home Loan Mortgage Corporation   The Federal Home Loan Mortgage Corporation also belongs to the Federal Home Loan Bank System but performs a different function than the 12 Home Loan Banks do. Freddie Mac provides a secondary market mainly for conventional mortgage loans—that is, mortgages that are not insured by the Federal Housing Administration nor guaranteed by the Veterans Administration. When the corporation was established in 1970, secondary market facilities for government-insured and government-guaranteed mortgages already were in place, but support for conventional home loans was lacking. Freddie Mac was created to fill this gap in the secondary market. It typically purchases mortgages from institutions originating the loans, thereby replenishing lenders' cash positions so they can write new loans. To a small extent, the Federal Home Loan Mortgage Corporation purchases mortgage loans to hold in its portfolio. More commonly, Freddie Mac purchases mortgage loans, places them in pools, and issues pass-through certificates backed by these loans.

The common stock of Freddie Mac is owned by the 12 Federal Home Loan Banks. Recognizing that ultimately the thrift institutions that are members of the Federal Home Loan Bank System have a claim on its income, Freddie Mac issued $600 million of participating preferred stock to these institutions in January 1985.

The Federal National Mortgage Association The Congress established the Federal National Mortgage Association in 1938 to provide a secondary market for federally underwritten mortgages. Fannie Mae was once part of the federal government, but it was separated in 1968 and now is fully owned by private investors (its shares are traded on the New York Stock Exchange). For many years Fannie Mae could deal only in mortgages underwritten by the Federal Housing Administration or guaranteed by the Veterans Administration; it received authority to buy and sell conventional mortgage loans in 1970, and it made its first purchase in 1972.

At midyear 1986, Fannie Mae held $94 billion in mortgages, making it the largest single investor in home loans in the country. In recent years, Fannie Mae has diversified its activities on both the asset and liability sides of its balance sheet. On the asset side, FNMA now invests heavily in adjustable rate and second mortgages and it recently began purchasing multi-family mortgages. Previously, Fannie Mae had focused on the purchase of long-term, fixed-rate, first-lien family mortgages. On the liability side, Fannie Mae now issues debt securities in foreign markets and foreign currencies, engages in swap transactions (discussed later), and offers several new types of debt securities. This sponsored agency also has issued a large amount of pass-through securities, which are not reflected on its balance sheet.

Farm Credit Banks The Farm Credit System has the most complex organizational structure of the five federally sponsored credit agencies. The System is divided geographically into 12 districts. Each district has a Federal Land Bank, a Federal Intermediate Credit Bank, and a Bank for Cooperatives. In addition, a Central Bank for Cooperatives participates in large loans or loans that span more than one district. These 37 banks, along with a large number of cooperative associations that own the banks, form the heart of the Farm Credit System. The Farm Credit Administration, an independent agency of the federal government, provides supervision at the national level. The regulatory role of the Farm Credit Administration was increased in 1985 by the Farm Credit Assistance Act that restructured the system. This same legislation also gave the Secretary of the Treasury greater authority to provide financial assistance to the Farm Credit Banks. This financial assistance would be advanced to the FCBs through the Farm Credit System Capital Corporation, another branch of the System restructured by the 1985 legislation to ensure the continued viability of the Farm Credit Banks and their lending associations.

The three types of Farm Credit Banks and their lending associations differ in the types of loans they make. The Federal Land Banks, through a total of about 300 land bank associations, issue primarily longer-term loans for the purchase of farms, farm equipment, or rural real estate. Most of these loans have variable interest rates. The Federal Land Banks and their lending associations account for about 65 percent of the total assets of the Farm Credit System. The Federal Intermediate Credit Banks advance funds to about 200 production credit associations and to other financial institutions, such as commercial banks, that make primarily short-term loans for production or operating purposes. They also write a small volume of loans for farm and rural homes and for farm-related businesses. The Federal Intermediate Credit Banks and their lending institutions account for about 22 percent of the total assets of the Farm Credit System.

The Banks for Cooperatives make loans of all types directly to cooperative organizations providing agricultural services. The services include marketing farm products, purchasing farm supplies, or operating public utilities. As with the other Farm Credit Banks, the Banks for Cooperatives are owned by the cooperative organizations that borrow from them.

At one time, the Federal Land Banks, the Federal Intermediate Credit Banks, and the Banks for Cooperatives each issued their own debt in the financial markets. In 1977, they issued their first consolidated debt (that is, a security that was the joint obligation of all 37 Farm Credit Banks), and since 1979 all debt issuance has been on a consolidated basis. The Farm Credit Banks tap the short-term markets for a large proportion of their funds because most of their loans have either short terms or variable interest rates.

Student Loan Marketing Association   The Student Loan Marketing Association was created by the Congress in 1972 to provide a secondary market for student loans guaranteed by the federal government. Sallie Mae also encourages the flow of credit to higher education by providing loans to institutions, known as warehousing advances, so that they can write additional student loans.

Most of the student loans purchased by Sallie Mae are granted under the Guaranteed Student Loan Program. These loans are originated by private lending institutions (such as commercial banks, thrift institutions, and educational institutions), and they are guaranteed either directly or indirectly by the federal government. Sallie Mae also purchases loans granted under other federal programs for higher education, such as the HEAL program (Health Education Assistance Loans) and the PLUS program (loans to parents of dependent undergraduate students and to independent students).

THE MARKET FOR THE SECURITIES OF THE FEDERALLY SPONSORED CREDIT AGENCIES

Federally sponsored credit agencies finance their loan programs and secondary market purchases primarily by issuing debt and pass-through securities in

143

the money and capital markets. These securities are not guaranteed by the federal government, but because of the ties of the sponsored agencies to the government, they are afforded certain privileges not available to most other issues:

- exemption from the requirement to register the issue with the Securities and Exchange Commission
- exemption of interest income from state and local taxes (except for issues of the Federal National Mortgage Association and the Federal Home Loan Mortgage Corporation)
- eligibility as collateral when commercial banks and thrift institutions borrow from the Federal Reserve's discount window and when thrift institutions borrow from a Federal Home Loan Bank
- eligibility for purchase by the Federal Reserve in open market operations
- eligibility as collateral for public deposits, including Treasury tax and loan accounts
- favorable status in the portfolios of depository institutions; for example, the shorter-term securities may be used to meet the liquidity requirements of thrift institutions belonging to the Federal Home Loan Bank System, and national banks may invest and deal in these securities without limit.

The sponsored agencies issue a variety of short-term securities in the money market, and they tap the longer-term markets through debentures. Those securities are sold in the marketplace with the assistance of a fiscal agent, which recommends to the sponsored agencies the offering rates on the securities and allocates the notes and bonds to securities dealers. Those dealers, in turn, distribute the securities to the public. The sponsored agencies meet the bulk of their financing needs through the issuance of traditional securities, but they also have used some of the more innovative techniques that have emerged in the U.S. financial system in recent years.

Financing in the Money Market   The federally sponsored credit agencies, as a group, issue about 20 percent of their debt with an original maturity of less than one year. Among the sponsored agencies, however, the financing patterns are quite different, with Fannie Mae and the Home Loan Banks doing relatively little financing in the money market and the other sponsored agencies conducting 25 to 35 percent of their financing with short-term instruments (Chart 1).

The divergent financing patterns are related to the nature of the assets and activities of each sponsored agency. The Farm Credit Banks and Sallie Mae hold primarily variable-rate assets, and thus issue larger amounts of short-term debt to limit their exposure to interest rate risk. Similarly, Freddie Mac purchases mortgages but typically holds them only for a short period until they can be formed into a pool and sold as a pass-through security. In recent years, however, the proportion of Freddie Mac's financing done with short-term instruments has

144

Chart 1

SHORT-TERM DEBT AS A PERCENT OF TOTAL DEBT, JUNE 1986

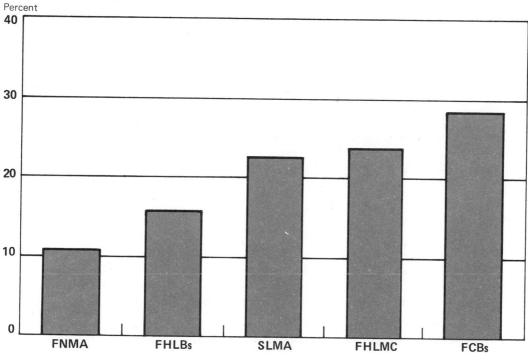

been reduced by its increased use of collateralized mortgage obligations (discussed later), a type of long-term obligation.

The Federal Home Loan Banks attempt to match the maturities of their assets and liabilities; thus, their participation in the money market varies with the demand of thrift institutions for short-term advances. An unexpected jump in the demand for longer-term advances also might be financed in the money market until the FHLBs can arrange a longer-term debt issue. Fannie Mae's debt management strategy in recent years has focused on lengthening the average maturity of its debt in order to match more closely the average maturity of its assets and limit its exposure to interest rate risk. For the most part, Fannie Mae is achieving this objective by issuing longer-term debentures and through innovative financing techniques such as interest rate swaps (discussed later). FNMA has increased its outstanding volume of short-term debt only slightly in recent years, and short-term debt as a proportion of total debt fell from about 15 percent in the early 1980s to about 11 percent at midyear 1986.

While the sponsored agencies issue a variety of short-term debt instruments, discount notes are by far the most popular. Like Treasury bills and commercial

TABLE III

**FEDERALLY SPONSORED CREDIT AGENCIES
DISCOUNT NOTES OUTSTANDING**

(June 30, 1986)

Sponsored agency	Amount Outstanding ($ millions)	Percent of Short-Term Debt	Percent of Total Debt	Average Remaining Maturity (days)
FHLBs	12,922	100.0	15.8	120
FNMA	6,993	69.9	7.6	87
FHLMC	2,992	100.0	23.8	35
FCBs	10,225	56.6	16.1	52
SLMA	1,082	30.9	7.0	55
Total	34,214	72.0	12.9	

paper, these securities do not pay explicit interest, rather they are issued at a discount from the par value paid at maturity. At midyear 1986, outstanding discount notes of the sponsored agencies totaled $34 billion, representing about 70 percent of their short-term debt (Table III). The maturities of discount notes range from overnight to 360 days, but frequently the sponsored agencies operate in a narrower maturity range. For example, the FHLMC usually issues discount notes with maturities of 30 days or less; the FHLBs, in contrast, do not issue discount notes with maturities under 30 days and frequently bunch their issuance around 3 and 6 months. The average maturities of outstanding discount notes at midyear 1986 are presented in Table III.

Discount notes are offered by the sponsored agencies on a daily basis through a group of five to ten dealer firms. The dealers are compensated with a fee that varies with the volume of funds issued and the maturity of the discount notes. The normal practice is for dealers to receive .05 percent (5 basis points, annual rate) of the volume of funds placed. Because the fee is at an annual rate, dealers receive smaller fees for short-term discount notes. The dealer groups maintain close contact with the ultimate investors, giving them the capability of raising funds on short notice. The heaviest investors in discount notes are money market mutual funds and commercial banks. Other institutional investors—such as insurance companies, pension funds, and thrift institutions—also purchase discount notes; purchases by individual investors are infrequent.

The sponsored agencies normally control the volume and maturity of discount notes by altering their offering rates. For example, if a particular borrower needed a large volume of funds with maturities under 30 days, it would increase

Table IV

OFFERING RATES ON DISCOUNT NOTES

(March 13, 1986)

FHLBs		FHLMC	
Maturity	Rate	Maturity	Rate
30 to 81	6.00	31	7.10
82 to 100	6.78	11 to 14	7.15
101 to 360	6.25		

SLMA		FCBs	
Maturity	Rate	Maturity	Rate
5 to 14	6.90	5 to 14	7.00
15 to 87	6.00	15 to 29	6.95
88 to 92	6.80	30 to 59	6.80
93 to 173	6.00	60 to 89	6.75
174 to 179	6.75	90 to 119	6.70
180 to 360	6.00	120 to 360	not offering

Note: Maturity is in number of days.
Source: Telerate, page 31.

the rates on its shortest issue and drop its rates on longer-term discount notes below that of other issuers, or it simply might not offer longer-term notes on that day.

An example of offering rates on sponsored agency discount notes in mid-March 1986 is presented in Table IV. The Federal Home Loan Banks were interested only in funds in the 82- to 100-day maturity range on this day. Their offering rates in the other maturity ranges were actually below Treasury bill rates. Freddie Mac was interested only in very short-term discount notes on this day, which is usually the case for this sponsored agency. Sallie Mae apparently wanted funds only in the limited maturity ranges offering 6-3/4 percent and above. The Farm Credit Banks were offering an attractive rate out to 119 days, but they were encouraging inflows into the short end of the maturity range.

The observed interest rate spreads between discount notes and Treasury bills vary with the volume of funds the sponsored agencies wish to raise in a particular maturity range. Normally, spreads will be in the range of 10 to 30 basis points, but they can be very narrow (even negative) if an issuer has little interest in new funds or wider than 30 basis points if the sponsored agency greatly needs funds. On the day shown in Table IV, 3- and 6-month Treasury bills were yielding between 6.60 and 6.65 percent. The Home Loan Bank spreads were very tight,

147

but on this day they already raised nearly all their desired funds at higher rates posted earlier and lowered their offering rates to slow the inflow of funds. In the desired maturity range of the other sponsored agencies, the spreads for the most part are in the 20 to 30 basis point range. The spreads for the Farm Credit Banks are wider than for the other sponsored agencies, stemming from investor concern over credit quality because of the poor financial condition of some farmers.

The sponsored agencies usually pay lower rates on their debt than private borrowers in the financial system. The lower rates on the securities of the sponsored agencies result partly from their unique features and partly from the strong financial condition of their issuers. In addition, the sponsored agencies, either directly or indirectly, have lines of credit with the Treasury Department (at the discretion of its secretary) should they experience difficulty in meeting their obligations. Beyond these factors, some investors believe that, although there is no explicit guarantee, the federal government would not allow a sponsored agency to default on a debt issue.

Aside from discount notes, the most prominent types of money market instruments issued by the sponsored agencies are the 6- and 9-month securities of the Farm Credit Banks. At midyear 1986, there was about $7.8 billion of such securities outstanding, representing about 40 percent of the short-term debt of the Farm Credit System and about 15 percent of short-term securities issued by all sponsored agencies. This volume of 6- and 9-month securities is down from earlier years because the Farm Credit Banks have been reducing their outstanding debt due to the weak loan demand from the depressed agricultural sector. During 1985, for example, the Farm Credit Banks ran off $5.5 billion of these securities. Also, in the fall of 1985 and into early 1986, the Farm Credit Banks eliminated the 9-month issue from the regular monthly offerings; on a few occasions, the FCBs have substituted 3-month securities for the suspended offerings of 9-month issues.

In contrast to discount notes, the 3-, 6-, and 9-month securities of the Farm Credit Banks are coupon bearing securities, and they are offered to investors only on a monthly basis through a group of about 150 dealers. As with discount notes, the major purchasers are commercial banks and money market mutual funds. Other institutional investors also are frequent purchasers, and individual investors sometimes acquire these instruments directly.

In ordinary times, the interest rate spreads between these short-term securities and Treasury bills were quite narrow—typically only a few basis points in magnitude (Chart 2).[2] In the fall of 1985, however, the spreads widened to nearly

---

[2] The market convention is to compare the quoted yields on these short-term securities with the coupon-equivalent rates on Treasury bills. However, the quoted yields on the Farm Credit securities are on a 360-day basis while the coupon-equivalent bill rate is on a 365-day basis. Thus, the spread

Chart 2

SPREAD BETWEEN THE YIELDS ON 6-MONTH SECURITIES OF THE FARM CREDIT BANKS AND 6-MONTH TREASURY BILLS

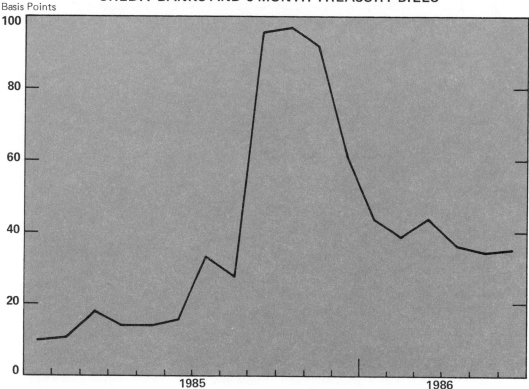

Note: The Farm Credit securities are priced at the end of the month shown on the chart and they settle at the beginning of the following month. The Treasury bill rate is a one-day quote on the day Farm Credit securities are priced. The bill rate is on a coupon-equivalent basis. The rate on the Farm Credit securities is multiplied by 365/360 to make it comparable to the Treasury bill quote.

100 basis points as investors became concerned with financial difficulties of farmers. After the passage of a bill that restructured the Farm Credit System and provided for potential financial assistance from the Treasury Department, these spreads narrowed to about 30 basis points—well below the high levels in the fall of 1985, but still well above the marginal levels evident when the quality of the Farm Credit System was unquestioned.

The Federal National Mortgage Association also issues money market instruments other than discount notes. Fannie Mae offers "residential financing

---

typically quoted by market participants is understated by an amount equal to 365/360 times the rate on the Farm Credit security. The data shown in Chart 2 are adjusted to account for this difference.

securities" on a daily basis through a group of securities dealers. These securities are coupon bearing instruments and have maturities of six months and one year. The interest rates on these securities are comparable to those on discount notes. At midyear 1986, Fannie Mae had $1.3 billion of residential financing securities outstanding, representing 13 percent of its short-term debt.

Fannie Mae also had $1.8 billion of debt outstanding under a master note program at midyear 1986. This security is designed for institutional investors with varying liquidity needs. The investors can vary the amount of funds held in the master note on a daily basis, usually in a range of 80 to 120 percent of an agreed amount. The interest rate on master notes is tied to the average auction rates on the 91-day Treasury bill and changes each week following the auction. (See the chapter on commercial paper for a more complete discussion of master notes.)

The Student Loan Marketing Association issues a variable-rate instrument, with an offering made once each month. This instrument has a 6-month maturity, and its rate is tied to the average auction rate (coupon equivalent basis) on new 6-month Treasury bills and changes each week when the Treasury auctions new securities. Usually the Sallie Mae yield is 35 basis points more than the bill rate. At mid-year 1986, Sallie Mae had $1.7 billion of these securities outstanding, representing about 50 percent of its short-term debt. Sallie Mae also raises funds through a master note program, much like Fannie Mae's program, and it has a small volume of repurchase agreements outstanding.

Longer-Term Securities of the Sponsored Agencies   The sponsored agencies fill their longer-term financing needs with debentures. The Federal Home Loan Banks, the Farm Credit Banks, and the Federal National Mortgage Association offer debentures to the public each month according to a fixed schedule, and they occasionally bring to market unscheduled offerings as well. Issuance by the Student Loan Marketing Association and the Federal Home Loan Mortgage Corporation is irregular. Most of the longer-term securities issued by the sponsored agencies have maturities in the range of one to ten years; maturities in excess of that are infrequent.

The interest rates on intermediate-term bonds issued by the sponsored agencies usually are 15 to 30 basis points higher than the rates on Treasury securities of similar maturity (Chart 3). As in the money market, these spreads are much tighter than those observed on corporate securities of comparable maturity.

On two recent occasions, however, the confidence of investors in the quality of sponsored-agency securities was shaken so that the interest rate spreads over Treasury securities widened (Chart 3). The first incident began in 1981 when the net income of the Federal National Mortgage Association weakened and investment analysts reported that the securities of Fannie Mae carried greater credit risk

Chart 3

AVERAGE SPREAD BETWEEN YIELDS ON SECURITIES OF THE FEDERALLY SPONSORED CREDIT AGENCIES AND ON TREASURY SECURITIES OF CORRESPONDING MATURITY

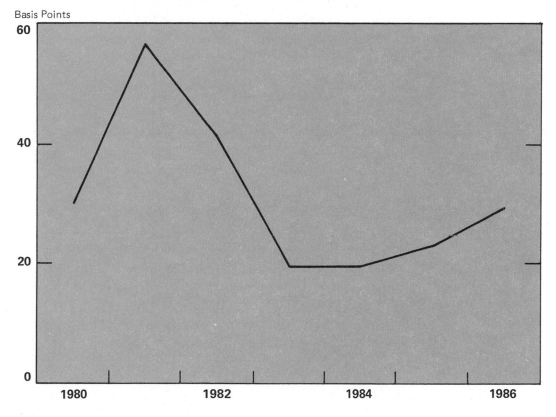

Basis Points

Note: Data are yearly averages for intermediate-term securities, which have maturities of more than one year up to five years. Only the securities of the Federal Home Loan Banks, the Federal National Mortgage Association, and the Farm Credit Banks are included.

than previously perceived. Interest rate spreads over Treasury securities on Fannie Mae's debt averaged about 80 basis points in 1981, and some issues came to market with spreads as high as 150 basis points. The risk consciousness of investors during this period affected the other sponsored agencies, and their interest rate spreads widened some even though their financial positions were sound. The concerns of investors were allayed in subsequent years as lower levels of interest rates and new strategies adopted by Fannie Mae improved its prospects for profitability.

In the fall of 1985 the interest rate spreads on the longer-term securities of the Farm Credit Banks widened to more than 125 basis points as the financial condition of many farmers deteriorated. This episode is not noticeable on the chart because the concern did not surface until late in the year and because the Farm Credit Banks slowed their issuance of longer-term securities under these circumstances. Also, in this case, the other sponsored agencies were little affected by the financial conditions in the agricultural sector.

While the federally sponsored credit agencies meet the bulk of their financing needs through the traditional offerings of money market instruments and debentures, they also have been involved in innovative transactions in an effort to broaden their investor base and to lower their overall interest expense. The Student Loan Marketing Association and the Federal National Mortgage Association have made efforts to broaden their investor base by issuing securities in foreign countries. These issues have been denominated both in dollars and foreign currencies; some issues have been "dual currency securities," which pay interest in a foreign currency but the face value is paid in dollars at maturity. To protect themselves from the risks of exchange rate fluctuations from such issues, Sallie Mae and Fannie Mae utilized another innovative financing technique, a currency swap.

Currency swaps involve two parties that issue debt in each other's currencies, then exchange their payment obligations so that each services debt in its home currency. In the case of the recent Sallie Mae and Fannie Mae yen issues, for example, those sponsored agencies could exchange their interest payment obligations with a Japanese firm that issued a comparable amount of debt denominated in dollars. This technique allows a borrower to raise funds in the market in which its interest expenses are lowest, regardless of the currency used in that market, without exposure to exchange rate fluctuations.

The currency swap is similar to the interest rate swap used extensively by Sallie Mae and to a lesser extent by Fannie Mae. An interest rate swap is a transaction in which two parties, one with fixed-rate debt and the other with variable-rate debt, agree to exchange interest-payment obligations, thereby converting their type of payment from fixed-rate to variable-rate or vice versa. With this type of transaction, the two parties usually find that their overall funding costs are lower than they would have been had they issued their preferred fixed or variable-rate instrument directly. Sallie Mae, a pioneer in the technique in the United States, wished to issue variable-rate debt because most of its assets carry variable interest rates. However, it had issued so much debt of that type that investors were willing to increase their holdings only at higher rates. Sallie Mae found that it could keep its funding costs low and still be protected from interest rate risk by issuing fixed-rate debt and engaging in an interest rate swap.

Table V

SECONDARY MARKET TRADING IN TREASURY AND AGENCY SECURITIES[1]

(Average Daily Volume, Millions of Dollars)

	Volume of Purchases and Sales	
	Treasury	Agency
1981	11,236	1,728
1982	14,697	2,018
1983	18,833	2,118
1984	24,273	2,623
1985	35,773	3,651
1986H1	43,278	3,559

[1] Trading volume does not include transactions with brokers and other dealers. The data on agency trading includes the transactions involving the securities of government-owned agencies.

The Secondary Market for Sponsored Agency Securities The secondary market for both the short-term and long-term securities of the sponsored agencies resembles closely the market for Treasury securities. Investors buy and sell sponsored agency securities in over-the-counter trading with the dealer firms that originally placed the securities in the primary market. Dealers also trade among themselves to obtain securities they have committed to deliver or to achieve some desired portfolio position; as in the Treasury market, most of the inter-dealer trading is conducted through brokers. In all trading, including transactions between dealers and with other customers, dealers do not charge commissions, rather they rely on the spreads between their bid (buying) and ask (selling) prices to compensate them for their services.[3]

Trading activity in sponsored agency securities is much smaller, both absolutely and relative to the volume of outstanding debt, than the high level of activity in the Treasury securities market (Table V).[4] However, the market in sponsored-agency debt should still be viewed as highly liquid. Treasury instruments are the most heavily traded securities in the world and provide a high

---

[3] Dealers also earn profits if the interest income from the securities they hold is greater than their cost of financing these securities (that is, they earn a "positive carry"). Dealers also attempt to earn capital gains (or avoid capital losses) on their portfolio of securities. For further discussion of a dealer market, see the chapters on treasury bills and repurchase agreements.

[4] The data in the table slightly overstate the volume of trading in sponsored agency securities because the debt of government-owned agencies—such as the Tennessee Valley Authority and the Federal Housing Administration—are included. These agencies no longer issue their own debt in the financial markets, but they still have some securities outstanding.

standard for comparison. Securities dealers report that sponsored agency debt trades much more actively than corporate bonds, although no data are available to confirm this.

Among the debt of the sponsored agencies, secondary market trading is concentrated mostly in short-term securities. In 1985, for example, 55 percent of all dealer transactions with other investors involved securities with one year or less remaining to maturity.[5] Longer-term securities of the sponsored agencies tend to be purchased by investors that will hold a security until maturity, such as pension funds or managers of a dedicated portfolio. Shorter-term securities, on the other hand, tend to be purchased by investors that do larger amounts of trading, such as money market mutual funds and commercial banks. Even the longer-term securities of the sponsored agencies are said to trade actively until a new security of a particular issuer appears on the market, which usually is one month later.

Pass-Through Securities and Collateralized Mortgage Obligations As previously mentioned, Freddie Mac and Fannie Mae issue a large volume of pass-through securities. These securities are not debt obligations of the issuer; rather they represent an ownership share in an underlying pool of mortgages. The holder of the certificate receives the monthly payments of principal and interest made by the homeowners. This instrument attracts investors from the capital markets that otherwise might not invest in mortgages. Pass-through securities are attractive to investors because their yield and credit quality are high. At midyear 1986, Freddie Mac and Fannie Mae combined had nearly $200 billion of pass-through securities outstanding (Table VI).

The major disadvantage of pass-through securities is that their maturity is highly uncertain; if homeowners prepay their mortgage loan (either because they refinance or because they move to a new house) the pass-through security is retired long before the expected date. Moreover, mortgage prepayments and the paydown of pass-through securities frequently increase when interest rates drop, precisely the time when investors wish to hold longer-term, fixed-rate assets.

The volume of pass-through securities issued by these sponsored agencies has increased sharply since late 1981 because of the introduction of Freddie Mac's guarantor program and Fannie Mae's mortgage-backed security program. Under these programs, mortgage investors can exchange whole mortgage loans for pass-through securities. The interest rates on these pass-through securities are one-half percentage point below the rate on the underlying mortgage loans;

---

[5] Included in this figure are longer-term securities issued in past years that now have one year or less remaining to maturity. Data are not available to focus only on securities that were issued originally in the money market.

Table VI

GROSS NEW ISSUES OF PASS-THROUGH SECURITIES

(Millions of Dollars)

	Total Gross Volume of New Issues		Swap-Related New Issues	
	FHLMC	FNMA	FHLMC	FNMA
1980	2,527	–0–	–0–	–0–
1981	3,529	718	2,305	718
1982	24,171	13,969	21,937	10,896
1983	19,692	13,341	15,538	8,922
1984	18,684	13,546	15,335	12,553
1985	38,850	23,651	25,618	22,147
1986H1[1]	71,448	46,718	42,618	40,452
Memo: Outstanding pass-through securities, June 1986	125,903	72,377	n.a.	n.a.

n.a.—not available.
[1] Annual rate.

the difference represents a fee to Freddie Mac and Fannie Mae for guaranteeing the pass-through security. These transactions are commonly referred to as mortgage swaps. From 1982 to mid-1986, about 75 percent of the new participation certificates issued by Freddie Mac and Fannie Mae were associated with swaps (Table VI). Mortgage investors engage in these transactions because the participation certificate has greater liquidity. Also, the participation certificate can serve as collateral in a repurchase agreement; thus, mortgage investors expand their borrowing capabilities by holding the pass-through securities rather than mortgage loans.

An important innovation in the sponsored-agency market that lessened the major disadvantages of pass-through securities was the collateralized mortgage obligation (CMO), introduced in 1983 by the Federal Home Loan Mortgage Corporation. As its name implies, this security is simply a debt issue backed with mortgages or pass-through securities. The unique feature introduced by Freddie Mac was the division of an issue into various classes, differing from one another in the way principal value is repaid. Table VII presents an example. The investors in the class A-1 securities receive interest payments as well as all of the

Table VII

**CHARACTERISTICS OF COLLATERALIZED MORTGAGE OBLIGATIONS OF THE
FEDERAL HOME LOAN MORTGAGE CORPORATION, SERIES A, JUNE 1983**

Characteristic	Class		
	A-1	A-2	A-3
Amount sold (millions of dollars)	215	350	435
Maximum average life (years)	3.2	8.6	20.4
Quoted yield (percent)	10.70	11.37	11.98
Spread over yield on comparable Treasury securities (basis points)[1]	39	52	84

[1] Spread over closest Treasury constant-maturity yield on June 7, 1983.

scheduled repayments and prepayments on the underlying mortgages; the investors in the other classes receive only interest payments until all class A-1 securities are retired. Because initially class A-1 securities receive the repayments on the underlying mortgages, their expected life is relatively short. After class A-1 bonds are retired, the class A-2 bonds receive both interest payments and mortgage repayments while class A-3 bonds continue to receive only interest payments. After class A-2 is retired, class A-3 receives both interest payments and mortgage repayments.

This innovation reduces (though it does not eliminate) the major disadvantage of uncertainty about maturity that is associated with mortgage pass-through securities. When a mortgage-related security is divided into various maturity classes, investors have a clearer expectation of when their security will be repaid.

CONCLUSION

The federally sponsored credit agencies were created to alter the flow of funds in cases in which the allocation of resources achieved through market forces was believed to be suboptimal. However, as the U.S. financial system becomes less regulated, the ability and the need of the sponsored agencies to influence the allocation of resources by serving as intermediaries may be lessened. With the removal of interest rate ceilings on deposits and the steady movement toward interstate banking, credit can flow much more easily to different regions of the country or to different markets where its productive use will be greatest. The development of new financial instruments also will facilitate an efficient flow of funds through the economy. In short, our financial system may be evolving to the point where the optimal allocation of resources can be attained without intervention sponsored by the federal government. If the resulting market solution to resource allocation is still viewed as suboptimal from a social point of view, some form of direct subsidy may be necessary to achieve the desired outcome.

For the time being, the sponsored agencies are important participants in the money and capital markets. Their financial resources are substantial, they have developed expertise in their areas, and they are well established among the borrowers and lenders in the credit markets that they serve. Their activities enhance the liquidity in these markets and foster the integration of the various components of the financial system.

12

MONEY MARKET MUTUAL FUNDS AND OTHER SHORT-TERM INVESTMENT POOLS

Timothy Q. Cook
Jeremy G. Duffield

Since the early 1970s numerous short-term investment pooling arrangements (STIPS) have emerged in the nation's financial system. The most well-known form is the money market mutual fund (MMF). While the various types of STIPs differ in some respects, such as the kind of asset held or the type of investor, they are all alike in their basic function which is to purchase large pools of short-term financial instruments and sell shares in these pools to investors. Because it typically takes at least $100,000 to purchase most money market instruments, STIPs allow investors to gain access to money market yields with a much smaller amount of money. STIPs also provide many investors greater liquidity, diversification, and a higher yield net of expenses than could be obtained by direct investment in the money market. This chapter discusses the four major types of STIPs: money market funds, short-term tax-exempt funds, short-term investment funds of bank trust departments, and local government investment pools. As of mid-1986 these four categories of STIPs held over $375 billion in money market instruments.

MONEY MARKET MUTUAL FUNDS[1]

The first MMF started offering shares to the public in 1972. The MMF industry experienced its first period of rapid growth in 1974 and early 1975 when money market interest rates rose well above the Regulation Q ceiling rates that depository institutions were permitted to pay on small time and savings deposits. By mid-1975 there were roughly 35 MMFs in operation with assets of almost $4 billion. The level of MMF assets remained in a range of $3 to $4 billion until early 1978, when interest rates again rose above Regulation Q ceiling rates. In the late 1970s and early 1980s very high levels of money market rates resulted in huge

---

[1] Data presented in this section is for taxable money market funds only.

Chart 1

MMF ASSETS

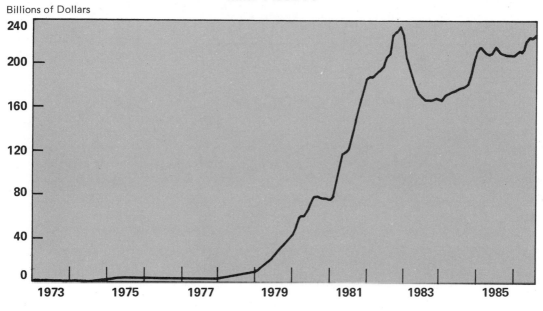

Billions of Dollars

240

200

160

120

80

40

0

1973   1975   1977   1979   1981   1983   1985

Source: Board of Governors of the Federal Reserve System.

differentials between the rates paid by MMFs and the rates that investors could earn on small time and savings deposits at depository institutions. Explosive growth in MMFs resulted; from the end of 1977 to November 1982 MMF assets rose from $4 billion to $235 billion (Chart 1).

To counter the outflow of savings balances from banks into MMFs, depository institutions were authorized to offer two ceiling-free accounts: the money market deposit account (MMDA) in December 1982 and the Super NOW account in January 1983. The MMDA account was especially popular, in part because it was initially offered at promotional rates that were well above those available at MMFs. From November 1982 to the end of 1983 MMF assets fell by $67 billion to a level of $168 billion. As shown in Chart 2, average MMDA rates fell below average MMF yields in August 1983, and from then through mid-1986 the differential between MMF and MMDA rates averaged about 50 basis points in favor of MMFs. MMF growth resumed in early 1984 and by mid-1986 MMF shares had returned to their late 1982 level. There were about 270 MMFs in mid-1986 with total shareholder accounts of over 14 million.

The history of MMF growth clearly indicates that ceiling interest rates at depository institutions contributed to this growth. That MMFs successfully survived the removal of these ceiling rates suggests that other developments were

159

Chart 2

THE SPREAD BETWEEN THE AVERAGE YIELD ON MMDAs AND MMFs
(Weekly Data, 3/16/83 to 5/20/86)

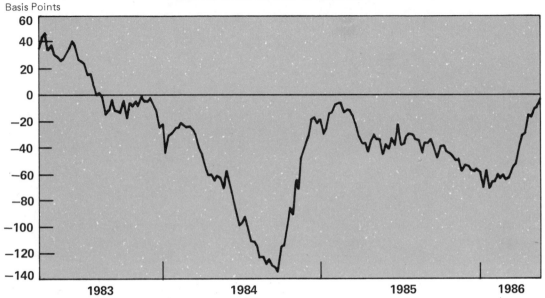

Source: MMF yields are from *Donoghue's Money Fund Report* of Holliston, Mass.
MMDA yields are from *Bank Rate Monitor* of North Palm Beach, Florida.

also important to their emergence in the 1970s as an important financial intermediary. One such factor was technological progress in the computer and telecommunications industries that enabled MMFs to provide intermediation in the money market at a low cost.[2] Computers play a pervasive role in the operations of MMFs and other STIPS. The unit cost of all the services performed by computers—storing data, making calculations, printing information—fell sharply in the 1970s. Equally important to MMFs was the development of sophisticated telecommunications systems such as Inward Wide Area Telecommunications Service ("800" numbers) and computerized switchboards. This technology was important because the vast majority of investors in MMFs do business over the phone, mostly by long distance. Less developed technology probably accounts for why MMFs did not emerge until the 1970s, even though the

---

[2] The argument that technological progress was an important determinant of MMF growth is provided in more detail in Cook and Duffield [1980].

1960s also experienced periods of large differentials between market rates and Regulation Q ceiling interest rates.

Another factor contributing to the growth of MMFs has been their use in conjunction with other products offered by mutual fund groups and brokerage companies. Investors often use MMFs as a parking place for cash reserves awaiting investment in longer term financial assets such as stocks and bonds. For example, the switching of mutual fund shares, which has grown rapidly in recent years, usually involves the exchange of MMF shares for some other type of share. Further, MMFs are generally the core vehicle in the popular "cash management accounts" offered by large brokerage firms. It seems likely that the renewed growth of MMFs since early 1984 has been due not only to their competitive rates, but also to the rapid growth over this period of the brokerage business and the entire mutual fund industry. (Excluding short-term funds, mutual fund assets grew from $113 billion at the end of 1983 to $356 billion in June 1986.)

Individuals are the largest investors in MMFs. MMFs are also used by a variety of institutional investors, including bank trust departments, corporations, and retirement plans. One category of the MMF industry, generally labelled "institutions-only" MMFs, has evolved to deal solely with this type of investor. There were 36 institutions-only MMFs in mid-1986 with total assets of $52 billion. Many institutions also invest in "broker-sponsored" and "general purpose" MMFs. (General purpose funds do not target any particular group, but are available to all investors.) The largest institutional users of MMFs are small and medium-sized bank trust departments, who use MMFs as a means of earning a market rate on the short-term reserves of their personal and employee benefit trust accounts. Some small, midsize, and even some larger corporations also use MMFs for cash management purposes.

The general operating characteristics of MMFs are fairly standard. Minimum initial investments usually range from $500 to $5,000, although a small number of funds require no minimum and institutions-only MMFs typically require minimums of $50,000 or more. Most funds have a checking option that enables shareholders to write checks, usually with a minimum of $500. Shares can also be redeemed at most MMFs by telephone or wire request, in which case payment by the MMF is either mailed to the investor or remitted by wire to the investor's bank account.

Because MMFs are no-load mutual funds, investors purchase and redeem shares without paying a sales charge. Instead, expenses of the funds are deducted daily from gross income before shareholder dividends are declared. The difference between the yield earned on a MMF's assets and the yield earned by shareholders is the MMF's expense ratio (defined as the ratio of total expenses on an annual basis to average assets). The expense ratio for most MMFs ranges from 0.4 to 1.0 percent. In 1985 the weighted-average expense ratio for the

Table I

COMPOSITION OF MMF ASSETS

(June 1986, in Billions)

	Amount	% of Total
U.S. Treasury bills	15.4	6.9
Other Treasury securities	6.9	3.1
Other U.S. securities	14.8	6.7
Repurchase agreements	32.2	14.5
Commercial bank CD[1]	12.7	5.7
Other Domestic CD[2]	4.2	1.9
Eurodollar CD[3]	22.1	10.0
Commercial Paper	98.6	44.4
Bankers' acceptances	10.9	4.9
Other	4.3	1.9
Total assets	222.0	100.0

[1] Commercial bank CDs are those issued by American banks located in the United States.
[2] Other domestic CDs include those issued by S&Ls and American branches of foreign banks.
[3] Eurodollar CDs are those issued by foreign branches of domestic banks and some issued by Canadian banks; this category includes some one-day paper.
Source: Investment Company Institute.

industry as a whole was 0.59 percent, and the median expense ratio was 0.75 percent.[3]

MMFs vary in the investment policies they follow. Some funds limit their investments to U.S. Treasury or Treasury plus Federal Agency securities. A larger number purchase a wide range of prime domestic money market instruments, including commercial paper, domestic CDs, and bankers acceptances. Other funds purchase both prime domestic instruments and Eurodollar CDs. Table I shows the aggregate composition of MMF assets in June 1986. At that time 44.4 percent of total MMF assets was commercial paper, 14.5 percent was repurchase agreements, 10.0 percent was U.S. Treasury securities, 10.0 percent was Eurodollar CDs, 7.6 percent was domestic CDs, and 4.9 percent was bankers acceptances. The average maturity of MMF assets ranged from 40 to 50 days in the year ending June 1986.

TAX-EXEMPT MONEY MARKET FUNDS

Tax-exempt money market funds are the tax-exempt equivalent to MMFs. Tax-exempt funds invest in securities issued by state and local government

[3] These figures are from *Lipper Directors' Analytical Data*, Lipper Analytical Securities, May 1986.

162

entities which pay interest income that is exempt from Federal income taxes. A small number of tax-exempt funds buy only the securities issued by governments within a particular state, such as California, Massachusetts or New York. These funds offer investors from those states interest income that is exempt from both Federal and state, and sometimes local, income taxes. The first short-term tax-exempt fund offered shares to the public in 1977. By mid-1986 there were 104 tax-exempt MMFs in operation with combined assets of $58 billion.

Because tax-exempt money market funds invest in tax-exempt securities, they appeal to investors in relatively high Federal income tax brackets. To consider the decision faced by such investors, suppose the yield earned by taxable MMFs is YT and the yield earned by tax-exempt MMFs is YTF. Then an investor with a marginal income tax rate of t will earn an after-tax yield of YT(1 − t) by investing in the taxable MMF and YTF by investing in the tax-exempt MMF. The tax rate, t*, at which an investor would earn the same after-tax rate in a taxable and tax-exempt MMF is:

$$t^* = 1 - (YTF/YT).$$

An investor with a marginal tax rate greater than t* would earn a higher after-tax yield in a tax-exempt money fund than in a taxable money fund. Chart 3 shows the behavior of t* in recent years. In the early 1980s a marginal tax rate of 40 to 45 percent was generally required to earn a higher after-tax yield in a tax-exempt MMF than in a taxable MMF. In 1985 and 1986, however, the marginal tax rate required to earn a higher yield in a tax-exempt MMF fell to a range of 30 to 40 percent. This decline reflects the rise in this period of the ratio tax-exempt to taxable money market yields. One likely reason for the rise in the ratio is pressure on short-term tax-exempt yields resulting from the substantial increase in this period in the supply of short-term tax-exempt securities. (See the chapter on short-term municipal securities.)

Tax reform legislation in 1986 reduced the highest federal marginal tax rates for individuals and corporations to 28 percent and 34 percent, respectively.[4] This reduction in the highest marginal tax rates should have the effect of raising the ratio of tax-exempt to taxable money market yields relative to its average level in the past, which in turn should raise the ratio of the yields paid by tax-exempt versus taxable MMFs.

In order to maintain a constant share value of $1.00, almost all tax-exempt money market funds (in addition to most taxable MMFs) use the "amortized cost"

---

[4] Under the 1986 tax legislation the marginal tax bracket for married couples filing joint returns starting in 1988 is 15 percent below $29,750 and 28 percent above that figure. However, the benefit of the 15 percent tax bracket is phased-out between $71,900 and $149,250 and personal exemptions are phased-out above $149,250. These phase-outs raise the top effective marginal tax rate to 33 percent.

Chart 3

**TAX RATE EQUATING AFTER-TAX YIELDS
ON TAXABLE AND TAX-EXEMPT MMFs**

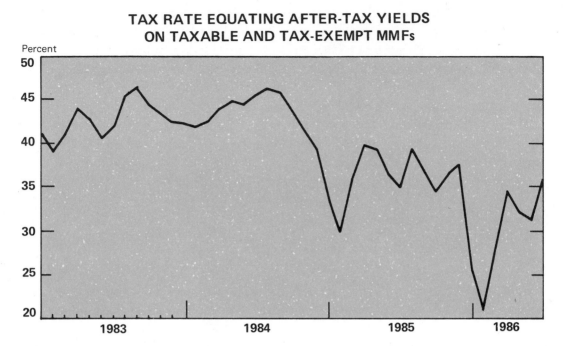

Source: Yields series are from *Donoghue's Money Fund Report* of Holliston, Mass.

method of valuation under which securities are valued at acquisition cost rather than market value. Under this method the interest earned on each security (plus any discount received or less any premium paid upon purchase) is accrued uniformly over the remaining maturity of the security. By declaring these accruals as a daily dividend to its shareholders, the fund is able to set a fixed price of $1.00 per share. According to Securities and Exchange Commission (SEC) regulations, funds using this method of valuation must maintain an average dollar-weighted maturity of no more than 120 days and must limit their investments to instruments that are of high quality and that have a remaining maturity of one year or less. Virtually all tax-exempt MMFs follow these regulations because of the importance they place on being able to offer investors a constant share value.

According to industry estimates, at least 50 percent of the securities held by tax-exempt MMFs are variable or floating rate instruments. These securities generally have a "demand" or "put" feature that allows the fund at certain times to receive the principal amount of the underlying securities either from the issuer or a third party. (The chapter on short-term municipal securities discusses this type of instrument in more detail.) SEC regulations specify conditions under which

164

these variable and floating rate instruments can be treated as short-term for the purpose of satisfying the maturity requirements to use the amortized cost method of valuation.[5] These regulations greatly expand the investment alternatives available to tax-exempt MMFs while still enabling them to use the amortized cost method of valuation and maintain a constant share value.

SHORT-TERM INVESTMENT FUNDS

Short-term investment funds (STIFs) are collective investment funds operated by bank trust departments. A collective investment fund is an arrangement whereby the monies of different accounts in the trust department are pooled to purchase a certain type of security, such as common stocks, corporate bonds, tax-exempt bonds, or, in the case of STIFs, short-term securities. The first STIF appears to have been started in 1968. By the end of 1974 there were over 70 STIFs with total assets of almost $3 billion. Like MMFs, STIFs began to grow rapidly when interest rates rose in the late 1970s, and by the end of 1979 there were 250 STIFS with over $32 billion in assets. STIFs continued to grow in the 1980s, and at the end of 1984 there were 343 STIFs with total assets of $75.9 billion.

STIFs function just like MMFs and offer the same advantages to holders of trust department accounts. In particular, the minimum investment is usually a negligible amount and funds can be put in and withdrawn without transactions fees.

Most bank trust departments without STIFs use MMFs for their trust accounts. The decision to set up a STIF or to use a MMF is largely dependent on the size of the trust department. The larger the trust department the more likely it is to have a STIF. Survey results from two sources using data from the late 1970s both indicate that trust departments with assets of less than $500 million are very unlikely to set up their own STIF; departments with assets of $500 million to $1 billion are much more likely to establish a STIF; and departments with assets of $1 billion or more are very likely to establish a STIF.[6]

Regulations on the portfolio of STIFS set by the Comptroller of the Currency require that: (1) at least 80 percent of investments must be payable on demand or have a maturity not exceeding 91 days, and (2) not less than 20 percent of the value of the fund's assets must be composed of cash, demand obligations, and other assets that mature on the fund's next business day. As a result of these regulations, STIFs hold a substantial amount of variable amount notes (also called

---

[5] See SEC Release No. IC-14983 (*Federal Register*, Vol. 51, No. 55, March 21, 1986) for a detailed description of these regulations.

[6] See Cook and Duffield [1979b, p.22] and American Bankers Association [1979, pp.16, 22]

Table II

ASSETS OF SHORT-TERM INVESTMENT FUNDS

(Year-end 1984)

	No. of Funds	No. of Banks	Assets (billions of $)	Total Accounts
Personal trust	136	110	13.9	212,709
Employee benefit	156	119	57.7	54,173
Keogh	23	20	0.2	8,721
Other	28	22	4.1	30,668
TOTAL	343	163[a]	75.9	306,271

a. Total does not equal sum because some banks have more than one STIF.
Source: 1984 Survey of Trust Assets of Insured Commercial Banks.

master notes), which are a type of open-ended commercial paper that allows the investment and withdrawal of funds on a daily basis and pays a daily interest rate tied to the current commercial paper rate. In addition, STIFS hold a large amount of standard commercial paper.

Most STIFs fall into two broad categories. The first is for the accounts of personal trusts and estates. These STIFs receive tax-exempt status under the condition that income earned by the fund is distributed to participating account holders. The second type of STIF is for the accounts of employee benefit plans that are exempt from taxation under the Internal Revenue Code. Under IRS regulations monies of these tax-exempt employee benefit accounts can not be mixed with monies of personal trust and estate accounts. Hence, if a bank trust department wishes to provide STIF services to both types of accounts, it must establish both types of STIFs.

Table II shows the aggregate numbers and total assets of each type of STIF as of year-end 1984. At that time 212,709 personal trust accounts had a total of $13.9 billion invested in STIFs, while 54,173 employee benefit accounts had a total of $57.7 billion invested in STIFs. There was also a small amount of funds invested in other STIFs not included in these two categories.

LOCAL GOVERNMENT INVESTMENT POOLS

Local government investment pools (LGIPs) are investment pools set up by individual states to enable local government entities—such as counties, cities, school districts, state agencies, etc.—to purchase shares in a large portfolio of money market instruments.[7] The primary purpose of state legislation establishing these pools has been to encourage efficient management of idle funds. Most pools are administered by the state treasurer's office, often in conjunction with the state investment board and a local government advisory council. In some exceptions to this general pattern, private organizations provide advisory and administrative services, usually under the sponsorship of the state or an association of local governments. For instance, the Illinois LGIP is administered by a bank trust department, and LGIPs in Massachusetts, North Carolina and Pennsylvania are run by investment management firms.

Table III

LGIP STATISTICS

(December 1985)

| | Assets ($ millions) | Average Maturity | Participants | | Established |
			No. of Active	% of Potential	
California	3,280	1 yr. 86 days	995	26.1	1977
Colorado	89	98 days	76	3.8	1985
Connecticut	76	40 days	75	17.3	1973
Florida	3,341	75 days	350	38.4	1977
Georgia	342	112 days	75	5.9	1981
Illinois	161	24 days	730	11.0	1974
Maryland	62	13 days	84	26.7	1982
Massachusetts	672	29 days	558	72.9	1977
Montana	246	82 days	96	10.0	1973
New Jersey	3,567	80 days	458	27.1	1978
North Carolina	294	26 days	374	39.5	1982
Oregon	863	N.A.	520	35.9	1974
Pennsylvania	578	39 days	930	25.1	1981
Tennessee	95	293 days	313	34.6	1979
Utah	418	147 days	325	66.1	1974
Virginia	33	30 days	37	9.5	1981
West Virginia	670	3 yrs.	1,317	82.3	1978
Wisconsin	688	81 days	281	11.2	1977
TOTAL	15,475		7,594		

Note: Colorado data is for June 1986.
Source: Telephone survey of LGIPs by Fidelity Investments, Boston.

---

[7] Most states do not permit investment by localities in MMFs. However, a few states allow their local units to purchase shares in MMFs whose investments meet the state's legal list of acceptable investments for localities. See Maynard and Wheatley [1986].

167

In most respects the operating characteristics of LGIPs are identical to those of MMFs. Funds may be invested by wire or check and withdrawn either by telephone request, with payment sent by wire, or check. Funds may generally be invested and withdrawn on a daily basis. Interest is earned daily net of the pool's expenses.

The first LGIPs were established in 1973 by Connecticut and Montana. By 1986 a total of 20 states had established LGIPs. Table III provides summary data on various characteristics of these LGIPs.[8] As of December 1985 there were 7,594 government units investing a total of $15.5 billion in LGIPs. Participation by eligible government units within a particular state is highly variable, ranging from as low as 3.8 percent to as high as 82.3 percent. LGIPs also follow widely differing maturity strategies. While many have average maturities as short as those of MMFs, some have average maturities of several months or longer.

CONCLUSION

Short-term investment pools revolutionized the money market by providing virtually all investors access to money market investments. When MMFs first emerged in the mid-1970s, a widespread view was that they were solely a reaction to interest rate ceilings at depository institutions, and that when these ceilings were removed MMFs and other STIPs would fade from view. Time has proved this view incorrect, as STIPs have continued to grow even in the absence of these ceilings. This growth reflects their ability to offer competitive money market yields and their widespread use in conjunction with other products offered by mutual fund groups, brokerage companies, and bank trust departments. Short-term investment pools will undoubtedly remain an important part of the money market in years to come.

References

American Bankers Association. *Collective Investment Funds Survey Report*, 1979. Washington, D. C.

Cook, Timothy Q. and Jeremy G. Duffield. "Average Costs of Money Market Mutual Funds." Federal Reserve Bank of Richmond, *Economic Review* (July/August 1979), pp. 32-39.

————. "Money Market Mutual Funds: A Reaction to Government Regulations or a Lasting Financial Innovation?" Federal Reserve Bank of Richmond, *Economic Review* (July/August 1979), pp. 15-31.

————. "Short-term Investment Pools." Federal Reserve Bank of Richmond, *Economic Review* (September/October 1980), pp. 3-23.

Maynard, David E. and Priscilla M. Wheatley. "At the Crossroads: Private Sector Perspectives on Public Sector Investing." *Government Finance Review* (February 1986), pp. 15-21.

---

[8] LGIPs in Minnesota and South Carolina are not included in the table.

13

SHORT-TERM INTEREST RATE FUTURES

Anatoli Kuprianov

Not long ago futures trading was limited to contracts for agricultural and other commodities. Trading in futures contracts for financial instruments began in the early 1970s, after almost a decade of accelerating inflation exposed market participants to unprecedented levels of exchange rate and interest rate risk. Foreign currency futures, introduced in 1972 by the Chicago Mercantile Exchange, were the first financial futures contracts to be traded. The first interest rate futures contract, a contract for the future delivery of mortgage certificates issued by the Government National Mortgage Association, began trading on the floor of the Chicago Board of Trade in 1975. Today financial futures are among the most actively traded of all futures contracts.

At present there are active futures markets for two different money market instruments: three-month Treasury bills and three-month Eurodollar time deposits. Treasury bill futures were introduced by the Chicago Mercantile Exchange in 1976, while trading in Eurodollar futures began late in 1981. Domestic certificate of deposit futures were also actively traded for a time but that market, while technically still active, became dormant for all practical purposes in 1986.

AN INTRODUCTION TO FUTURES MARKETS

A futures contract is a standardized, transferable agreement to buy or sell a given commodity or financial instrument on a specified future date at a set price. In a futures transaction the buyer (sometimes called the *long*) agrees to purchase and the seller (or *short*) to deliver a specified item according to the terms of the contract. For example, the buyer of a Treasury bill contract commits himself to purchase at some specified future date a thirteen-week Treasury bill paying a rate of interest negotiated at the time the contract is purchased. In contrast, a *cash* or *spot* market transaction simultaneously prices and transfers physical ownership of the item being sold. A *cash commodity* (cash security) refers to the actual physical commodity (security) as distinguished from the futures commodity.

169

Futures contracts are traded on organized exchanges. The basic function of a futures exchange is to set and enforce trading rules. There are thirteen futures exchanges in the United States at present. The principal exchanges are found in Chicago and New York. Short-term interest rate futures trade on a number of exchanges; however, the most active trading in these contracts takes place at the International Monetary Market (IMM) division of the Chicago Mercantile Exchange (CME).

Market Participants   Futures market participants are typically divided into two categories: hedgers and speculators. *Hedging* refers to a futures market transaction made as a temporary substitute for a spot market transaction to be made at a later date. The purpose of hedging is to take advantage of current prices in future transactions. In the money market, hedgers use interest rate futures to fix future borrowing and lending rates.

Futures market *speculation* involves assuming either a short or long futures position solely to profit from price changes, and not in connection with ordinary commercial pursuits. A dentist who buys wheat futures after hearing of a nuclear disaster in the Soviet Union is speculating that wheat prices will rise, while a grain dealer undertaking the same transaction would be hedging unless the futures position is out of proportion with anticipated future wheat purchases.

Characteristics of Futures Contracts   Three distinguishing characteristics are common to all futures contracts. First, a futures contract introduces the element of time into a transaction. Second, futures contracts are standardized agreements. Each futures exchange determines the specifications of the contracts traded on the exchange so that all contracts for a given item specify the same delivery location and a uniform deliverable grade. Traded contracts must also specify one of a limited number of designated delivery dates (also called *contract maturity* or *settlement* dates). The only item negotiated at the time of a futures transaction is price. Third, the exchange clearinghouse interposes itself as a counterparty to each contract. Once a futures transaction is concluded, a buyer and seller need never deal with one another again; their contractual obligations are with the clearinghouse. The clearinghouse, in turn, guarantees contract performance for both parties.

The first of these characteristics is not unique to futures contracts. A forward contract, like a futures contract, is a formal commitment between two parties specifying the terms of a transaction to be undertaken at a future date. Unlike futures contracts, however, forward contracts are not standardized; rather, they are custom-tailored agreements. As a general rule forward contracts are not transferable and so cannot be traded to a third party.

Trading in futures contracts is facilitated by contract standardization and the clearinghouse guarantee. Contract standardization reduces transaction costs. The clearinghouse guarantee removes credit risk, or risk that a party to the contract will fail to honor contractual commitments. These two characteristics make all contracts for the same item and maturity date perfect substitutes for one another so that a party to a futures contract can always liquidate a futures commitment (or *open position*) before maturity by making an offsetting transaction. For example, a trader with a long position in Treasury bill futures maturing in March of 1987 can liquidate his position any time before the last day of trading by selling an equal number of March Treasury bill futures. In practice, most futures contracts are liquidated in this way before they mature. By one estimate two percent of all futures contracts are held to maturity on average, although delivery is more common in some markets.[1]

Margin Requirements   A contract for the future delivery of an item gains value to one of the parties to the contract and imposes a liability on the other when futures prices change. A rise in Treasury bill futures prices, for example, gives all traders who are long in bill futures the right to buy Treasury bills at a price below the currently prevailing futures price; equivalently, they have the right to invest money at an interest rate higher than the current market rate. Traders with short positions, on the other hand, are committed to sell bills at a price lower than that which they would be required to pay if they wished to buy the contract back at the new futures price.

In the early days of trading in time contracts, as they were called in the nineteenth century, traders adversely affected by price movements often disappeared as the delivery date drew near. In response, futures exchanges adopted the practice of requiring a performance bond, called a *margin requirement*, of all buyers and sellers. They also began requiring all traders to recognize any gains or losses on their outstanding futures positions at the end of each trading session, a practice called *marking to market*.

All futures exchanges now require members to maintain margin accounts. Brokers who execute orders on behalf of customers are required to collect margin deposits from them before undertaking any trades. Minimum margin requirements are set by the exchanges. Brokers can, and most do, require their customers to maintain margins higher than the minimum levels set by the exchange. Any gains or losses realized when the contracts are marked to market at the end of a trading session are added to or subtracted from a trader's margin account. If the margin account balance falls below a specified minimum, called

---

[1] See Little [1984, p. 43].

the *maintenance margin*, the trader faces a *margin call* requiring the deposit of additional margin money, called the *variation margin*, to his account.

Futures Exchanges   The right to conduct transactions on the floor of a futures exchange is typically limited to exchange members, although trading privileges can be leased to another party. Members also have voting rights, which give them a voice in management decisions. Membership privileges can be bought and sold; the exchanges make public the most recent selling and current offer price for a membership.

Exchange members can be grouped into two categories. *Commission brokers* (also known as *floor brokers*) execute orders for nonmembers and other customers. Some floor brokers are employees of commission firms while others are independent operators who execute trades for other firms. The second type of exchange member is the *floor trader*, or *local*. Locals are independent operators who trade for their own account.[2]

The Role of the Exchange Clearinghouse   Each futures exchange operates a clearing organization, or clearinghouse, that records all transactions and insures all buy and sell trades match. The clearinghouse also assures the financial integrity of the contracts traded on the exchange by guaranteeing contract performance and supervising the process of delivery for contracts held to maturity.

Clearing member firms act as intermediaries between traders on the floor of the exchange and the clearinghouse, assisting in recording transactions and collecting required margin deposits. Clearing member firms are all members of the exchange, but not all exchange members are clearing members. All transactions taking place on the exchange floor must be cleared through a clearing member firm. Traders who are not directly affiliated with a clearing member must make arrangements with one to act as a designated clearing agent.

Clearing member firms are responsible for collecting margin deposits from their customers and depositing required margins with the clearinghouse. The clearinghouse holds clearing members responsible for losses incurred by their customers. Any time a trader fails to meet a margin call his position is immediately liquidated, with the resulting losses taken from his margin account. If losses exceed funds available in a customer's margin account the clearing member firm is required to make up the difference to the clearinghouse.

---

[2] Different types of floor traders can be distinguished based on the trading strategies they use most often; see Rothstein and Little [1984] for a description. Silber [1984] presents a comprehensive analysis of marketmaker behavior in futures markets.

Futures Commission Merchants A Futures Commission Merchant (FCM) is an intermediary that handles orders for the sale or purchase of a futures contract from the general public. An FCM can be a person or a firm. Some FCMs are exchange members employing their own floor brokers; others rely on independent brokers to handle trades ordered by their customers. An FCM is responsible for collecting the required margin deposit from customers before acting to execute a trade. The FCM must in turn deposit the required margin with its clearing agent. All FCMs must be licensed by the Commodity Futures Trading Commission (CFTC), which is the government agency responsible for regulating futures markets.

TREASURY BILL FUTURES

Treasury bill futures contracts are traded in the United States on two Chicago exchanges: the International Monetary Market (IMM) and the MidAmerica Commodity Exchange. Both contracts specify delivery of thirteen-week (91-day) bills. The IMM T-bill contract, which is the most actively traded of the two by a large margin, is described below.

Contract Specifications Upon maturity the IMM contract requires the seller to deliver a U.S. Treasury bill with a $1 million face value and thirteen weeks left to maturity. Contracts for delivery during the months of March, June, September, and December are traded on the exchange. At any one time contracts for eight different delivery dates are traded. A new contract begins trading after each delivery date, making the furthest delivery date for a new contract twenty-four months away.

Price Quotation Treasury bills do not pay explicit interest. Instead, they are sold at a discount relative to their redemption or face value. The difference between the purchase price of a Treasury bill and its face value determines the interest earned by a buyer. Treasury bill yields are typically quoted on a discount basis, that is, as a percentage of face value rather than of actual funds invested.[3]

Price quotations for T-bill futures contracts are based on an index devised by the IMM. The index is calculated by subtracting the Treasury bill discount yield from 100. For example, if the discount yield on a traded T-bill futures contract is 9.75 percent, then the index value is $100 - 9.75 = 90.25$. Index values move in the same direction as the future purchase price of the deliverable bill; a rise in the index value, for example, means that the price a buyer must agree to pay to take future delivery of a T-bill has risen.

The minimum price fluctuation permitted on the trading floor is one basis

---

[3] See the chapter on Treasury bills for details on yield calculations.

point (.01 percent), which comes to $25 on a contract specifying the delivery of a 91-day Treasury bill with a $1 million face value. Thus, the price of a T-bill futures contract may be quoted as 94.25, or 94.26, but not 94.255. The IMM eliminated maximum daily price limits for all its interest rate futures contracts in December of 1985.

A sample of a newspaper clipping reporting Treasury bill futures prices is reproduced in Box 1.

Box 1

FOLLOWING DAILY FUTURES MARKET ACTIVITY

Many newspapers report information on daily trading activity in futures markets. The clipping for IMM Treasury bill futures reproduced below is taken from the October 3, 1986, edition of the *Wall Street Journal.*

TREASURY BILLS (IMM)—$1 mil.; pts. of 100%

	Open	High	Low	Settle	Chg	Discount Settle	Chg	Open Interest
Dec	94.83	94.84	94.78	94.81	− .02	5.19 +	.02	26,133
Mr87	94.77	94.78	94.73	94.75	− .02	5.25 +	.02	6,510
June	94.59	94.59	94.55	94.56	− .02	5.44 +	.02	1,626
Sept	94.28	94.28	94.24	94.26	− .01	5.74 +	.01	668
Dec	93.89	93.90	93.87	93.89	− .02	6.11 +	.02	313
Mr88	93.53	93.54	93.51	93.53	− .02	6.47 +	.02	312

Est vol 3,554; vol Wed 7,750; open int 35,624, +632.

Each row gives price and trading volume data for a different contract delivery month. Delivery months for currently traded contracts are listed in the first column.

The next four columns show the opening price, high and low prices, and the closing or settlement price for the previous day's trading.

Column six gives the change in the contract settlement price over the last two trading sessions.

The seventh column reports the interest rate implied by the most recent settlement price, calculated by subtracting the settlement price from 100.

Column eight reports the change in the interest rates implied by the two most recent settlement prices. Note that the figures in this

---

column are equal in magnitude but opposite in sign to the change in settlement price displayed in the sixth column.

The last column lists *open interest* for each contract delivery month. Open interest refers to the number of outstanding contracts. Each unit represents both a buyer and a seller with an outstanding futures commitment, or open position. Notice that open interest is greatest for the nearest delivery month and declines steadily for successively distant delivery months. This pattern is typical, except when delivery for the nearby contract is impending and market participants begin to close out their positions.

Total trading volume and open interest for all contract delivery months are given in the last line. Trading volume refers to the total number of contracts for all contract delivery months traded on a particular day. Each transaction included in the count reflects both a purchase and sale of a futures contract. Note that the clipping includes data on total trading volume for each of the previous two trading sessions.

Total open interest, reported in the last line, is simply the sum of the open interest for each contract month listed in the rightmost column. The final entry on the bottom line reports the change in open interest over the previous two trading sessions.

Delivery Requirements   The Treasury auctions thirteen- and twenty-six week bills each Monday (except for holidays and special situations) and issues them on the following Thursday. Fifty-two week bills are auctioned every four weeks. These auctions are held on a Thursday and the bills are issued on the following Thursday. To insure an adequate supply of deliverable bills, the IMM schedules T-bill futures delivery dates for the three successive business days beginning with the first day of the contract month on which a thirteen-week bill is issued and a one-year bill has thirteen weeks to maturity. This schedule permits delivery requirements for the T-bill futures contract to be satisfied with either a newly issued thirteen-week bill or an original-issue twenty-six or fifty-two week bill with thirteen weeks left to maturity. The method used to determine the final delivery price is described in Box 2.

EXAMPLE OF A TREASURY BILL FUTURES TRANSACTION

Suppose that on October 2, 1986, a trader buys one December 1986 Treasury bill futures contract at the opening price of 94.83. Once the transaction is complete the trader is contractually obligated to buy a 1 million dollar (face value) thirteen-week Treasury bill yielding 100 − 94.83 = 5.17 percent on a discount basis on the contract delivery date, which is December 18, 1986. At the time of the initial transaction, however, the trader pays only a commission and deposits the required margin with his broker.

Effects of price changes   The *Wall Street Journal* entry in Box 1 shows that futures prices fell two basis points during that day's trading session, meaning that the discount rate on bills for future delivery rose after the contract was purchased. Since each one basis point change in the T-bill index is worth $25 dollars the trader would lose $50 if he were to sell the contract at the closing price.

The practice of marking futures contracts to market at the end of each trading session means that the trader is forced to realize this loss even though he does not sell the bill; thus, he has $50 subtracted from his margin account. That money is then transferred to a seller's margin account. After the contract is marked to market, the trader is still obliged to buy a Treasury bill on December 18, but now at a discount yield of 5.19 percent (the implied futures discount yield as of the close of trading).

Final settlement   If the trader chooses to hold his contract to maturity the contract is marked to market one last time at the close of the last day of trading. All longs with open positions at that time must be prepared to buy the deliverable bill at a purchase price determined by the closing futures index price.

The final settlement or purchase price implied by the IMM index value is determined as follows. First, calculate the total discount from the face value of the bill using the formula

$$\text{Discount} = \frac{\text{Days to Maturity} \times ((100 - \text{Index}) \times .01) \times \$1,000,000}{360},$$

where $((100 - \text{Index}) \times .01)$ is the futures discount yield expressed as a fraction. Second, calculate the purchase price by subtracting the total discount from the face value of the deliverable bill. Note that this is essentially the same procedure used to calculate the purchase price of a bill from the quoted discount yield in the spot market, the only difference being the use of the futures discount rate implied by the index value in place of the spot market rate.

Suppose that the final index price is 94.81; then, the settlement price for the first delivery day is

$$\$986,880.83 = \$1,000,000 - \frac{91 \times .0519 \times \$1,000,000}{360}.$$

This calculation assumes that the deliverable bill will have exactly 91 days to maturity, which will always be the case on the first contract delivery day except in special cases when a bill would otherwise mature on a national holiday.

Because buying a futures contract during the last trading session is essentially equivalent to buying a Treasury bill in the spot market, futures prices tend to converge to the spot market price of the deliverable security on the final day of trading in a futures contract. Thus, the final futures discount yield should differ little, if at all, from the spot market discount yield at the end of the final trading day.

Market History The IMM introduced the three-month Treasury bill futures contract in January of 1976. At the time the contract was introduced, trading in interest rate futures was still a relatively new development. Trading in the first interest rate futures contract, the Board of Trade's Government National Mortgage Association (GNMA) certificate contract, had begun only a few months earlier. The Treasury bill contract was the first futures contract for a money market instrument.

Dealers in U.S. government securities were among the first market participants to actively use Treasury bill futures. Other money market participants entered into futures trading more slowly. By the time the IMM contract was two years old, however, trading activity had begun to accelerate rapidly.

This trend can be seen in Charts 1 and 2, which plot two different measures of market activity for the IMM contract from the inception of trading in 1976 through the end of 1984. The first measure, plotted in Chart 1, is total monthly

177

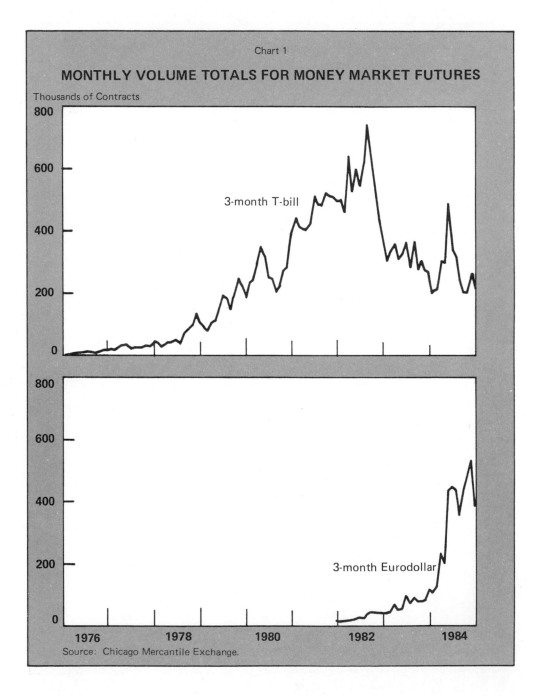

Chart 1

MONTHLY VOLUME TOTALS FOR MONEY MARKET FUTURES

Thousands of Contracts

3-month T-bill

3-month Eurodollar

1976   1978   1980   1982   1984

Source: Chicago Mercantile Exchange.

178

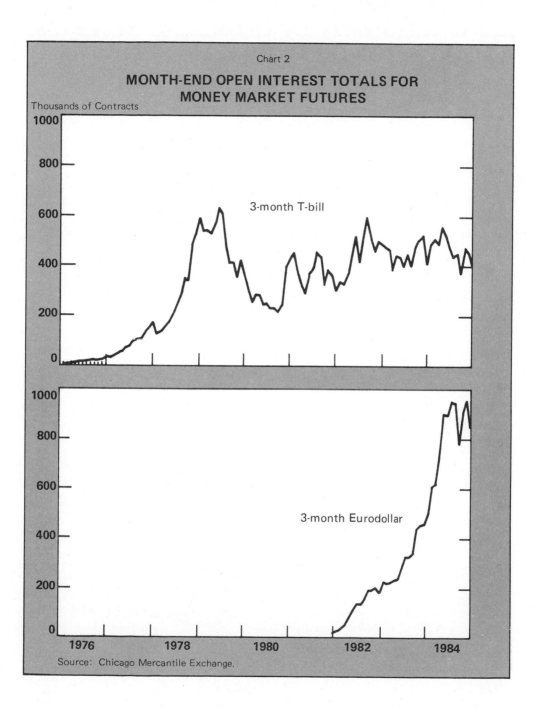

Chart 2

MONTH-END OPEN INTEREST TOTALS FOR MONEY MARKET FUTURES

Thousands of Contracts

3-month T-bill

3-month Eurodollar

1976   1978   1980   1982   1984

Source: Chicago Mercantile Exchange.

179

trading volume, which is a count of the total number of contracts (not the dollar value) traded for all contract delivery months. Each recorded trade reflects one buyer and one seller.

Chart 2 plots total month-end open interest for all contract delivery months. Month-end open interest is a count of the number of unsettled contracts as of the end of the last trading day of a given month. Each contract included in the open interest count reflects both a buyer and a seller with an outstanding futures commitment.

EURODOLLAR FUTURES

Eurodollar futures contracts are actively traded on two exchanges. In the United States, a three-month Eurodollar time deposit contract is traded at the IMM. A similar contract is also traded at the London International Financial Futures Exchange (LIFFE). The IMM contract is described below.

Contract Specifications   Technically, the buyer of a Eurodollar contract is required to place $1,000,000 in a three-month Eurodollar time deposit paying the contracted rate of interest on the contract maturity date. This delivery requirement exists only in principle, however, because the Eurodollar contract is *cash settled*. Cash settlement means that actual physical delivery never takes place; instead, any net changes in the value of the contract at maturity are settled in cash on the basis of spot market Eurodollar rates. Thus, cash settlement can be viewed as a final marking to market of the contract with the settlement amount based on the difference between the previous day's closing price and the final settlement price.

Price Quotation   Price quotations for Eurodollar futures are based on a price index similar to that used for Treasury bill futures. Unlike Treasury bills, Eurodollar time deposits (as well as domestic and Eurodollar CDs) pay explicit interest. The rate of interest paid on the face amount of such a deposit is termed an *add-on yield* because the depositor receives the face amount of the deposit plus an explicit interest payment when the deposit matures. In the case of Eurodollar time deposits, the add-on yield is commonly called the London Interbank Offered Rate (LIBOR), which is the interest rate at which major international banks offer to place Eurodollar deposits with one another. Like other money market rates, LIBOR is an annualized rate based on a 360–day year. The IMM Eurodollar futures price index is 100 minus the LIBOR for Eurodollar futures.

Determination of Settlement Price   When a futures contract contains provisions for physical delivery, market forces cause the futures price to converge to the spot market price as the delivery date draws near. This phenomenon is called *convergence*. In the case of a cash-settled contract, the futures exchange

180

forces the process of convergence to take place by setting the price of outstanding futures contracts equal to the spot market price at the end of the last day of trading.

To determine the final settlement price for its Eurodollar futures contract, the Mercantile Exchange clearinghouse randomly polls twelve banks actively participating in the London Eurodollar market at two different times during the last day of trading: once at a randomly selected time during the last 90 minutes of trading and once at the close of trading. The two highest and lowest price quotes from each polling are dropped and the remaining quotes are averaged to arrive at the LIBOR rate used for final settlement. The final settlement price is 100 minus the average of the LIBOR rates for the two sample times.

As with Treasury bill futures, every change of one basis point in the Eurodollar futures index price is worth twenty-five dollars. Thus, if the IMM price index rises 10 basis points during the last trading session all shorts have $250 per contract subtracted from their margin accounts while the longs each receive $250 per contract. Once the contracts are marked to market for the last time, buyers and sellers are relieved of the responsibility of actually placing or taking the deposits specified by the contract.

The IMM Eurodollar contract is the first futures contract traded in the United States to rely exclusively on a cash settlement procedure. The LIFFE Eurodollar contract also relies principally on cash settlement, although it does have provisions for physical delivery.[4]

Market History Trading in the IMM Eurodollar contract began in December, 1981. The LIFFE introduced its Eurodollar contract a few months later in September of 1982. Both markets are currently active. Trading activity in the IMM contract is much heavier than in the LIFFE contract, however.[5] Charts 1 and 2 display monthly time series of total trading volume and open interest for the IMM Eurodollar contract through the end of 1984.

Three factors have contributed to the popularity of Eurodollar futures. First, most major international banks rely heavily on Eurodollar market for short-term funds. To maintain ready access to this market, many of these banks have become active market makers in Eurodollar deposits. Eurodollar futures provide a means of hedging interest rate risk arising from these activities.

Second, major international corporations have come to rely increasingly on Eurodollar markets for borrowed funds. Borrowing rates for these corporations are

---

[4] Tompkins and Youngren [1983] contains a detailed comparison of the IMM and LIFFE contracts.

[5] As of the end of trading on October 2, 1986, for example, total volume and open interest for the IMM contract were 44,378 and 217,542 contracts, while trading volume for the LIFFE contract was 3,454 and open interest was 23,541.

THREE-MONTH TREASURY BILL AND EURODOLLAR TIME DEPOSIT FUTURES: IMM CONTRACT SPECIFICATIONS

	Treasury Bill	Eurodollar Time Deposit
Contract Size	$1,000,000	$1,000,000
Deliverable Grade	U. S. Treasury bills with thirteen weeks to maturity	Cash settlement with clearing corporation
Delivery Months	March, June, September, December	March, June, September, December
Price Quotation	Index: 100 minus discount yield	Index: 100 minus add-on yield
Minimum Price Fluctuation	.01 percent (1 basis point = $25)	.01 percent (1 basis point = $25)
Trading Hours (Chicago Time)	7:20 a.m.-2:00 p.m. (last day-10:00 a.m.)	7:20 a.m.-2:00 p.m. (last day-9:30 a.m.)
Last Day of Trading	The day before the first delivery date	Second London business day before the third Wednesday of delivery month
Delivery Days	Three successive business days beginning with the first day of the contract month on which a thirteen-week T-bill is issued and a one-year bill has thirteen weeks to maturity	Last day of trading

Source: Chicago Mercantile Exchange.

typically based on the three- or six-month LIBOR. When loans are priced this way, Eurodollar futures offer a means of hedging borrowing costs.

Finally, Eurodollar and domestic CD futures display almost identical price characteristics, which means that the two contracts are virtually perfect substitutes as hedging instruments.[6] The physical delivery requirements for CD futures proved to be awkward in comparison with the cash-settled Eurodollar contract, however, causing U.S. banks, once among the heaviest users of CD futures, to rely instead on Eurodollar futures to hedge domestic borrowing costs. In fact, the steep rise in trading volume in the Eurodollar contract during 1984 evident in Chart 1 coincides with a decline in CD futures trading volume beginning at about the same time. Thus, it appears that the success of the Eurodollar contract has contributed to the demise of trading in CD futures.

---

[6] Faux [1984] found the correlation between Eurodollar and CD futures prices to be .993.

USES OF INTEREST RATE FUTURES: HEDGING AND SPECULATION

Hedging Theory In the most general terms hedging refers to the act of matching one risk with a counterbalancing risk so as to reduce the overall risk of loss. Futures hedging was traditionally viewed narrowly as the use of futures contracts to offset the risk of loss resulting from price changes. To illustrate, consider the example of an investor with holdings of interest-bearing securities. If market interest rates rise, the value of those securities will fall. Since futures prices tend to move in sympathy with spot market prices, taking on a short position in interest rate futures produces an opposing risk. Traders with short positions in interest rate futures profit when interest rates rise because the contracts give them the right to sell the underlying security at the old, higher price, meaning that they can buy back the contracts at a profit.

This traditional view emphasized risk avoidance—futures hedging was seen solely as providing a form of insurance against price risk. The contemporary view of hedging, on the other hand, emphasizes the relative efficiency of futures markets. Buying or selling futures contracts is a good temporary substitute for planned spot market transactions because futures contracts are more liquid than cash securities and transaction costs are generally lower in futures markets. From this perspective, the hedging transaction described above can be viewed as a temporary substitute for selling existing holdings of interest-bearing securities and buying shorter-term securities whose value would be less affected by interest rate changes. Either transaction would reduce the risk faced by the investor, but the futures hedge does so at a lower cost.

Hedging as profit-maximizing behavior The principal shortcoming of the traditional concept of hedging is that it does not explain the hedging behavior of profit-maximizing firms. Although all firms must bear some risk inherent to the normal conduct of business, it is widely recognized that firms seek to maximize profits, and not to minimize risk. While risk minimization is not generally consistent with profit-maximizing behavior, cost minimization is. This is not to deny that hedging transactions are undertaken to reduce risk; hedging is one tool used in implementing a broader policy of risk management. The hedging behavior of profit-maximizing firms is best understood, however, when hedging is viewed as a temporary, low-cost alternative to planned spot market transactions rather than as a form of price insurance.[7]

The emphasis that modern hedging theory places on transaction costs is especially useful in understanding the hedging behavior of money market

---

[7] The concept of hedging as profit-maximizing behavior was developed by Working [1962]. Telser [1981, 1986] takes a similar view, arguing that futures markets exist primarily because they minimize transaction costs, and not because futures contracts can be used to insure against price risk.

participants. In the money market, investors interested only in minimizing risk need not hedge; they can simply hold a portfolio composed solely of T-bills that are close to maturity. Most investors, however, are willing to bear some additional risk in exchange for a higher expected rate of return. Hedgers in the money market selectively buy and sell interest rate futures to fix future borrowing and lending rates when they perceive it to be to their advantage to do so, and not to minimize risk per se.[8]

Portfolio hedging theory Portfolio hedging theory views futures contracts in the context of a hedger's entire portfolio of cash holdings. With this approach, cash holdings are treated as fixed and the expected returns of the unhedged portfolio are compared with those of a hedged portfolio. To the extent that futures prices are correlated with the value of the unhedged portfolio, a hedge can reduce portfolio risk. Final hedging positions are determined by the desired risk-return tradeoff, which may not be the risk-minimizing combination.[9]

Basis Risk *Basis* refers to the difference between the spot market price of the security being hedged and the futures price. In portfolio hedging applications, basis can also refer to the relationship between the value of the portfolio and the price of a futures contract. *Basis risk* refers to the risk hedgers face as a result of unexpected changes in basis.

In a *perfect hedge* any gains or losses resulting from a change in the price of the item being hedged is offset by an equal and opposite change in futures prices. Perfect futures hedges are rarely attainable in practice because futures contracts are not custom-tailored agreements. Contract standardization, while contributing to the liquidity of the futures markets, practically insures that those contracts will not be perfectly suited to the needs of any one hedger. As a result, hedgers are exposed to basis risk.

At least two sources of basis risk can be identified. First, because standardized delivery dates for futures contracts rarely coincide with planned transaction dates, most hedgers must unwind their futures positions before the contract delivery date. Futures prices do not always move in perfect conformity with spot prices before the contract maturity date, however, most often for fundamental economic reasons but sometimes for reasons that are not fully understood. Thus,

---

[8] Although these hedging concepts have gained widespread acceptance among market participants and regulatory agencies such as the CFTC, bank regulatory agencies define permissible hedges in terms of risk reduction. Federally insured banks and savings and loan associations are permitted to buy and sell futures for their own accounts only when the transactions can be shown to reduce overall risk; see Koppenhaver [1984] for more details.

[9] Powers and Vogel [1981, chapter 14] contains an introductory discussion of portfolio hedging theory. Figlewski [1986] contains a formal development of the portfolio approach to hedging, including methods for determining a risk-minimizing hedge.

any changes in the value of the futures contracts held as a hedge may not fully reflect changes in the spot price of the item being hedged at the time the hedge is lifted. If the date of a planned spot market transaction coincided exactly with the corresponding futures contract delivery date, delivery of the underlying cash instrument would permit a hedger to avoid this source of basis risk.

Second, in most cases the grade of the commodity being hedged differs from the deliverable grade specified by the futures contract. Price differentials between different commodity grades can vary, exposing hedgers to basis risk. This problem is not limited to commodity futures, moreover. Interest rate differentials on bank deposits, reflecting different risk premiums, can vary even among major money-center banks.

As long as changes in futures prices are highly correlated with changes in underlying cash prices a futures hedge can reduce overall risk. Hedging cannot eliminate basis risk, however. For this reason, it is often said that hedging replaces price risk with basis risk.

Cross Hedging Futures markets do not exist for all financial instruments. *Cross hedging* refers to the use of a futures contract for the delivery of one security as a hedge against an anticipated future transaction in a different security. An example of a popular cross hedge in the money market is the use of Eurodollar futures to hedge transactions in domestic CDs.

Futures prices tend to be more highly correlated with the price of the deliverable security than with other securities; as a result, a cross hedge will carry more basis risk than a regular hedge. When choosing a futures contract for a cross-hedging application, hedgers try to pick the futures contract for which price changes are most highly correlated with price changes of the security being hedged.

Examples of Interest Rate Hedging Strategies A wide variety of interest rate hedging strategies have been devised in the few years since interest rate futures were first introduced. Interest rate futures can be used to establish interest rates on anticipated future investments and borrowing rates on future loans. Financial intermediaries, such as banks, use interest rate futures to protect their balance sheets from adverse effects of changes in market rates. Examples of different hedging strategies are briefly described below.

The Long Hedge A long hedge involves buying futures contracts, or assuming a long futures position. Investors use long hedges to protect against falling interest rates by fixing interest rates on future investments. One way to think of a long hedge is as a transaction that lengthens the effective maturity of holdings of interest-bearing securities. This is illustrated by the following example.

Suppose a corporate cash manager is instructed to invest $10 million in Treasury bills until the firm anticipates needing the funds again in six months. The manager can fix the rate of return earned over this period in advance either by buying six-month bills or by simultaneously buying three-month bills and bill futures. The latter strategy of putting on a long futures hedge creates a *synthetic* six-month Treasury bill.

To take a simplified example suppose the date is September 18, 1986, exactly 91 days before the first delivery date for December Treasury bill futures. Six-month bills can be purchased at a discount yield of 5.42 percent. Creating a synthetic six month bill would require the simultaneous purchase of a three-month Treasury bill and a futures contract for the delivery of a three-month bill on December 18. Three-month bills sell at a 5.23 percent discount yield and the discount yield for December bill futures is 5.36 percent. Buying an actual six-month bill turns out to be the more profitable alternative in this example (all numbers used in this example, incidentally, reflect actual closing prices for September 18, 1986); however, putting together a synthetic Treasury bill can sometimes produce a higher yield than buying a longer-term bill in the spot market.[10] Another potential advantage to the futures hedge is that it can easily be lifted if market rates begin to rise.

A drawback to using the futures strategy comes from exposure to basis risk. In the above example the date of the initial transaction was chosen so as to fall exactly 91 days before the maturity date of December Treasury bill futures contracts. This does not always happen in practice.

The Short Hedge   The money manager in the above example could have used another method to create a synthetic six-month bill. Instead of buying three month bills and a futures contract for delivery in three months he could buy nine-month Treasury bills and simultaneously sell March 1987 bill contracts. Selling the futures contracts effectively shortens the maturity of the nine-month bills to six months. This last strategy is an example of a short hedge. A short hedge involves selling interest rate futures to protect the value of cash holdings of interest bearing securities or to fix borrowing costs. The following example shows how a corporation might use Eurodollar futures to fix a borrowing rate on a future loan.

Overseas affiliates of multinational firms frequently take out loans with borrowing costs tied to LIBOR. Consider a firm that expects to need such a loan in a month. The firm faces the risk that borrowing rates may rise before the loan is taken out. The corporate treasurer can hedge against this risk by shorting Eurodollar futures. Since taking out a loan amounts to selling an interest-bearing

---

[10] See Werderits [1983], for example.

security, selling interest rate futures contracts serves as a temporary substitute for taking out the loan now and investing the proceeds until the funds are needed. If interest rates rise, the cost of satisfying delivery requirements for the futures contract falls while the contracted delivery price remains the same. The gain from the futures position offsets increased borrowing costs.

Hedging Interest Rate Risk Financial intermediaries, such as banks and securities dealers, fund their holdings of earning assets largely through debt. Traditionally, financial intermediaries have used short-term sources of funds to finance holdings of longer-term assets. This condition is described as a *positive gap*. When an institution has a positive gap, changes in interest rates affect funding costs faster than asset returns. This means that any rise in interest rates will hurt future earnings, while a fall in rates produces windfall profits. The risk to net earnings caused by changes in interest rates is termed interest rate risk.

Financial intermediaries have begun to use interest rate futures to hedge interest rate risk. A positive gap can be hedged by either shortening the effective maturity of asset holdings or by fixing future borrowing rates. Readers interested in learning more about gap hedging strategies are referred to Brewer [1985], Kaufman [1984], and Kawaller [1983].

Risks Associated with Hedging

Risk of Margin Calls Hedgers, like all traders who take on futures positions, face the risk of margin calls. In the case of a hedging transaction, any decline in the value of a futures position is normally offset by gains from a cash position. Gains on the cash position are typically not realized immediately, however, while futures contracts are marked to market at the end of each trading session. The practice of marking futures contracts to market every day, while helping to insure the financial integrity of futures contracts, can place strains on a hedger's cash flow.

Liquidity Risk Although futures contracts are more liquid than the underlying security as a general rule, liquidity can be a problem in some markets. CD futures provide a good example. As of September 4, 1986, trading volume in CD futures was zero while total open interest was twenty-eight contracts. In such a market, it can at times be literally impossible to execute market orders for the purchase or sale of a contract. Hedgers who venture into such markets should be prepared to satisfy delivery requirements.

Liquidity can also be a problem for futures contracts with delivery dates more than a year away. Trading activity in futures contracts is heaviest in contracts for the nearby delivery month. Trading in the most distant contracts is typically very thin, indicating that those markets are less liquid. Liquidity can also be a problem for contracts a few days away from settlement. Unless a hedger plans delivery, it is best to either lift the hedge or roll it over (close out the existing futures position and buy or sell another futures contract) into the next contract delivery month before the last week of trading in a contract.[11]

The Role of Speculators Speculators have been active participants in futures markets since the earliest days of futures trading. Futures markets have proven attractive to speculators for at least two reasons. First, fractional margin requirements permit speculators to effectively leverage their positions to a greater degree than might otherwise be possible. Second, lower transaction costs and greater liquidity make futures contracts an attractive alternative to cash transactions for speculators as well as hedgers.

The early history of futures trading is filled with accounts of market squeezes—attempts at price manipulation effected by dumping or withholding commodity supplies on futures delivery dates—and traders who defaulted on their obligations when price changes created losses. Most often, speculators were blamed for these abuses. In addition, commodity producers often held speculators responsible for declines in commodity prices. These perceived speculative abuses produced several attempts to ban futures trading entirely.[12]

In response to these events, the futures exchanges devised ways to insure the orderly functioning of futures markets. Delivery requirements were designed so as to minimize the danger of market squeezes.[13] Margin requirements and the daily marking-to-market of contracts were adopted to eliminate credit risk from futures contracts. Speculators in futures markets are still sometimes blamed for large price fluctuations; for the most part, however, they have come to be viewed as playing a useful role in futures markets through their willingness to assume price risk, thereby making the markets more liquid for hedgers.

PRICE RELATIONSHIPS BETWEEN FUTURES AND CASH MARKETS

As a general rule futures prices tend to be highly correlated with the spot price of the deliverable security. All futures hedging strategies rely on this price

---

[11] Ronalds [1986] discusses contract life cycles for a number of financial futures.

[12] Hieronymus [1971; chapter 4] tells of the arrest of nine prominent members of the Chicago Board of Trade following the enactment of the Illinois Elevator bill in 1867. That bill classified any contract for the sale of grain for future delivery as gambling, except in cases where the seller actually owned physical stocks of the commodity being sold. The sections of the bill classfying futures contracts as gambling were repealed in the next session of the Illinois legislature, however, and the exchange members never came to trial.

[13] Paul [1985] discusses the design of contract settlement provisions.

relationship: it is because futures and spot prices are highly correlated that futures contracts can serve as temporary substitutes for cash transactions.

Price relationships between futures and underlying spot markets can be explained using arbitrage pricing theory, which is based on the premise that two different securities that can serve as perfect substitutes should sell for the same price. To apply this principle to the pricing of futures contracts, note that buying a futures contract substitutes for buying and holding the underlying security. Arbitrage pricing theory would thus predict that the futures price should just equal the price of the underlying security plus any net carrying costs.

The Cost of Carry Pricing Relation   The cost of financing and storing a commodity or security until delivery is called the *cost of carry*. For agricultural and other commodities cost of carry includes financing costs, storage, and any transaction costs. The convention in financial markets is to apply the term net carrying cost to the difference between any interest earned on the security and the cost of borrowing to finance its purchase.

The cost of carry pricing relation holds that the price of a futures contract should be determined by the spot price plus net carrying costs. Formally, the relation is given by

$$F = S + c,$$

where F is the market futures price, S is the current spot price of the deliverable security, and c is the cost of carry.

By definition, the difference between the futures and spot price is basis. Thus, basis should theoretically be determined by the cost of carry when the item being hedged is the same as the deliverable security. Understanding the cost of carry model is important in designing hedge strategies because it allows the hedger to anticipate certain changes in basis over the life of a hedge.

Convergence   Carrying costs fall as the futures settlement date approaches because the time period a cash position must be held grows shorter. This causes futures prices to converge to underlying spot market prices as the delivery date draws near. On the final day of trading in a futures contract a futures transaction is essentially equivalent to a spot transaction, so futures prices should differ little from spot prices. Changes in carrying costs can thus explain the phenomenon of convergence. Because of convergence, basis tends to decline systematically over the life of a hedge.

Cash and Carry Arbitrage   To see why futures prices should conform to the cost of carry model, consider the arbitrage opportunities that would exist if they did not. Suppose, for example, that the price of gold futures exceeded the current spot price of gold plus the cost of carry. Arbitragers could earn riskless profits by buying gold in the spot market, simultaneously selling gold futures, and subsequently delivering the gold on the futures settlement date. This type of transaction is known as *cash and carry* arbitrage because it involves buying the cash commodity and carrying it until the futures delivery date.

If the futures price were below the spot price, arbitragers would have the incentive to sell any cash holdings of gold (or short gold in the cash market if possible), buy gold futures, and then take delivery to replenish inventories. In either case, arbitrage activity should force futures prices to adjust to the current spot price plus the cost of carry.

Now consider a cash and carry transaction in the Treasury bill market. Applying the cost of carry pricing relation to the pricing of bill futures is a straightforward exercise because T-bills are discount instruments that do not pay explicit interest. The cost of carry (c) for a Treasury bill is therefore just the interest expense associated with funding the purchase of the bill over the period it is held. For the sake of simplicity suppose that the next delivery date for Treasury bill futures is exactly thirteen weeks away. If the current futures price exceeds the cost of buying a twenty-six week bill plus the carrying cost for the thirteen week holding period, arbitragers can earn riskless profits by simultaneously buying twenty-six week bills, selling nearby Treasury bill futures, and then delivering the bills when the contracts mature. In the opposite case a profitable arbitrage would involve selling cash holdings of twenty-six week bills, buying Treasury bill futures, and accepting delivery in thirteen weeks. A more detailed description of how Treasury bill carrying costs are determined follows.

The Implied Repo Rate A *repurchase agreement* (more commonly called a *repo* or RP) is a transaction involving the sale of a security, usually a Treasury security, with a commitment on the part of the seller to repurchase the security after a stated length of time. Repurchase agreements can be viewed as short-term loans collateralized by securities holdings. The interest rate paid by borrowers in the RP market is called the *repo rate*. Because repurchase agreements are a primary funding source for dealers in government securities, the Treasury bill repo rate is typically used to calculate net carrying costs for Treasury bill futures.

The *implied repo rate* (irr) is a measure of carrying costs implicit in the futures-spot price relationship. It is formally defined as the difference between the invoice or delivery cost F implied by the futures price and the current spot price S, converted to an annualized rate of return. The formula for calculating the implied repo rate is

$$irr = \frac{F - S}{S} \times \frac{360}{t}.$$

The implied repo rate actually measures the rate of return that could be earned by buying a Treasury bill and simultaneously selling a futures contract with a delivery date t days away. It measures implied interest expense in the sense that it reveals the borrowing rate at which the gross return to a cash and carry arbitrage transaction would just equal the cost of financing that transaction.

Comparing implied repo rates with actual rates amounts to comparing theoretical futures prices, as determined by the cost of carry model, with actual futures prices. An implied repo rate above the actual three-month repo rate would indicate that futures contracts are relatively overpriced because implied interest expense would be greater than actual interest expense. An implied repo rate below the actual rate, on the other hand, would indicate that futures contracts are underpriced. Gendreau [1985] presents indirect evidence suggesting that arbitrage keeps actual and implied repo rates for Treasury bills in alignment.

Two final observations are in order. First, the effect that margin calls can have on anticipated financing costs has been ignored in this discussion; Stigum [1983; chapter 14] and Kidder [1984] explain how this affects the calculations. Second, although this discussion has centered on applying implied repo rate calculations to the pricing of Treasury bill futures, the concept can also be applied to the pricing of other types of futures contracts; see Kidder [1984] and Rebell [1984] for more examples.

References

Brewer, Elijah. "Bank Gap Management and the Use of Financial Futures." Federal Reserve Bank of Chicago, *Economic Perspectives* 9 (March/April 1985), pp. 12-21.

Faux, Richard G., Jr. "Hedging Eurodollar Risk." In *The Handbook of Financial Futures*, edited by Nancy H. Rothstein and James M. Little. New York: McGraw-Hill Book Company, 1984, pp. 247-55.

Figlewski, Stephen. *Hedging with Financial Futures for Institutional Investors*. Cambridge, Mass.: Ballinger Publishing Company, 1986.

Gendreau, Brian C. "Carrying Costs and Treasury Bill Futures." *Journal of Portfolio Management* (Fall 1985), pp. 58-64.

Hieronymus, Thomas A. *Economics of Futures Trading*. New York: Commodity Research Bureau, Inc., 1971.

Kaufman, George G. "Measuring and Managing Interest Rate Risk: A Primer." Federal Reserve Bank of Chicago, *Economic Perspectives* 8 (January/February 1984), pp. 16-29.

Kawaller, Ira G. "Liability Side Gap Management: Risks and Opportunities." Chicago Mercantile Exchange, *Market Perspectives* 1 (August 1983).

Kidder, William M. "The Implied Repo Rate." In *The Handbook of Financial Futures*, edited by Nancy H. Rothstein and James M. Little. New York: McGraw-Hill Book Company, 1984, pp. 447-66.

Koppenhaver, G. D. "Trimming the Hedges: Regulators, Banks, and Financial Futures." Federal Reserve Bank of Chicago, *Economic Perspectives* 8 (November/December 1984), pp. 3-12.

Little, James M. "What Are Financial Futures?" In *The Handbook of Financial Futures*, edited by Nancy H. Rothstein and James M. Little. New York: McGraw-Hill Book Company, 1984, pp. 35-66.

Paul, Allen B. "The Role of Cash Settlement in Futures Contract Specification." In *Futures Markets: Regulatory Issues*, edited by Anne E. Peck. Washington, D.C.: American Enterprise Institute for Public Policy Research, 1985.

Powers, Mark, and David Vogel. *Inside the Financial Futures Markets*. New York: John Wiley and Sons, 1981.

Ronalds, Nicholas. "Contract Life Cycles for Selected CME Markets." Chicago Mercantile Exchange, *Market Perspectives* 4 (August 1986).

Rothstein, Nancy H., and James M. Little. "The Market Participants and Their Motivations." In *The Handbook of Financial Futures*, edited by Nancy H. Rothstein and James M. Little. New York: McGraw-Hill Book Company, 1984, pp. 115-37.

Silber, William L. "Marketmaker Behavior in an Auction Market: An Analysis of Scalpers in Futures Markets." *Journal of Finance* (September 1984), pp. 937-53.

Stigum, Marcia. *The Money Market*. Rev. ed. Homewood, Illinois: Dow Jones-Irving, 1983.

Rebell, Arthur L. "Numerical Relationships of Cash and Futures: Keys to Analysis of Hedge and Speculative Strategies." In *The Handbook of Financial Futures*, edited by Nancy H. Rothstein and James M. Little. New York: McGraw-Hill Book Company, 1984, pp. 467-91.

Telser, Lester G. "Why There Are Organized Futures Markets." *Journal of Law and Economics* 24 (April 1981), pp. 1-22.

————. "Futures and Actual Markets: How They Are Related." *The Journal of Business* 59 (April 1986), pp. 5-20.

Tompkins, Robert G., and Steven A. Youngren. "A Comparison of IMM and LIFFE Eurodollar Futures." Chicago Mercantile Exchange, *Market Perspectives* 1 (June/July 1983).

Werderits, John R. "Synthetic Money Market Instruments: A Short-Term Investment." Chicago Mercantile Exchange, *Market Perspectives* 1 (October 1983).

Working, Holbrook. "New Concepts Concerning Futures Markets and Prices." *American Economic Review* 52 (June 1962), pp. 432-59.

14

OPTIONS ON SHORT-TERM INTEREST RATE FUTURES

Anatoli Kuprianov

Options are contracts that give their owners the right, but not the obligation, to buy or sell a specified item at a set price on or before a specified date. An active over-the-counter market in stock options has existed in the United States for about a century. Options began to be traded on organized exchanges in 1973 when the Chicago Board Options Exchange (CBOE) was organized and began listing standardized stock options. Soon after the start of trading on the CBOE, the American, Pacific, and Philadephia stock exchanges also began listing standardized stock options. As interest in options trading among institutional investors and other financial market participants became evident the number of exchange-traded options grew rapidly. Today several different types of standardized options trade on virtually all major futures and stock exchanges, including stock options, other financial options such as foreign currency options, commodity options, and futures options.

Futures options are options on futures contracts. Currently traded money market futures options include options on three-month Treasury bill and three-month Eurodollar time deposit futures. The most active trading in both Treasury bill and Eurodollar time deposit futures options takes place at the International Monetary Market (IMM) division of the Chicago Mercantile Exchange (CME), although Eurodollar futures options also trade on the London International Financial Futures Exchange (LIFFE). Options on actual three-month Treasury bills are listed for trading by the American Stock Exchange (ASE), but this market is not active.

TERMINOLOGY AND DEFINITIONS

A *call option* gives the buyer the right, but not the obligation, to buy a specified item at a stipulated price called the *exercise* or *strike* price. The *underlying instrument*, or item specified by the option contract, can be a security such as a common stock or a Treasury bond, a specified amount of a commodity, or a futures contract. Call options are bought and sold for a market-determined price termed the *premium* or *call price*. In exchange for the premium, the seller (or *writer*) of a call option obligates himself to sell the underlying instrument at the strike price at the option of the buyer. When the buyer (or *holder*) of the option chooses to purchase the underlying instrument he is said to *exercise* the option.

A call option is said to be *in-the-money* when the market price of the underlying instrument is above the strike price and *out-of-the-money* when the market price of the underlying instrument falls below the strike price. When a call option is in-the-money the buyer has the right to purchase the underlying instrument at a price below the market price. The holder of an in-the-money *American* option can exercise it at any time before expiration date. In contrast, a *European* option can only be exercised on the expiration date.

Before the expiration date, out-of-the-money options will typically sell at a positive premium because of the possibility that the price of the underlying instrument will rise before expiration. At expiration the buyer will exercise the option if it is in-the-money or let it expire unexercised if it is out-of-the-money. An out-of-the-money call option has no value at expiration, since buyers will not purchase the underlying instrument at a price above the current market price. The value of an in-the-money call option at expiration is the current market price of the underlying instrument minus the strike price.

The buyer of a *put option* receives the right to sell a specified security at the strike or exercise price stipulated by the contract. In exchange for a cash premium (*put price*), the seller of a put option becomes contractually obliged to buy the underlying security at the strike price at the option of the holder. A put option is in-the-money when the market price of the underlying instrument is below the strike price and out-of-the-money when the market price is above the strike price.

Exchange-traded or *standardized* options, like futures contracts, are standardized contracts traded on organized exchanges. An option contract is completely specified by the description of the underlying instrument, strike price, and the expiration date. An exchange-traded option always specifies a uniform underlying instrument, one of a limited number of strike prices, and one of a limited number of expiration dates. Strike price intervals and expiration dates for traded contracts are determined by the exchange. Contract performance for exchange-traded options, as with futures contracts, is guaranteed by a clearing corporation that interposes itself as a third party to each option contract. The clearing corporation becomes the seller to each buyer and the buyer to each seller, thereby removing the risk that the seller of an option might fail to meet contract obligations.

Contract standardization together with the clearing corporation guarantee facilitates options trading. A holder or seller of an exchange-traded option can always liquidate an open position in an option before expiration by making an offsetting transaction. For example, a holder of a Treasury bill futures call option can offset his position by selling a T-bill futures call with the same strike price and expiration date; the net profit or loss from such a transaction is determined by the difference between the premium originally paid for the call and the price received when it is sold. Similarly, the holder of a put option can liquidate his position by selling a put with the same strike price and expiration date. As with futures contracts, most positions in standardized options are liquidated before the expiration date with an offsetting transaction rather than being held for the purpose of selling or buying the underlying instrument.

Unlike futures contracts, buyers of put and call options are not required to deposit funds in a margin account because their risk of loss is limited to the premium paid for the option. Sellers of put and call options are required to maintain margin accounts, however, since they face a considerable risk of loss, as will become evident when the payoffs to different option positions are examined below.

Finally, *over-the-counter* (OTC) options are custom-tailored agreements for which option specifications (the underlying instrument, amount, strike price, exercise rights, and expiration date) are all negotiated by the two parties to the contract. OTC options are usually sold directly rather than through an exchange. Major commercial and investment banks often write custom-tailored interest rate options for their commercial customers. A bank, for example, might write a *cap*, or series of interest rate put options, for a commercial customer to fix a maximum interest rate on a floating-rate loan tied to short-term interest rates.

OPTIONS ON SHORT-TERM INTEREST RATE FUTURES

Put and call options on Treasury bill and Eurodollar futures are actively traded at the IMM in trading areas, or *trading pits* as they are called, located next to the trading pits for the underlying futures contracts.[1] Exercising a futures option results in either a long or short futures position. When a holder exercises a futures call option he buys the underlying futures contract at the strike price, or takes on a *long futures position*. To completely liquidate his resulting futures position, the buyer must undertake an offsetting futures transaction. The writer of a call option must in turn sell, or take on a *short futures position* in, the underlying futures contract when it is exercised. When a futures put option is exercised the holder takes on a short futures position and the writer a long position.

The primary advantage of futures options over options for actual securities

---

[1] These futures contracts are described in the previous chapter.

stems from the liquidity of futures contracts. Because futures markets tend to be more liquid than underlying cash markets, offsetting a position resulting from the exercise of an option is usually easier with futures options than with options on actual securities. This can be especially important to put and call writers, who usually enter into options agreements to earn fee income rather than with the ultimate goal of buying or selling the underlying instrument.

IMM money market futures options are American options. ASE Treasury bill options, in contrast, are European-type options for actual Treasury bills. LIFFE Eurodollar futures options are American options specifying LIFFE Eurodollar time deposit futures contracts as the underlying instrument.

At present trading activity in IMM Treasury bill futures options is relatively light but greatly surpasses trading in ASE bill options, which is almost nonexistent. IMM Eurodollar futures options are very actively traded while volume in LIFFE Eurodollar futures options, although significant, is considerably smaller. Contract specifications for IMM money market futures options are described in the Box.

CONTRACT SPECIFICATIONS FOR OPTIONS ON IMM MONEY MARKET FUTURES

Options on Treasury Bill Futures   IMM Treasury bill futures options were first listed for trading in April of 1986. The underlying instrument for these options is the IMM three-month Treasury bill futures contract. Expiration dates for traded contracts fall approximately three to four weeks before the underlying futures contract matures.[1] IMM futures options can be exercised any time up to the expiration date.

Strike Price Intervals   Strike price intervals are 25 basis points for IMM index prices above 91.00 and 50 basis points for index prices below 91.00. Strike prices are typically quoted in terms of basis points. Thus, the strike prices for traded Treasury bill futures options can be 90.50 or 92.25, but not 90.25 or 92.10.

Price Quotation   Premium quotations for Treasury bill futures

---

[1] The precise rule used to determine IMM Treasury bill futures options expiration dates is as follows. The expiration date is the business day nearest the underlying futures contract month that satisfies the following two conditions. First, the expiration date must fall on the last business day of the week. Second, the last day of trading must precede the first day of the futures contract month by at least six business days.

options are based on the IMM index price of the underlying futures contract. As with the underlying futures contract, the minimum price fluctuation is one basis point and each basis point is worth $25. Thus, a quote of 0.35 represents an options premium of $875 (35 basis points x $25). The minimum price fluctuation for put and call premiums is one basis point. There is no upper limit on daily price fluctuations.

Options on Eurodollar Futures   IMM options on Eurodollar futures began trading in March, 1985. Eurodollar options expire at the end of the last day of trading in the underlying Eurodollar futures contract. Since the Eurodollar futures contract is cash settled the final settlement for Eurodollar options follows the cash settlement procedure adopted for Eurodollar futures.

To illustrate, suppose the strike price for a bought Eurodollar futures call option is 91.00 and the final settlement price for Eurodollar futures is 91.50. Exercising the call option at expiration gives the holder the right, in principle, to place $1,000,000 in a three-month Eurodollar deposit paying an add-on rate of nine percent. But since the contract is settled in cash, the holder receives $1250 (50 basis points x $25) in lieu of the right to place the Eurodollar deposit paying nine percent.

Strike Price Intervals   Strike price intervals for Eurodollar futures options are the same as Treasury bill strike price intervals.

Price Quotation   Premium quotations for Eurodollar options are based on the IMM index price of the underlying Eurodollar futures contract. As with the underlying futures contract, the minimum price fluctuation is one basis point and each basis point is worth $25.

PAYOFF DIAGRAMS

The difference between options and the underlying futures contracts becomes evident once the *payoff diagrams* for each contract are compared. The payoff diagrams depicted in Figures 1 through 3 show how profits and losses from different futures and options positions held to expiration vary as underlying futures prices change.

Futures Contracts   Figure 1 displays payoff diagrams for unhedged long and short futures positions. The horizontal axis in these diagrams measures the price,

Figure 1

PAYOFFS FOR UNHEDGED FUTURES CONTRACTS

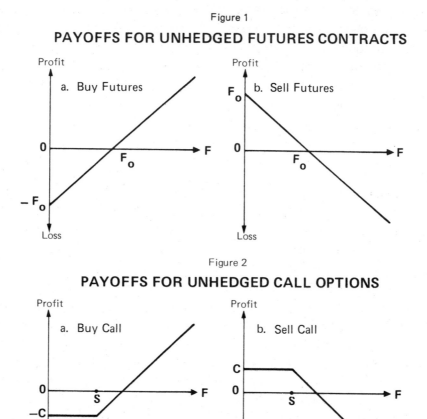

Figure 2

PAYOFFS FOR UNHEDGED CALL OPTIONS

Figure 3

PAYOFFS FOR UNHEDGED PUT OPTIONS

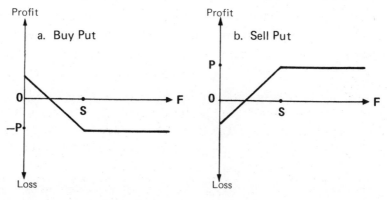

F, of the futures contract while the vertical axis measures any profits or losses stemming from changes in futures prices. To simplify the analysis, transaction costs, such as brokerage fees, are ignored in drawing these diagrams. The buyer of a futures contract earns or loses one dollar for each dollar the price of the contract rises or falls. Thus, the payoff can be depicted by a 45 degree line showing a zero profit at the original purchase price, denoted by the point F_0 in Figure 1a. A trader with an unhedged short position is in the opposite position, profiting when futures prices fall and losing money when prices rise.

Futures Call Options   Figure 2a shows the payoff diagram for an unhedged, or *naked*, bought call option held to expiration. In return for the payment of the call premium, C, the buyer receives the right to buy the underlying futures contract at the strike price S. At expiration an out-of-the-money option has no value. A buyer holding an out-of-the-money call option will allow the option to expire unexercised, earning a total net profit of -C; that is, he loses the call premium paid at the time the option was purchased. When the price of the underlying futures contract is above the strike price the buyer can exercise the option, buy the underlying futures contract at the strike price, and liquidate his futures position at a profit. The buyer's net profit in this second case is the difference between the market price of the futures contract, F, and the strike price, S, less the premium paid for the call, C.

To take an example, suppose that a buyer pays a premium of $800 for a December 1986 Treasury bill futures call option with a strike price of 94.50 (IMM index price).[2] This option is in-the-money when December Treasury bill futures prices rise above 94.50. If the price of a Treasury bill futures contract is 95.00, the buyer can exercise the option and immediately liquidate his futures position at a $1,250 (50 basis points x $25) profit. His net profit is $450 ($1,250 − $800).

Figure 2b shows the payoff at expiration earned by the seller of a call option. His profit will be the full amount of the call premium C if the option is not exercised; that is, if the price of the underlying futures contract on the expiration date is below the strike price. If the price of the underlying futures contract is above the strike price, however, the option will be exercised and the writer will be required to sell the underlying futures contract at the strike price S. Liquidating the resulting futures position requires buying the contract back at the higher market price F. Thus, the writer's net profit if the option is exercised is the call premium C minus the difference (F − S). The net profit is negative if the premium C is less

---

[2] The IMM index price for Treasury bill futures is 100 minus the futures discount yield to be paid on the deliverable bill. Each one basis point change in the index price corresponds to a $25 change in the price of the deliverable bill. See the previous chapter for more details.

than the loss (F − S) incurred from selling the underlying futures contract at the strike price.

Futures Put Options Figure 3a shows the payoff diagram for a bought put option held to expiration. The buyer pays a put premium P in exchange for the right to sell the underlying futures contract at the strike price S. He will allow the option to expire unexercised if the price of the underlying futures contract is above the strike price. In this case, he loses the put premium. When the underlying futures price is below the strike price the put holder can exercise the option, sell the underlying futures contract, and liquidate the resulting futures position at a profit. The put holder's net profit in this second case is the amount by which the strike price S exceeds the market price F of the underlying futures contract, minus the put premium.

As an example, suppose that a buyer pays a premium of $525 for a put option on December Treasury bill futures with a strike price of 95.00. If the price of the underlying futures contract is 94.90 the put holder can earn $250 (10 basis points x $25) by exercising the option, selling Treasury bill futures at 95.00, and then liquidating his position through an offsetting purchase at 94.90. His net profit (loss in this case) is $250 − $525 = − $275.

Finally, Figure 3b shows the payoff at expiration earned by the seller of a put option. If the option is out-of-the-money (that is, if the market price of the underlying futures contract is above the strike price) at expiration, the seller earns a profit equal to the full put premium, P. Otherwise, the option will be exercised and the writer will be forced to buy the underlying futures contract at a price above the market price. Liquidating the resulting futures position results in a loss, which may more than offset the premium earned from writing the option.

As the payoff diagrams in Figures 2 and 3 make clear, buying a put does not offset a long call position. Instead, the holder of a call option can liquidate his position only by selling a call with the same expiration date and strike price. Similarly, the holder of a put can liquidate his position by selling a put with the same contract specification.

HEDGING WITH INTEREST RATE FUTURES OPTIONS

An option hedge combines an option with a cash position in the underlying instrument in such a way that either the underlying instrument protects the option against loss or the option protects the underlying instrument against loss. Buying a put option, for example, protects against a large loss resulting from a long position in the underlying instrument.

Options on futures can be used to hedge cash market positions because futures prices tend to be highly correlated with prices of the deliverable securities. Some futures options, such as the IMM Eurodollar futures option, expire on the same day the underlying futures contract matures. Exercising a futures option on the maturity date of the underlying contract amounts to exercising an option on the actual cash instrument.

The Difference Between a Futures and an Options Hedge The basic difference between hedging with options and hedging with futures is that options enable hedgers to limit losses from adverse price movements while leaving open the opportunity to profit from favorable price changes. A futures hedge, in contrast, just fixes the price at which a planned future transaction takes place— the hedger is protected from the risk of loss if the value of his cash market holdings falls, but loses the opportunity to profit if those holdings appreciate.

Thus, options can be thought of as providing a form of price insurance. Like any other form of insurance, however, buyers are required to pay a premium for protection against loss, which means that although they have the opportunity to profit if the value of their underlying cash position rises the returns to a position hedged with options will be smaller on average than the returns to an unhedged position.

Over-the-counter put and call options on short-term interest rates are sometimes called *caps* and *floors*, terms that derive from descriptions of the basic hedging strategies each type of option can be used to structure. Buying an interest rate put option caps or establishes a maximum borrowing rate on a floating-rate loan tied to short-term interest rates. Buying a call option sets a floor or minimum yield on a future investment.

Interest rate caps and floors can also be created using options on interest rate futures, as is illustrated by the following two examples.

Creating Interest Rate Floors A futures call option establishes a maximum purchase price for the underlying instrument. Since the price of an interest-bearing security varies inversely with market interest rates, establishing a maximum purchase price on an interest-bearing security amounts to fixing a minimum yield on the anticipated investment. The following example illustrates the mechanics of an options hedge undertaken to fix an investment floor.

On August 15 a corporate treasurer learns that his firm will receive a cash inflow of $1 million in three months. Such funds are typically invested in three-month Treasury bills. The treasurer can fix a minimum yield on the anticipated investment either by buying a Treasury bill futures contract or by buying a Treasury bill futures call option. Call options on December Treasury bill futures expire on November 14, which turns out to coincide exactly with the date the hedger in this example anticipates receiving the cash inflow.

IMM Treasury bill futures can be bought at a price of 94.71 on August 15, implying a futures discount yield of 5.29 percent. Treasury bill futures call options with a strike price of 94.75 (implying a discount yield of 5.25 percent) sell for a premium of 21 basis points, or $525. The results of a futures and an options hedge are compared below under two different assumptions about market rates of return prevailing on the date of the planned investment.

Results of the Futures Hedge First, consider the rate of return fixed by a futures hedge. If the corporate treasurer could buy a Treasury bill futures contract maturing on November 14, when he plans to invest in T-bills, the hedge would be perfect and the rate of return fixed by the futures hedging strategy would be known with certainty. However, the nearest maturity date for a Treasury bill futures contract falls in December. Uncertainty about the exact relationship between futures and spot Treasury bill prices on the date of the anticipated cash inflow introduces the risk, known as *basis risk*, that the yield produced by the hedge may differ from the expected yield.[3] For the sake of simplicity this source of risk will be ignored in this example; specifically, it will be assumed that the futures discount yield always equals the actual yield on a thirteen-week Treasury bill on November 14. Under this assumption the futures hedge will always result in an effective discount yield of 5.29 percent on the planned investment. Although this convenient relationship could not be expected to hold in reality, the error this assumption introduces is unimportant for purposes of this simple example.

Calculating the Investment Floor Suppose that interest rates fall after August 15 and the discount yield on Treasury bill futures contracts declines from 5.29 percent to 5.00 percent at the November 14 expiration date. Since the resulting price of the underlying futures contract, 95.00, is above the strike price of 94.75, the option can be exercised and the resulting futures position liquidated at a profit of 25 basis points, or $625. This profit is partially offset by the 21 basis point call premium, reducing the net profit to 4 basis points. Again assuming no basis risk so that the discount yield on thirteen-week Treasury bills is 5.00 percent, the effective hedged discount yield in this case is 5.04 percent. This outcome produces a discount yield 4 basis points higher than the unhedged yield, but 25 basis points lower than the 5.29 percent yield that could have been fixed by the futures hedge.

Notice that in this example 5.04 percent is the minimum discount yield the hedger would face, no matter how low interest rates turn out to be on the expiration date. This is because—in the absence of basis risk—any additional

---

[3] Basis risk is discussed in greater detail in the previous chapter.

decline in the discount Treasury bill yield below 5.00 percent would be exactly offset by additional profit from the hedge. In actual practice basis risk would make the calculation of an absolute floor impossible, although an expected floor could be estimated.

Results of the Options Hedge When Interest Rates Rise   Now consider the rate of return produced by the option hedging strategy if interest rates rise before the planned investment date. Suppose that on November 14 the price of an IMM Treasury bill futures contract falls to 94.45, implying a discount yield of 5.55 percent. In this case the price of the underlying futures contract is below the strike price of 94.75, so the option will be permitted to expire unexercised. Assuming once more that the spot price equals the futures price, the discount yield for a thirteen-week Treasury bill bought in the spot market is 5.55 percent. For the hedger, the net effective yield is 5.34 percent (5.55 percent minus the 21 basis point call premium), which is 5 basis points higher than the yield that would have been earned using a futures hedge.

This second case illustrates the potential advantage an options hedging strategy has over a futures hedge. While the interest rate floor established by the options hedge is lower than the rate fixed by the futures hedge, the options hedge permits the hedger to earn a higher yield if interest rates rise by enough to offset the cost of the call premium.

Interest Rate Caps   Buying a put option on an interest rate futures contract sets a minimum price the cash security can be sold for at a future date. Fixing a minimum price on an interest-bearing security is equivalent to fixing a maximum interest rate, however, so that an interest rate futures put option can be used to fix a maximum borrowing rate, or cap. If interest rates fall before the loan is taken out, the hedger loses part or all of the put premium, but can borrow at the lower market rate.

To take a specific example, suppose that on October 15 a large corporation makes plans to take out a three-month, $1 million loan in two months. The firm's bank typically charges 100 basis points over the three-month LIBOR for such loans. The firm can protect itself against the risk of a rise in interest rates before the loan is taken out either by selling Eurodollar futures or by buying a Eurodollar futures put option.

For purposes of this example assume that options on Eurodollar futures expire on December 15, the exact date the planned loan is to be taken out. As of October 15, December Eurodollar time deposit futures trade at a price of 93.99 on the IMM, implying a futures LIBOR of 6.01 percent. A put option on December Eurodollar futures with a strike price of 93.75 sells for a premium of 6 basis points.

The results of a futures hedge and a hedge structured using the put option are compared below.

Result of a Futures Hedge IMM Eurodollar futures mature on the same day options on those contracts expire. Thus, the firm in this example can put together a perfect futures hedge. Such a hedge would lock-in a borrowing rate of 7.01 percent (6.01 percent fixed by the sale of the futures contract plus the 100 basis point markup charged by the lending bank).

Calculating the Interest Rate Cap Now consider the result of the option hedge when interest rates rise before the loan is taken out. Suppose that the three-month LIBOR is 6.30 on the expiration date, so that the final settlement price for Eurodollar futures is 93.70. The underlying futures contract price is 5 basis points below the 93.75 strike price, so the option can be exercised and the underlying position settled in cash to earn a $125 profit. Since IMM Eurodollar futures options expire on the same day the underlying futures contract matures and that contract is cash settled, this profit is paid directly to the hedger. The profit from exercising the option is more than offset by the 6 basis point put premium, however. The net loss from the hedge is thus 1 basis point. The resulting effective borrowing rate is 7.31 percent (6.30 market LIBOR, plus the 1 basis point net hedging cost, plus the 100 basis point markup), 30 basis points higher than the effective borrowing rate that could have been fixed with a futures hedge and 1 basis point higher than the unhedged borrowing rate.

The interest rate cap of 7.31 percent is attained whenever the underlying contract settlement price hits the strike price. Notice that no matter how high interest rates were to rise, effective borrowing costs would never go above this level because any further increase in market rates would be exactly offset by the additional profits gained from exercising the put option.

Result of the Options Hedge When Interest Rates Fall Finally, consider the effective borrowing cost resulting from the option hedge if the three-month LIBOR were to fall to 6.00 percent on the expiration date. If LIBOR is 6.00 percent the settlement price for December Eurodollar futures will be 94.00, which means that a put option with a strike price of 93.75 is out-of-the-money. The interest rate paid on the loan in this case is 7.00 percent, but the net effective cost is 7.06 percent because of the loss of the put premium.

Notice that in both of the cases considered above the borrowing rate produced by the options hedge was higher than either the unhedged borrowing rate or the rate that could have been fixed with a futures hedge. This points to an important characteristic of options hedges. The premium paid on an option protects the hedger from heavy losses due to large price fluctuations while permitting gains in the form of lower borrowing costs or higher investment rates in cases where favorable price movements occur. When only small price movements occur, however, any benefit from holding the option may be more than offset by the cost of the option premium. Thus, unless large price movements are realized, an options hedge can easily prove to be more costly than a futures hedge.

Although options on interest rate futures have only been actively traded for a short time, a large number of interest rate option hedging strategies have been developed. At present, the heaviest commercial users of money market futures options are commercial and investment banks that write caps and floors for their customers and then hedge their resulting net over-the-counter positions with standardized interest rate futures options.[4]

PRICE RELATIONSHIPS BETWEEN FUTURES OPTIONS AND FUTURES CONTRACTS

As noted earlier, an out-of-the-money option will typically have value before the expiration date because of the possibility that the option could go in-the-money before it expires. The difference between the strike price and the market price of the underlying instrument is called the *intrinsic value* of the option. An option's intrinsic value is the gain that could be realized if it were exercised. Any excess of the option premium above its intrinsic value is called the *time value* of the contract. The time value of an option is greater the longer the time to expiration because an option with a longer life has a greater chance of going deeper in-the-money before it expires. As the expiration date draws nearer time value declines; once the expiration date arrives, the time value of an option is zero and the only value the option has is its intrinsic value.

To illustrate, the table presents call prices, underlying futures prices, and time values for IMM Eurodollar futures options with different expiration dates as of the end of trading on November 6, 1986. The first row in the table gives data for options on December Eurodollar futures. As of the end of trading on November 6,

SELECTED EURODOLLAR FUTURES CALL OPTION PREMIUMS

Expiration Month	Strike Price	Premium	Futures Price	Intrinsic Value	Time Value
December	93.50	0.53	94.02	0.52	0.01
March	93.50	0.62	94.02	0.52	0.10
June	93.50	0.60	93.85	0.35	0.25

---

[4] For a more detailed description of the development of interest rate options markets see Bank for International Settlements [1986, chapter 3].

a Eurodollar call option on a December 1986 futures contract with a strike price of 93.50 sold for a premium of 53 basis points. The price of the underlying futures contract at the end of the same trading session was 94.02, so this option was in-the-money. The intrinsic value of the December option was 52 basis points; thus, the difference between the call premium and its intrinsic value is one basis point, or $25. As noted above, the time value of the options for successively distant expiration dates grows larger.

A comprehensive discussion of factors determining options prices is beyond the scope of this article. However, two concluding observations are in order. First, the deeper an option is in-the-money, the greater the proportion of the option premium is due to intrinsic value and therefore the more closely price movements in the underlying futures contracts are reflected by changes in the option premium. Thus, in-the-money options provide hedgers with greater risk reduction than out-of-the-money options. Second, all other things equal, the time value of an option is greater the more volatile are underlying futures prices. This is because more volatile underlying futures prices make it more likely an option will go deeper in-the-money before it expires.

Readers interested in a formal theoretical development of the pricing formula for options on futures contracts are referred to Black [1976]. Less technically oriented readers will find Koppenhaver's [1986] introductory exposition useful. Emanuel [1985] shows how to apply the Black formula to the pricing of Eurodollar futures options.

References

Bank for International Settlements. *Recent Innovations in International Banking*. Basle, Switzerland, April 1986.

Black , Fisher. "The Pricing of Commodity Contracts." *Journal of Financial Economics* 3 (January/March 1976), pp. 167–79.

Emanuel, David. "Eurodollar Volatility and Option Pricing." Chicago Mercantile Exchange, *Market Perspectives* 3 (April 1985).

Koppenhaver, G. D. "Futures Options and Their Use by Financial Intermediaries." Federal Reserve Bank of Chicago, *Economic Perspectives* 10 (January/February 1986), pp. 18–31.

Kramer, Samuel L., Lyn Miller Senholz, and Carl O. Helstrom, III. *Options Hedging Handbook*. Cedar Falls, IA: Center for Futures Education, Inc., 1985.

Mates , Christopher I. "Cap Rate Loans: 'Put' a Stop to Runaway Interest Expense: Part 1." Chicago Mercantile Exchange, *Market Perspectives* 3 (June 1985).

Mates , Christopher I. and James E. Murphy. "Investment Floors and Fences Using T-bill Options." Chicago Mercantile Exchange, *Market Perspectives* 4 (April, 1986).

INDEX

INDEX